本 书
国家社科基金重点项目
"基于多模态库的中国大学生英语学术交流能力的自动评测研究"
（项目编号：20AYY013）
阶 段 性 成 果

影响中国英语学习者
语音评测的显著特征研究

程 欣／著

Criterial Features
in the Assessment
of Chinese EFL
Learners' Pronunciation

南京大学出版社

图书在版编目(CIP)数据

影响中国英语学习者语音评测的显著特征研究 / 程欣著. —南京：南京大学出版社，2022.8
ISBN 978-7-305-25467-3

Ⅰ.①影… Ⅱ.①程… Ⅲ.①英语—语音—教学研究—中国 Ⅳ.①H311

中国版本图书馆CIP数据核字(2022)第039314号

出版发行	南京大学出版社		
社　　址	南京市汉口路22号	邮　编	210093
出 版 人	金鑫荣		

书　　名 影响中国英语学习者语音评测的显著特征研究
著　　者 程　欣
责任编辑 董　颖

照　　排	南京紫藤制版印务中心
印　　刷	广东虎彩云印刷有限公司
开　　本	880×1230　1/32　印张9　字数245千
版　　次	2022年8月第1版　2022年8月第1次印刷
ISBN	978-7-305-25467-3
定　　价	53.00元

网　　址：http://www.njupco.com
官方微博：http://weibo.com/njupco
官方微信：njupress
销售咨询热线：(025)83594756

＊ 版权所有，侵权必究
＊ 凡购买南大版图书，如有印装质量问题，请与所购图书销售部门联系调换

前　言

长期以来,语音评测在二语口语测试中处于边缘地位。这导致语音评测理论匮乏、研究不足、标准模糊,无法为评分员提供有效的语音评分指导。近年来,语音研究的蓬勃兴起为语音评测研究提供了新的契机,但学界对能有效区分学习者语音水平的语音特征,以及它们与各语音维度分项评分的关系尚不明确。因此,此类研究将为建设更有效的语音评分量表,开发自动评测工具,以及完善语音评测理论奠定坚实的基础。

根据前人在语音学、口语测评和二语习得等相关领域内的研究,广义的"语音"包含了音段、韵律和流利度三个维度。语音的教学和评测受到两种构念的影响,分别是"本族语原则"和"可懂性原则"。因此,对学习者语音特征的实证研究多聚焦于某个维度的语音特征与口音、可懂性和可理解度之间的关系。然而,囊括各维度上语音特征与语音水平之间关系的研究数量很少。已有的研究发现,与口音和可理解度密切相关的语音特征虽不尽相同,但大量重叠;对音段和超音段特征在语音评测中的作用大小没有统一定论。此外,口语测试效能模型还显示,语音评测作为口语评测的一部分,除了受到学习者语音特征的影响,还受到评分员、评分量表、口语任务种类和学习者母语背景等多方面的影响。因此,本研究对各变量进行了严格的控制,着眼于中国英语学习者的语篇朗读评测,旨在发现并验证影响中国英语学习者语音总体印象评分和精细分项评分的显著语音特征,以期为后续建设精细的语音评测量表提供实证依据。

具体来说,本研究拟回答三个研究问题:1) 在基于文献的语音特征中，哪些与语音评测结果密切相关？2）这些语音特征如何区分高、中、低三个语音水平组？3）哪些语音特征对音段、韵律和流利度三个维度的语音精细分项评分最具预测性？

为回答这些研究问题，本研究采用文献研究与语料库数据分析相结合的研究方法。首先，通过对语音理论、语音评测标准和语音实证研究中所涉及的语音特征进行甄选，选出涉及音段、韵律及流利度三个维度的共 42 个语音特征。随后，通过分析英语学习者朗读语料中的这些语音特征与语音评分之间的关系，对其区分性和显著性进行验证。研究中使用的语料选自《中国英语学习者朗读语料库》，是中外评分员总体印象评分高度一致的 89 篇学习者语料（分属高、中、低三个语音水平组），其中三名专家评分员对这些语料进行了音段、韵律及流利度三个维度的精细分项评分。对语音特征的分析分两个步骤进行。第一步，分别从高、中、低语音水平组中选取最典型的 10 篇语料（10＊3），进行基于文献的所有 42 个语音特征的标注和分析。使用"相关分析"统计方法分析这些语音特征与语音总体印象评分及三个维度上精细分项评分的相关度，挑选出与评分呈显著相关的特征。第二步，在所有 89 篇语料（含第一阶段中的 30 篇）中，标注和分析已经过第一阶段验证的语音特征。使用"单因素方差分析"统计方法研究它们在区分语音高、中、低水平组时的作用；使用"逐步线性回归分析"方法建立各维度的语音特征对三个精细分项语音评分的预测模型。

本研究的主要发现和启示如下：

首先，在基于文献的 42 个语音特征中，有 16 个特征与语音总体印象评分显著相关，它们可被分别归类为音段、韵律和流利度三个维度；同时，它们也分别与音段、韵律和流利度的精细分项评分显著相关。音段特征包括音段准确性（*单音替换、元音替换、起始辅音替换*）和*不完全爆破*两类；韵律特征由语调（*调群错误、陈述句边界非降调使用、整体音域*）、重音（*句重音错误、调核重音错误、调核重音时长突显度*）和节奏（*重音节拍*）三个小类特征组成；流利度特征则包括语速和停顿频率类特征（*总停顿频率、从句/词*

组边界和*词组内部停顿频率*)。此外，另有一个音段特征(*增音*)虽与总体印象评分的相关性不具有统计学意义，但却与音段的精细分项评分显著相关。

研究发现的这些与语音评分密切相关的语音特征表明，语音评测受到口语任务的影响，在难度较低的朗读任务中，为了提高语音水平的区分度，评分员不可避免地会采取"本族语原则"进行评分。因此，研究者认为，在语音评测中应对"可懂性原则"和"本族语原则"两个构念采取兼容并蓄的态度，并在制定具体的评分量表时充分考虑口语任务对其的影响，而不能一味奉行"可懂性原则"的评分构念，完全摒弃"本族语原则"。

其次，针对总体印象评分，不同的语音特征在区分语音高、中、低水平组时具有不同的作用。首先，能够有效区分所有语音水平组(高-中、高-低、中-低)的特征是*语速和重音节拍*；其次，音段准确性(如*单音替换、元音替换、起始辅音替换*)、*不完全爆破*，以及*句重音错误*是区分中、低语音水平组的重要特征；而其他的超音段特征则更能区分语音高、中(如停顿频率和调核重音的相关特征)和高、低水平组(如语调的相关特征)。

该研究结果对音段和超音段特征在语音水平感知和评分中所起的作用有了新的诠释。研究认为，音段和超音段特征对语音水平感知和评分的影响随学习者语音水平阶段的变化而有所不同，不能简单而论。这启示我们，在二语语音教学中，应把掌握重音节拍的英语节奏和提高语速放到贯穿始终的重要地位，同时针对不同语音水平的学习者应采用不同的语音教学重点。对语音水平较低的学习者，应重点提高音段准确性、掌握不完全爆破技巧；对超音段层面的教学也不应忽视，尤其是语速、节奏和句重音的准确性。对语音水平较高的学习者，则应更多关注超音段层面，如减少停顿，并更好掌握语调和调核重音的使用。此外，在朗读语音评分量表的建设中，能够适用所有语音评测水平档的语音特征是存在的，但不是传统量表中的"语音"(音段)、"语调"，而是语速和节奏。对于其他的语音特征，应根据它们在区分语音高、中、低水平组时所具有的不同作用编写适合不同语音水平档的评分描述语。

最后,针对精细分项评分,研究发现,*单音替换*、*不完全爆破*以及*增音*能一起预测音段的精细分项评分,其中,音段准确性特征(即*单音替换*)的预测力最为显著;在韵律维度,节奏特征(即*重音节拍*)对韵律的精细分项评分贡献最大,*重音节拍*和*调核重音错误*两特征相结合,能够更有效地预测韵律评分;在对流利度的评分中,*语速*和*停顿频率*都起到重要作用,但*语速*的权重更高。

这些结果显示了不同语音特征对各维度精细评分具有不同程度的作用,是建设精细的语音评测分项量表的基础。在发展诊断性评测和计算机辅助语音评测时,应在音段、韵律和流利度三个维度上分别赋予*单音替换*、*重音节拍*和*语速*更多的关注和权重。

综上所述,本研究不仅有助于推进语音和评测理论的发展,而且对二语语音教学和评测具有重要指导价值。研究发现为建设更精细有效的二语语音评分量表提供了实证依据,对发展诊断性的语音评测、改进计算机辅助语音训练和自动语音评测系统都具有积极的意义。

Preface

Due to a long-time marginalization of pronunciation in the communicative framework for L2 spoken assessment, there was insufficient research on pronunciation assessment. The existing rating scales for L2 pronunciation have suffered from a weakness of vague descriptors in the rating criteria, and failed to provide an effective guide for raters. In recent decades, pronunciation research has experienced a resurgence of interest, and much attention has been brought to the development of L2 pronunciation assessment. However, much remains unknown about what phonological features could differentiate between pronunciation rating levels, and how salient they were in raters' judgement of different dimensions of pronunciation proficiency.

According to literature, "pronunciation" in the broad sense includes three aspects, segmentals, prosody and fluency. Pronunciation pedagogy and assessment have been influenced by the "nativeness principle" and the "intelligibility principle." As a result, previous studies have mostly focused on phonological features of one aspect and their relation to accentedness, intelligibility and/or comprehensibility. Only a few included phonological features of all three aspects. They found a large overlapping of phonological features representing accentedness and comprehensibility, and drew different conclusions of the role segmental and suprasegmental features played.

This study was exploratory in nature, aiming to identify and validate the criterial features in Chinese EFL learners' pronunciation for assessment purposes, in the hope of providing empirical evidence for a more concrete set of descriptors in the construction of holistic as well as analytic pronunciation scales. More specifically, there are three research questions in this study.

1. What phonological features identified in previous literature contribute to the ratings of the Chinese EFL learners' pronunciation?

2. What role do the phonological features play in distinguishing the holistic rating levels of Chinese EFL learners' pronunciation?

3. What are the differential contributions of the phonological features to the analytic ratings of Chinese EFL learners' pronunciation?

To answer these questions, a mixed-method approach was adopted, combining the intuition/theory-based and empirically-based approaches. First, a total of 42 phonological features from three dimensions (segmentals, prosody and fluency) were identified, based on pronunciation theories, empirical studies and rating scales. Then, they were empirically validated using a data-based approach. Eighty-nine speech samples were taken from the Read English Speech Corpus of Chinese Learners, which shared high agreement in the holistic ratings by both Chinese and native-speaker raters, and could be divided into three levels of pronunciation proficiency (high, medium, low). Three phonetically trained raters rated these speech samples analytically in terms of segmentals, prosody and fluency. The analysis of the phonological features underwent two phases. In

Phase I, ten samples in each level group were taken (10 * 3) for a speech coding of all the 42 features derived from previous literature. Correlation analyses were conducted to investigate the relationship between these phonological features and the holistic as well as analytic pronunciation ratings. Those which significantly correlated with the pronunciation ratings were validated and selected in preparation for the more in-depth analysis in the Phase-II study. In Phase II, all the 89 speech samples (including the 30 samples analyzed in Phase I) were coded in terms of the phonological features validated in Phase I. The features were then analyzed, using ANOVA to explore how different features could distinguish holistic pronunciation rating levels, and using multiple linear regression to investigate their relative importance in predicting the analytic pronunciation ratings. The current study yielded the following major findings.

First, the study identified 16 out of the 42 phonological features derived from previous literature as criterial features in the assessment of Chinese EFL learners' overall pronunciation proficiency. They covered three dimensions of pronunciation, namely segmentals, prosody and fluency. The verified features from each dimension also significantly contributed to their corresponding analytic ratings. One more segmental feature (*phoneme insertion*) was found to significantly correlate with the segmental ratings but not with the holistic ratings. The validated criterial features revealed an advantage of many native-like features, hence suggesting with caution that in assessing pronunciation in reading-aloud production, a conceptualization combining both intelligibility and accentedness should be considered.

Second, in terms of the holistic ratings, phonological

features were found to play different roles in distinguishing levels of pronunciation proficiency. Two features, *articulation rate* and *overall stress timing*, were able to successfully differentiate between all the levels (high-medium, high-low, medium-low). While features of segmental accuracy (*phoneme substitution*, *vowel substitution*, *onset consonant substitution*), *incomplete plosion* and *sentence stress errors* were found to mainly function between the medium and low levels, other suprasegmental features characterized the high level, are able to discriminate between the high and medium levels (features related to pause frequency and nuclear stress), and the high and low levels (intonation features). This finding supports a view that the focus of pronunciation instructions on segmentals versus suprasegmentals may vary as a function of learners' pronunciation level, so as the descriptors in pronunciation rating scales. As is suggested, while consistent attention should be paid to rate and a stress-timing rhythm across all the pronunciation levels, learners and teachers might need to shift their focus gradually from segmental accuracy and sentence stress placement to pausing, intonation and nuclear stress pattern along the levels.

Third, in terms of the analytic ratings of different dimensions of pronunciation, a combination of *phoneme substitution*, *incomplete plosion* and *phoneme insertion*, were found to account for the segmental ratings, with the feature of segmental accuracy (*phoneme substitution*) as the best predictor; the prosodic ratings were best predicted by *overall stress timing* and *nuclear stress errors*, with the rhythmic feature (*overall stress timing*) having a greater contribution; finally, the best predictor of perceived fluency was *articulation rate*, followed by *pause frequency*. The findings of the relative importance of the phonological features in assessing the three different dimensions of pronunciations help the construction of analytic scales in the pronunciation assessment. They also suggest that in automated pronunciation scoring, all the three dimensions of pronunciation should be taken into consideration, with a relatively higher weight given to segmental accuracy, rhythm and articulation rate, respectively.

In a nutshell, the present study has significant implications for pronunciation conceptualization, pedagogy and assessment. The findings provided empirical support for the construction of more concrete descriptors in the holistic as well as analytic pronunciation rating scales, and were of crucial importance to the development of diagnostic pronunciation assessment, computer-assisted pronunciation training and automated scoring.

Acknowledgements

I would like to express my gratitude to many people for inspiring and encouraging me during the long doctoral years, and for supporting and helping me unselfishly. Without their help and love, I would not be able to complete this dissertation.

I am most grateful to my two supervisors, Professor Haixiao Wang and Professor Hua Chen.

Professor Wang is the person who directed me into this doctoral program, and has supported my research interest throughout the process. He has always been very nice and patient with me, spending long hours reading my proposals and drafts, and arranging time for our meetings from his busy schedule. What impressed me most was his expert advice when I had doubts about the feasibility of my research, and gave me faith to move on. He provided detailed comments on the drafts, helping me improve the structure and polish the language. Our discussion of all aspects of the dissertation was enormously helpful.

Professor Hua Chen is the one who ushered me in the research of pronunciation. She was so kind to invite me to join her research team, and encouraged me to attend various conferences on pronunciation and testing, which motivated me to start this research. Whenever I had difficulty with my study or work, she offered help in every possible way. Her expertise in phonetics and phonology provided me with invaluable help in the completion of my doctoral study. She was also strict with me, pushing me and inspiring me with her own diligence and passion in the research.

I also feel indebted to Professor Yenren Ding, who attended almost all of my progress report meetings, discussed my research proposals, and helped improve the language and logic in my proposals and in this dissertation as well. His suggestion of "writing the thoughts down" has been proved to be the most effective in the drafting of the dissertation.

I owe special thanks to Professor Feng Chen for his statistical advice. He helped me out of the numerous complex statistical methods, and convinced me of the validity of using traditional statistical methods such as ANOVA and Regression in this dissertation.

Special gratitude also goes to Professor Chuanbin Ni who gave me insightful suggestions at the initial phase of my research, to Professor Gussenhoven who warmly welcomed my audition of his classes in phonetics and phonology when he lectured at Nanjing University, and to the three raters, Associate Professors Zhaoxia Tian, Jin Yang and Xingping Sun, who participated in the rater interviews and offered their insights of pronunciation rating.

I am grateful to other professors and doctors at Nanjing University as well. Professor Wenyu Wang and Associate Professor Shi Zhu have patiently listened to my confusion and offered me advice on statistical analysis. Associate Professor Yan Zhang gave me practical advice on dissertation composition.

I would like to thank Ph.D. candidate Juqiang Chen who

provided me with the latest version of the Praat script to extract fundamental frequency from the speech samples, Ph. D. candidate Dongyue Xie and Ph.D. candidate Han Zuo who helped to look for literature in need for my dissertation. I would also like to thank my dear classmates in the doctoral program, particularly Dr. Ran Bi and Ph.D. candidate Ning Cao, who went through the ups and downs with me during the doctoral years, and cheered me up when I was in frustration.

And finally, I am grateful to my mother for doing much of the housework and taking care of me and my family for so many years. I also thank my husband for taking charge of the study of our son in the last several months during my writing of this dissertation.

Table of Contents

前言 ··· ⅰ
Preface ··· ⅴ
Acknowledgements ··· ⅹ

Chapter One INTRODUCTION ································· 001
  1.1 Background ·· 001
  1.2 Need for the study ··· 003
  1.3 Outline of the dissertation ··· 004

Chapter Two LITERATURE REVIEW ···························· 006
  2.1 Definition of key concepts ··· 006
      2.1.1 Pronunciation
      2.1.2 Criterial features
  2.2 Second language pronunciation assessment ·········· 010
      2.2.1 Competing paradigms
      2.2.2 Factors influencing the pronunciation assessment
      2.2.3 Automated scoring
  2.3 Criterial features in L2 pronunciation assessment ······ 034
      2.3.1 The Mixed-method approach to identify criterial features
      2.3.2 Phonological categories derived from theories
      2.3.3 Phonological categories derived from rating scales
      2.3.4 Phonological features derived from empirical studies
      2.3.5 Summary of the phonological features identified
           in the literature

2.3.6 Relative contribution of the phonological features

Chapter Three METHODOLOGY ·············· 098
3.1 Research questions ·············· 098
3.2 Speech corpus ·············· 099
    3.2.1 RESCCL
    3.2.2 The speech samples for this study
    3.2.3 Read English Speech Corpus of Native American Speakers
3.3 Phase-Ⅰ study ·············· 109
    3.3.1 Speech samples in Phase Ⅰ
    3.3.2 Speech coding in Phase Ⅰ
    3.3.3 Data analysis in Phase Ⅰ
3.4 Phase-Ⅱ study ·············· 132
    3.4.1 Speech coding in Phase Ⅱ
    3.4.2 Data analysis in Phase Ⅱ
3.5 Summary ·············· 135

Chapter Four RESULTS AND DISCUSSION Ⅰ: The Validation of Criterial Features ·············· 136
4.1 Segmental features ·············· 136
4.2 Prosodic features ·············· 140
    4.2.1 Intonation features
    4.2.2 Stress features
    4.2.3 Rhythmic features
4.3 Fluency features ·············· 148
4.4 Discussion ·············· 151
    4.4.1 Features that significantly contributed to the pronunciation ratings
    4.4.2 Features that failed to significantly contribute to the pronunciation ratings

Chapter Five   RESULTS AND DISCUSSION Ⅱ : Distinguishing the Holistic Rating Levels ·················· 168
5.1　Segmental features ······················· 169
5.2　Prosodic features ························ 173
　　5.2.1　Intonation features
　　5.2.2　Stress features
　　5.2.3　Rhythmic feature
5.3　Fluency features ························ 181
　　5.3.1　Speed
　　5.3.2　Breakdown features
5.4　Discussion ······························ 187
　　5.4.1　Features distinguishing all the levels
　　5.4.2　Features distinguishing between the lower levels
　　5.4.3　Features distinguishing between the high and lower levels
　　5.4.4　The feature failing to distinguish across holistic rating levels
5.5　Summary ······························· 198

Chapter Six   RESULTS AND DISCUSSION Ⅲ : Predicting the Analytic Ratings ························ 199
6.1　Segmental features ······················· 199
　　6.1.1　Checking the assumptions for regression
　　6.1.2　The regression model for the segmental ratings
6.2　Prosodic features ························ 204
　　6.2.1　Checking the assumptions for regression
　　6.2.2　The regression model for the prosodic ratings
6.3　Fluency features ························ 208
　　6.3.1　Checking the assumptions for regression
　　6.3.2　The regression model for the fluency ratings
6.4　Discussion ······························ 212
　　6.4.1　Segmental predictors

        6.4.2   Prosodic predictors
        6.4.3   Fluency predictors
    6.5   Summary ·· 216

Chapter Seven   CONCLUSION ······································· 217
    7.1   Major findings ·· 217
        7.1.1   The validation of the criterial features
        7.1.2   The role of the criterial features in distinguishing the holistic rating levels
        7.1.3   The differential contribution of the criterial features to the analytic ratings
    7.2   Implications ··· 220
        7.2.1   Implications for the conceptualizations of pronunciation
        7.2.2   Implications for pronunciation teaching
        7.2.3   Implications for pronunciation testing
    7.3   Limitations ·· 224
    7.4   Suggestions for future research ······························ 226

References ·· 227
Appendix A: Text of the read dialogues ························ 259
Appendix B: Categorization of the within-sentence pauses ······ 261
Appendix C: Locations of boundary tones examined for tone deviation ··· 263
Appendix D: Syllables possible to be stressed in the read text
··· 265
Appendix E: Possible locations for accented syllables and sampled tonic/weak syllables ··································· 267

List of Abbreviations and Symbols

ALP	average length of all silent pauses
ALPA	average length of silent pauses at clause boundaries
ALPB	average length of silent pauses at phrase boundaries
ALPC	average length of silent pauses within phrases
AR	articulation rate
CIF	consonant insertion at the word-final position
DE	phoneme deletion errors
DL	average length of disfluencies
DN	number of disfluencies
ICP	incomplete plosion
IPD	intonation phrasing deviation
Lexical S/U	average ratio of stressed to unstressed vowel duration in sample bi-syllabic words
NE	nuclear stress errors
OPR	overall pitch range as the distance between f0 maximum and f0 minimum on the vowels of stressed syllables
OST	overall stress timing as the duration ratio of unstressed to stressed syllables
PF	frequency of all silent pauses
PFA	frequency of silent pauses at clause boundaries
PFB	frequency of silent pauses at phrase boundaries
PFC	frequency of silent pauses within phrases
PI	phoneme insertion
PWV	pairwise variability
PWV-A	pairwise variability in type-A foot (with short stretches of weak syllables)

PWV-B	pairwise variability in type-B foot (with long stretches of weak syllables)
SCT	consonant substitution types in stressed syllables
SCTcoda	consonant substitution types at the coda position in stressed syllables
SCTonset	consonant substitution types at the onset position in stressed syllables
SE	sentence stress errors
ST	phoneme substitution types in stressed syllables
SVT	vowel substitution types in stressed syllables
TFD	failure to use the falling tone as expected
TFD1	failure to use falling tones at default boundaries (in simple statements)
TFD2	failure to use falling tones at non-default boundaries (in questions)
TRD	failure to use the rising or level tone as expected
TRD1	failure to use rising or level tones at non-default boundaries (in statements)
TRD2	failure to use rising or level tones at default boundaries (in questions)
T/Wdur	duration ratio of tonic to weak syllables
T/Wf0	f0 ratio of tonic to weak syllables
T/Wint	intensity ratio of tonic to weak syllables
Varco-C	normalized standard deviation of consonantal intervals
Varco-V	normalized standard deviation of vocalic intervals
VIF	vowel or syllable insertion at the word-final position
%V	average proportion of the duration of vocalic intervals

Chapter One
INTRODUCTION

1.1 Background

Once dubbed as "the Cinderella of language teaching" (Kelly, 1969, as cited in Isaacs, 2018, p. 273), pronunciation has been marginalized in the field of second language teaching, research and assessment for almost half a century, despite its vital role as the "first-level hurdle" for learners to master (Iwashita, Brown, McNamara, & O'Hagan, 2008, p. 44). This history of pronunciation has often been depicted as a "pendulum" (Isaacs, 2018, p. 273; Kang & Ginther, 2018, p. 1), swinging back and forth in L2 pedagogical practices, and subsequently resulting in a fluctuation in its assessment.

Since linguistic Naturalism took its place in the late 1960s, language learning has been viewed as a natural process, through exposure to sufficient comprehensible input; therefore, explicit pronunciation instruction was considered ineffective for learners to improve pronunciation proficiency, and even might hinder their communicative competence (Krashen, 1982). Together with the emerging model of communicative competence (Canale & Swain, 1980), this view contributed to the fall of pronunciation in the circle of language teaching, research and assessment for the following decades. In Canale & Swain's model

(1980), and the Communicative Language Ability framework by Bachman (1990), pronunciation falls under grammatical competence and refers to knowledge of phonological rules. The pairing of "phonology" with "graphology" in this influential framework lacks logic, and seems to be a residue from the skills-and-components models of the early 1960s (Isaacs, 2014).

This under-conceptualization of pronunciation in communicative models has led to evident repercussions in pronunciation assessment. According to the research timeline (Isaacs & Harding, 2017), there was a dearth of literature, particularly in the area of L2 pronunciation assessment. From Lado's suggestion to an indirect written pronunciation test in his book *Language Testing* (1961) to the emergence of automated scoring of L2 speech (Bernstein, 1999), the only published research article related to pronunciation testing was Buck's paper (1989).

Not until the mid-1990s, pronunciation witnessed a revival of interest in applied linguistics. Part of the reason was a shift in conceptualizing pronunciation from the "perception of accentedness to broader aspects of performance, primarily intelligibility and comprehensibility" (Kang & Ginther, 2018, p. 1). Munro and Derwing's (1995) seminal paper on intelligibility, comprehensibility and foreign accent, for the first time, delineated the distinction and relationship between these different dimensions of pronunciation, and paved way for numerous studies in this respect.

Research on pronunciation assessment, however, was left behind until about a decade ago. It was spurred by the need to revise the pronunciation scales in some of the high-stakes international English proficiency tests such as IELTS, and the important role pronunciation plays in the fast development of automated scoring of speech (Isaacs, 2018). Most literature in this respect concerns the construct validity (Isaacs, 2008), the development of rating scales (Isaacs & Trofimovich, 2012; Isaacs, Trofimovich, & Foote, 2018) and the understanding of various linguistic features (Crowther, Trofimovich, Saito, & Isaacs, 2018; Isaacs & Trofimovich, 2012; Iwashita et al., 2008; Kang, 2010) underlying raters' judgements of the L2 pronunciation.

1.2 Need for the study

Motivated by the revived attention to pronunciation in the field of both applied linguistics and pronunciation assessment, the present study aims to identify and validate criterial features in assessing Chinese EFL learners' pronunciation.

The need for the study first lies in the difficulty of raters in assessing pronunciation. Previous literature has consistently reported that raters lacked confidence in assessing pronunciation (Brown & Taylor, 2006; Isaacs, 2014; Levis, 2006), not only because teachers had inadequate knowledge of pronunciation (Levis, 2006), but also because there was a lack of concrete pronunciation rating scales to guide them in the rating process (Harding, 2018). A better understanding of the relationship between pronunciation production and perception is the key to the construction of a more concrete set of descriptors, which can better differentiate between rating levels.

Also, this study of the criterial features in assessing L2 pronunciation is essential for the development of automated pronunciation scoring and computer-assisted pronunciation training (CAPT), which aims to provide learners with a range of diagnostic information. While pronunciation assessment in high-stakes exams have received much attention in research (e.g., Brown & Taylor, 2006; Isaacs, Trofimovich, Yu, & Chereau, 2015), the pronunciation assessment for formative and diagnostic purposes are neglected. In an effort to meet this need, this study focuses on the relationship between the phonological features, and the judgements of not only overall pronunciation proficiency, but also different dimensions of pronunciation. It is hoped that the findings of this study can help to target particular pronunciation difficulties for learners at different pronunciation proficiency levels.

Moreover, this study contributes to the proposed phonological syllabus for English as an international language (EIL) (Jenkins, 2000, 2002), since the holistic pronunciation ratings in this study were based on both native and nonnative perceptions of L2 pronunciation proficiency. While previous studies have found some differences between the perceptions of native and nonnative raters, what features constitute their common judgment of L2 pronunciation remain unclear, which, from the perspective of World-Englishes, is of equal importance.

1.3 Outline of the dissertation

The dissertation is composed of seven chapters. Chapter one presents the background and the need for the study. Chapter two reviews literature related to pronunciation assessment and criterial features contributing to the pronunciation rating. The research questions and methodology are described in Chapter three, followed by results and discussions in Chapter four, five and six, corresponding to each of the research questions. Finally, Chapter seven reports the major findings of the current study and discusses the implications and limitations of the study.

Chapter Two
LITERATURE REVIEW

This chapter contains four parts. The key concepts in the study are defined first. Then follows a review of literature on the second language (L2) pronunciation assessment and the criterial features of L2 pronunciation. Finally, the features identified in the previous literature are summarized for further analysis.

2.1 Definition of key concepts

This section presents the definition of two key concepts, *pronunciation* and *criterial features*.

2.1.1 Pronunciation

In the field of phonetics and phonology, *pronunciation* is an umbrella term to cover both segmental and suprasegmental aspects of speech (Cruttenden, 2001). *Segmental* refers to the articulation of sound segments (individual vowels and consonants); *suprasegmental* denotes "longer stretches of utterance hierarchically constructed and constrained from syllables, to feet, words, phonological words, rhythmic or breath groups, and sentences modulated by superimposed stresses and intonation" (Cesar-Lee, 1999, p. 11). Therefore, in most pronunciation handbooks, such as Reed & Levis (2015), the term *pronunciation* encompasses elements "from sounds to syllables, to word stress to rhythm to intonation" (p. xvii).

However, the term *pronunciation* is not used or defined consistently across pronunciation or speaking rating scales (Isaacs & Trofimovich, 2012; Zhong, 2019).

In the TOEFL Internet-based test (iBT) Independent Speaking Rubrics, *pronunciation* refers only to the articulation of sound segments, since the term is paralleled with other phonological terminologies such as "intonation" and "pacing" in the descriptors of the Delivery Scale. For example, the Band 3 descriptor for the TOEFL iBT (Educational Testing Service, 2014) reads, "speech is generally clear, with some fluidity of expression, though minor difficulties with pronunciation, intonation, or pacing are noticeable and may require listener effort at times …". In contrast, *pronunciation* in the descriptors of the IELTS speaking test apparently includes both segmental and suprasegmental features such as stress, intonation, and rhythm (Isaacs, 2014), when the term "a range of pronunciation features" is used (British Council, IDP: IELTS Australia and University of Cambridge ESOL Examinations, n.d.), although not elaborated in the descriptors.

Unlike rating scale descriptors, the term used in pronunciation research is defined generally in a consistent way to include both segmental and prosodic features (Anderson-Hsieh, Johnson & Koehler, 1992; Chen & Li, 2017; Derwing & Munro, 2005; Harding, 2017; Isaacs & Harding, 2017; Isaac & Trofimovich, 2017; Isaac et al., 2015; Jenkins, 2002; Saito, Trofimovich,& Isaacs, 2015; Yates, Zielinski, & Pryor, 2008), with only a few referring solely to segmental accuracy (Brown, Iwashita, &

McNamara, 2005; Koren, 1995).

In some of the latest pronunciation studies (Isaacs, 2018; Saito & Plonsky, 2019), the term "pronunciation" also includes fluency-related features. This is mainly for two reasons. First, like stress and pitch, fluency-related features such as speaking rate and pausing are considered to fall in the category of suprasegmentals (Kang, 2010; Trofimovich & Baker, 2006), which is defined in phonetics and phonology to refer to "a vocal effect which extends over more than one sound segment in an utterance, such as a pitch, stress or juncture pattern" (Crystal, 2003, p. 446). Second, fluency has been found to have a moderate to strong correlation with comprehensibility (Derwing, Munro, & Thomson, 2008; Derwing, Rossiter, Munro, & Thomson, 2004; Isaacs & Thomson, 2013; Isaacs & Trofimovich, 2012; Saito et al., 2015); therefore, raters reported that it was hard to assess pronunciation " in isolation from other elements of the speaking construct, particularly fluency" (Harding, 2017, p. 26). Actually, two scales conflate pronunciation and fluency features within the "Delivery" criterion—the TOEFL speaking scale (Educational Testing Service, 2014) and the Trinity College London Integrated Skills in English Examination (ISE) (Trinity College London, 2015).

Following the latest trend, "pronunciation" in this research refers to both segmental features that describe the articulation of individual consonant and vowel sounds, and suprasegmental features that are properties of units of speech larger than the individual segments, including such prosodic features as stress, intonation and rhythm, and fluency-related features as well, for example, rate and pausing.

2.1.2 Criterial features

In the context of second language testing, the term *criterial features* is defined as "the properties of learner English that are characteristic and indicative of L2 proficiency at each of the levels and that distinguish higher levels from lower levels" (Hawkins & Filipovic, 2012, p. 11). In L2 speaking assessment, *criterial features* are those representing the speaking construct and characterize candidates' spoken performances at each of the proficiency levels (Fulcher, 2003; Iwashita et al., 2008). Therefore, the term has been widely adopted in the construction of rating scales (Fulcher, 1996; Knoch, 2011).

Generally, there are two types of criterial features, global and specific. The global one refers to the human intuitions of candidates' global proficiency, while the specific one describes a wide range of parameters based on expert rating or detailed speech analysis of candidates' performance. For example, Jin and Mak (2012, p. 24) reviewed the development of a similar concept, "distinguishing features," in rating speaking performance, with a focus from the general fundamental feature of "native speaker," through the functional "can do statements" at different levels, to the specific linguistic features of language in the operational speaking rating scales. The "native speaker" feature and "can do statements" belong to the global type of criterial features that can differentiate between levels of speaking performance, while the linguistic properties of learner language are specific criterial features, including various grammatical, phonological and vocabulary features

(Iwashita et al., 2008).

In L2 pronunciation teaching and assessment, Saito and Plonsky (2019) proposed a framework for L2 pronunciation measurement, in which they clarified the distinctions between the global and specific constructs of L2 pronunciation. The global constructs include raters' perception of comprehensibility, intelligibility, accentedness, clarity and perceived fluency; the specific constructs are made up of various segmental and suprasegmental features derived either from expert rating or acoustic analysis.

In this research, the term *criterial features* only refers to the specific phonological features that contribute to the ratings of L2 pronunciation proficiency.

2.2 Second language pronunciation assessment

This part is to describe the second language pronunciation assessment, which provides the context of this study. First, the competing paradigms in the field of pronunciation research are reviewed. After that, a number of facets that can influence the score of pronunciation proficiency (e.g., the rater, the rating scale, the task, the test taker) are discussed, followed by a description of automated scoring of pronunciation.

2.2.1 Competing paradigms

As is introduced by Levis (2005), two conflicting principles have greatly influenced pronunciation research and pedagogy, the "nativeness principle" and the "intelligibility principle" (p. 370).

The nativeness principle holds that the goal of

pronunciation for L2 learners is to reduce a foreign accent and achieve native-like pronunciation. This view treats L1 as a bad habit and advocates great effort in pronunciation teaching to eliminate the L1 trace; therefore, L2 pronunciation should be assessed by the native norm. The nativeness principle dominated the paradigm in pronunciation instruction before the 1960s in the west. It continued to exert great influence in English pronunciation teaching and assessment in China until the beginning of the 21st century, despite extensive research proving that there is a critical period for acquiring pronunciation, and that it is neither realistic (Flege, Munro, & MacKay, 1995) nor necessary (Jenkins, 2000) to achieve an accent-free pronunciation.

The intelligibility principle suggests that L2 learners only need to achieve a pronunciation proficiency that would enable them to be easily understood by their interlocutors. This view has been endorsed by most applied linguists as well as researchers of L2 pronunciation with the development of World Englishes as the guide for pronunciation instruction and assessment (Harding, 2013; Isaacs & Trofimovich, 2012).

Based on the intelligibility principle, Jenkins (2000, 2002) proposed the lingua franca core (LFC), a set of phonological features that are essential for successful communication between speakers of various L1 backgrounds. She suggested that pronunciation teaching should focus on these core features to facilitate understanding rather than waste too much energy on accent reduction, as it does not necessarily improve intelligibility. Compelling as it is, the LFC has not yet been adopted as a standard either in the instructional or assessment context, due to limited empirical evidence (Isaacs, 2014).

In the development of pronunciation assessment or L2 speaking proficiency scales, researchers seem to agree that the intelligibility principle should provide the basis for construct definition (Harding, 2018; Isaacs & Trofimovich, 2012; Levis, 2005). However, how this construct should be defined, operationalized and related to other dimensions of pronunciation continue to pose a challenge for test developers. One relevant problem is that, in many scales, intelligibility is used in its broad sense, referring to what Derwing and Munro (1997) defined as comprehensibility, "judgments on a rating scale of how difficult or easy an utterance is to understand" (p. 2). The problem of such a conflation reflects a confusion about the significant findings from Munro and Derwing's (1995) study. They originally revealed only a weak correlation between accentedness and intelligibility, and a relatively strong relationship between accentedness and comprehensibility. In other words, L2 learners with a strong accent may still be less comprehensible, despite being intelligible. The confusion of intelligibility with comprehensibility in rating scales might lead to a downgrade of the role accent plays in communication.

The second issue concerning the application of the intelligibility principle in assessment is the question of who is to be used as "touchstones" (Lado, 1961, p. 79) in evaluating whether the speech is intelligible. More complicatedly, while some researchers consider intelligibility as a static property of the listener, others see it as a dynamic process between the speaker and the listener in an interactive context (Rajadurai, 2007). Rater/listener effects have been proved significant by research (Carey, Mannell, & Dunn, 2011), and will be elaborated on later in this chapter.

A further issue worthy of consideration is the relationship between intelligibility and acceptability. It has been found that intelligibility does not guarantee acceptability (Isaacs, 2008), and errors that do not seriously impair intelligibility may also have negative effects on listeners' judgments (Van den Doel, 2006). As was argued by Szpyra-Kozlowska (2014), an accented speech that was comfortably understood depended on not only its comprehensibility but also acceptability. According to Levis (2006), acceptability refers to "the norms associated with standard forms, and by extension, the norms associated with social power" (p. 253). This view might explain why the US English accent was favoured by most listeners from various L1 backgrounds when they were asked to judge the acceptability of the different English accents for international communication (Chang, 2008). In the Chinese context, research has confirmed that Chinese college students and teachers' attitudes towards Chinese-accented English have become more positive across the first decade of this century. However, 42% of the students and 58% of the teachers in China preferred a standard English pronunciation or to sound more native-like, as shown in a large-scale nationwide questionnaire survey (He & Zhang, 2010). The authors, hereby, advocated the continued adoption of Standard Englishes as the teaching model in China.

Taken together, what constitutes the global L2 pronunciation proficiency remains open to debate. Therefore, when assessing L2 learners' overall pronunciation proficiency, this study does not single out a particular construct; instead, it follows Saito and Plonsky's (2019) practice and uses raters' holistic Judgment, i.e., raters' intuition about L2 learners' pronunciation proficiency, which might be a cluster of comprehensibility, accentedness, intelligibility, and fluency, without giving specified instructions. This practice, as Saito and Plonsky (2019) have argued, was empirically supported, since a significantly strong correlation ($r = 0.74 \sim 0.92$) had been found not only between accentedness and comprehensibility (Crowther, Trofimovich, & Isaacs, 2016; Crowther et al., 2018; Trofimovich & Isaacs, 2012), but also between comprehensibility and fluency (Derwing et al., 2004). The linguistic features underlying these different constructs are often overlapping (Bergeron & Trofimovich, 2017; Saito et al., 2015). It is then reasonable to argue that these different constructs of pronunciation are closely related, and could be considered as a whole in the context of pronunciation assessment.

2.2.2 Factors influencing the pronunciation assessment

Tests of spoken language are performance-based in nature; therefore, factors that systematically affect the performance are worthy of investigation (O'Sullivan, Saville, & Weir, 2002). As pronunciation is an integral part of speaking proficiency, models of second language speaking test performance (e.g., Fulcher, 2003; McNamara, 1996; Skehan, 1998) can be used to describe the relationship between test scores and test variables in assessing pronunciation.

Among the models of oral test performance, Fulcher's (2003) is the most comprehensive and exhaustive one. This model (Figure 2.1) provides a detailed description of various variables that influence the score of a speaking test and its inferences about the test taker. More specifically, the score and its inferences reflect how a test taker's peformance meets the

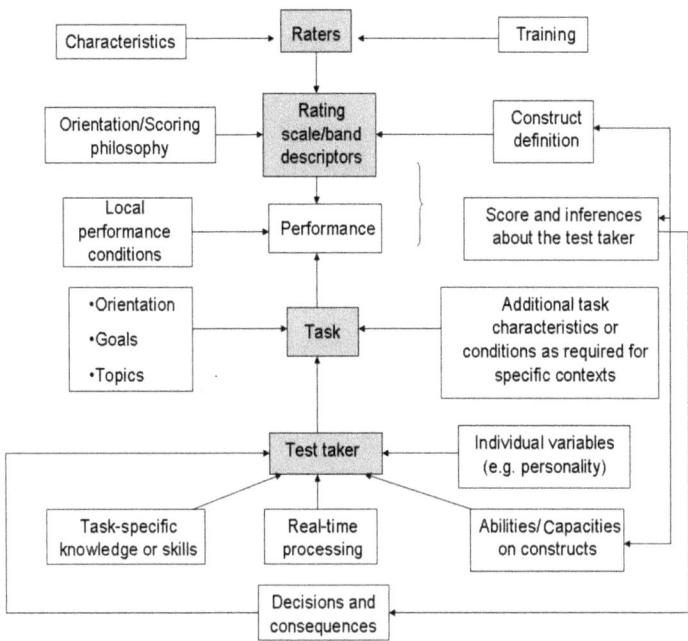

Figure 2.1 An expanded model of speaking test performance (Fulcher, 2003: 115)

band descriptors in the raters' judgment. The test taker's performance is placed in the centre of the model, influenced by four major factors, as shown in the four shaded boxes, including raters, rating scales, tasks, and test takers. The model also shows various sub-variables that serve these four major factors. As indicated by Fulcher (2003), rater training and rater characteristics play a role in how raters use the rating scale. Besides, the scoring philosophy and the construct definition of the rating scale are important in the rating process. In the case of the task, task orientation, goals, topics and any other task characteristics or conditions as required for specific contexts may exert effects on the performance. Finally, the model also illustrates the variables influencing the test taker, such as individual variables like personability, test takers' capacities on the rating constructs, their real-time processing ability, and the task-specific knowledge or skills they have.

As this dissertation addresses the criterial features in L2 learners' performance in the hope of providing evidence for a clearer definition of the construct and more detailed band descriptors in the pronunciation rating scales, it is important to review the literature on the factors demonstrated in the model that may cause score variation. Each of the four grey-shaded factors on performance in Fulcher's model is to be discussed in turn in the remainder of this section.

2.2.2.1 Raters

As shown in Flucher's (2003) model, raters play an important role in the rating process, and affect the final score of learner performance. For this reason, numerous studies have explored the rater effect on the ratings of various dimensions of speech. Generally, previous research has focused on two respects—raters' familiarity with the L2 speech and rater cognition.

2.2.2.1.1 Raters' familiarity with the L2 speech

Raters' familiarity with the L2 speech may be caused by raters' L1 background and rater experience.

When discussing the effect of raters' L1 background, Bent and Bradlow (2003) proposed the idea of "the interlanguage speech intelligibility benefit" (p. 1602), which suggests that the listeners from particular language backgrounds are more tolerant of particular nonnative speaking accents. However, empirical research seems to result in contradicting findings. On the one hand, such interlanguage intelligibility benefit was found in a number of studies. For example, in Major, Fitzmaurice, Bunta, and Balasubramanian's (2002) research, Spanish listeners benefited from their L1 background. They scored better on a listening comprehension test of a lecture in Spanish-accented English, though the Chinese listeners in the experiment did not. Kang, Vo and Moran (2016) also confirmed the effect of listeners' L1 on the perception of Vietnamese-accented English speech. They found that listeners who shared the same L1 with the speakers (Vietnamese) perceived the speech significantly more comprehensible and less accented than the nonnative English-speaking listeners of other L1s. On the other hand, studies are reporting no intelligibility benefit for the listeners on the speech produced in their own accent. Munro, Derwing and Morton (2006) examined the ratings of intelligibility, comprehensibility, and accentedness from listeners of different L1 backgrounds on L2 English speech, and found no significant difference across listener groups. Similarly, Kim's (2009) study showed that native and nonnative English-speaking teachers shared similar severity patterns across different oral tasks. Even more complicatedly, in the research on L2 German, O'Brien (2016) found that native listeners were more lenient than L2 German listeners in rating comprehensibility, but the same in rating accentedness. Though it is still not clear whether or to what extent raters' L1 backgrounds affect their pronunciation rating, one thing is certain that nonnative raters are as qualified as native raters in assessing L2 oral proficiency as they also presented high internal-consistency in their ratings (Kim, 2009).

The L1 background of the raters may also lead to

differences in what constitutes their judgments. Riney, Takada and Ota (2000) found that Japanese raters relied more on suprasegmental features (intonation), and native English raters focused more on segmentals when they rated the comprehensibility of Japanese learners' English speech. Kang, Vo and Moran (2016) found just the opposite when native American and Vietnamese listeners rated the Vietnamese accented English. Interestingly, when the listeners were from an L1 background that the speakers did not share, they prioritized suprasegmental features (stress) as the native listeners. Thus, more research into what constitutes the shared judgements by raters from different L1 backgrounds seems to be urgent.

Other than L1 background, research has also centred around the effect of rater experience. However, the terminology and operationalization of "experience" vary in different research. It is usually defined in two ways. For one thing, it refers to whether or not the raters are linguistically trained. Experienced raters might be called experts, including phoneticians, speech therapists (e.g., Cucchiarini, Strick, & Boves, 2002), and experienced ESL/EFL teachers (e. g., Rossiter, 2009). For another, experience can also be defined as the degree of listeners' exposure to (e.g., Kennedy & Trofimovich, 2008) or familiarity with L2 speech (e.g., Carey et al., 2011). There is sometimes an overlapping on the two definitions, since experienced ESL teachers tend to have more exposure to L2 speech. Previous research comparing expert raters and naïve raters has led to mixed results. While Hadden (1991) found non-teachers were more lenient than ESL teachers in rating Chinese students' English proficiency in an extemporaneous task, Barnwell (1989) reported just the opposite finding that the naïve raters were harsher than trained ACTFL oral interviewers in ratings of L2 oral communication. With regard to pronunciation assessment, the effect of rater experience seems complex. In terms of the overall pronunciation rating, examiners who were familiar with the candidates' interlanguage rated pronunciation higher than those with no or little exposure to the L2 speech (Browne & Fulcher, 2017; Carey et al., 2011). However, when it comes to more specific ratings, rater experience has been found to only influence the intelligibility of the L2 speech (measured by listener transcription of the L2 speech), with more experienced listeners understanding more than their inexperienced counterparts (Browne & Fulcher, 2017; Kenney & Trofimovich, 2008), but have little impact on their comprehensibility and accent ratings (Bergeron & Trfimovich, 2017; Kenney & Trofimovich, 2008).

Due to the inconsistency in previous research findings, the present study employs only college EFL teachers as raters since they are most likely to be the raters in actual performance tests and various forms of diagnostic assessments in the Chinese context. This study also includes raters from both Chinese mainland and native English-speaking countries (the U.S. and Australia) who have years of teaching experience in China and are very familiar with Chinese-accented English. Different from previous studies involving raters from different L1 backgrounds (e.g., Kang & Moran, 2016; Riney, Takagi, & Inutsuka, 2005), the current study focuses on the shared perception of both the native and non-native raters by analyzing only the speech samples ranked into the same levels by both groups. In doing so, we could better understand the similarities between different rater groups from a lingua franca perspective, since raters are likely to come from various L1 backgrounds.

2.2.2.1.2 Rater cognition

Even when raters share the same L1 background and similar teaching experience, their rating severity can also differ (He & Zhang, 2008; Xu & Zeng, 2015), and what constitutes their ratings may vary (Brown, 2000; Douglas & Selinker, 1992). Literature on rater cognition is extremely limited in the rating of oral proficiency (Brown et al., 2005). It has been reported that in the rating process, raters tended to focus not only on the criteria specified in the scales, but also on the aspects of performance that were not explicitly included in the scales, or on self-generated features not mentioned in scoring rubrics (Brown, 2000; Douglas, 1994; Meiron, 1998, as cited in Brown et al., 2005, p. 7; Wang, 2000). Pollitt and Murray (1996) also found that performance characteristics were weighed differently by raters at different levels of proficiency, which means the features that differentiated between different proficiency levels might not be the same.

The number of studies targeting rater cognition in pronunciation assessment is small. Limited literature has revealed a few problems raters have when rating pronunciation. One is concerned with raters' confidence in rating. Brown and Taylor (2006) investigated examiners' views and experience of the revised IELTS Speaking test (the 2001 scale), and reported that many raters lacked confidence in assessing pronunciation, which might be attributed to the vague band descriptors in the rating scales and the inadequate expertise in pronunciation teaching (Levis, 2006). Fortunately, the confidence level was found to be significantly raised when raters applied the revised pronunciation scale with more detailed band descriptors combining both global constructs such as intelligibility and listener effort and phonological features, though the relationship between them was not clearly mentioned (Yates et al., 2008).

The second problem is related to the norm issue. In Brown and Taylor's (2006) study, some examiners expressed worries when using the IELTS Pronunciation Scale about the effect of familiarity with a certain type of pronunciation and the confusion on issues related to questions like intelligible to whom, what native-speaker speech was, and what kinds of regional variations were acceptable. Such norm issues were also found in the study of Chen and Li (2017), in which they surveyed Chinese raters' views on rating pronunciation in the nationwide TEM (Test for English Majors) Oral tests and CET Spoken tests (CET-SET). Over half of the raters claimed that the Chinese accent in test takers' English speech would have a negative effect on the pronunciation rating, thus, showing a strong inclination to the traditional native-speaker norm in the assessment. At the same time, the rest of the raters under investigation tended to attach more importance to intelligibility in assessing pronunciation.

Finally, like Meiron's (1998, as cited in Brown et al., 2005, p. 7) and Brown's (2000), research on pronunciation assessment also found that raters might use self-generated features not mentioned or not explicitly mentioned in the relevant scoring rubric. For example, raters reported the difficulty in isolating pronunciation from fluency constructs (e.g., Brown & Taylor, 2006; Yates et al., 2008), the influence of lexico-grammatical aspects (Isaacs & Trofimovich, 2012), and even communicative skills (Chen & Li, 2017) in assessing pronunciation.

Previous research on rater cognition indicates that raters need to be guided by a more detailed pronunciation scale with descriptions of various phonological features at different levels, raising such questions as what features raters consider crucial in assessing pronunciation.

2.2.2.2 Rating Scales

As discussed in Section 1.1, pronunciation is theoretically marginalized in the communicative framework for L2 speaking assessment; therefore, the existing rating scales[①] for L2 pronunciation present noticeable shortcomings (Isaacs, 2014). The most distinctive weakness is the vague or general descriptors in the rating criteria, which failed to provide sufficient guide for raters in the rating process.

For instance, in the nine-level IELTS Pronunciation subscale (IELTS, 2018), levels four, six, eight, and nine use such descriptors as "limited range," "range," "wide range," and "full range of pronunciation features," respectively. There is no specification on what phonological features that constitute level distinctions and how they associate with intelligibility (Isaacs et al., 2018). Take TOEFL iBT integrated speaking rubrics (Educational Testing Service, 2014) for another

---

① The rating scales reviewed in this section include the Phonological scale in Common European Framework of Reference for Languages (CEFR), which is not simply a rating scale, but a reference for language learning, teaching and assessment.

example. In the five-level "Delivery" subscale, relativistic descriptors are used for the focal construct "intelligibility": "considerable listener effort" (level one), "problems with intelligibility" (level two), "overall intelligibility" as "good" (level three), or "high" (level four). Although such descriptors are used with specific linguistic features like "pacing," "pronunciation" (referring only to segmental production), and "intonation," there is no indication of the extent to which these features relate to intelligibility at different levels (Isaacs et al., 2018). In Harding's (2017, p. 29) usability study of the CEFR Phonological scale (Council of Europe, 2001), raters reported that the descriptors were "short and lacking in detail," with ambiguous terms such as "natural" (level B2).

With regard to the English pronunciation rating scales used in China, CET-SET and TEM Oral Test included, almost all adopt a holistic scale and over-concise descriptors (Gao, 2007), focusing only on segment accuracy and intonation, and using relativistic descriptors such as "not accurate/natural", "generally accurate/natural" and "accurate/natural" (Syllabus for TEM 4-Oral, 2014).

The recent flourish of pronunciation research has led to some profound revisions of old scales and the construction of new scales. In the new versions of the Cambridge ESOL common scale for speaking (Cambridge English, 2016) and TEM-4 Oral Test Pronunciation subscale (TEM-4 Oral, 2014), nativeness has been abandoned as a criterion. Intelligibility is emphasized as a core construct in the former two scales, though the question of "intelligible to whom" remain unsolved.

Moreover, in the revision process report of the CEFR

Phonological scale, Piccardo (2016) proposed three scales, including one general phonology scale and two analytic scales, sound articulation, and prosody (intonation, stress, and rhythm). This was the first time, to the knowledge of the researcher, that analytic scales had been developed for pronunciation learning, teaching, and assessment.

What should also be noted is a data-driven method in the construction of a three-level L2 English "Comprehensibility scale guidelines" (Isaacs & Trofimovich, 2012). In this study, they identified the linguistic features that correlated with the comprehensibility ratings of L2 picture-narrative speech. Altogether 19 auditory and acoustic measures of pronunciation, fluency, lexicogrammar, and discourse were analyzed. Then the statistical analysis was converged with raters' introspective reports on the variables affecting their judgments. From both quantitative and qualitative analysis, a set of linguistic features were found to best distinguish between three levels of comprehensibility. Based on this preliminary scale, Isaacs et al. (2018) further constructed a more sophisticated six-level comprehensibility scale for formative assessment purposes, which consisted of four subscales, with pronunciation and fluency as primary, and vocabulary and grammar as optional. Of course, their scale was designed for international university students from mixed L1 backgrounds, and comprehensibility seems to be a larger concept that includes more than pronunciation, so it might not be applicable to other assessment contexts. However, this scale development approach brings insights for future work, particularly in respect of pinpointing the criterial features in the L2 speech.

2.2.2.3 Task

Task effect is evident in multiple aspects of L2 speech, from pronunciation to grammar and lexicon. Over the years, many theoretical models have been proposed to explain how various aspects of task contribute to L2 speech production, such as Capability Continuum Model (Tarone, 1983), Trade-off Hypothesis (Skehan, 1998), and Cognition Hypothesis (Robinson, 2001).

Tarone's model emphasized task formality, suggesting that L2 speech may vary between a pidgin-like vernacular and a careful target-like style in tasks of different degrees of formality. Both Skehan (1998) and Robinson (2001) focused on the cognitive complexity of the tasks. While Skehan proposed a tradeoff between linguistic complexity and accuracy since cognitively complex tasks cause higher processing demands, Robinson (2001) argued that speakers tended to produce more elaborate language in the more complex task in order to meet the expectations. Their studies show that different tasks affect multiple aspects of L2 production, from pronunciation (Tarone, 1983) to grammar and lexicon (Robinson, 2001; Skehan, 1998).

In L2 pronunciation research, Saito and Plonsky (2019) reviewed two major types of tasks that varied in their cognitive demands, the controlled tasks such as read-aloud tasks and spontaneous tasks such as picture narratives and oral interviews. In the former task type, L2 learners focus primarily on pronunciation, while in the latter task format, their pronunciation is tested when they use the language mainly for meaning. Similar to Skehan's (1998) view, Saito and Plonsky

(2019) suggested that L2 pronunciation forms are likely to be more target-like when elicited from controlled tasks than from spontaneous tasks because of the lack of planning time, the increased cognitive demands and linguistic processing in the latter. According to Spada and Tomita (2010), controlled speech tasks are better suited to measure more explicit and conscious knowledge of L2 pronunciation forms; in contrast, spontaneous speech tasks can elicit more unconscious and unmonitored use of L2 pronunciation in communication.

Perhaps for this reason, guided by Bachman's communicative language ability framework (1990), the bulk of recent pronunciation research on the relationship between linguistic correlates and the evaluation of L2 pronunciation in terms of accentedness and comprehensibility has adopted the spontaneous task in the research design, almost unanimously the picture-narrative task (Bergeron & Trofimovich, 2017), in which L2 speakers describe a sequence of ordered images.These studies resulted in a similar finding that a wide range of phonological measures correlated with accentedness and comprehensibility were overlapping; while accentedness may only be associated with phonology, comprehensibility involves more linguistic dimensions such as grammar and lexis (Isaacs & Trofimovich, 2012; Saito et al., 2015; Saito, Trofimovich, & Isaacs, 2016; Trofimovich & Isaacs, 2012). Although Crowther et al. (2018) researched the task type effect on the linguistic measures that differentiate comprehensibility from accentedness, the three tasks they applied were all spontaneous tasks, namely a picture narrative task, an IELTS long-turn task (an individual speech on an assigned topic), and a TOEFL iBT integrated task (an oral response to both listening and reading stimuli). Their findings seemed to suggest that the distinction between the two constructs was task specific; the more demanding the spontaneous tasks were, the more interrelated the two constructs were. Considering that the distinction between the two constructs only lies in the lexicogrammar dimension, there is a reason to believe that the constructs do not considerably distinguish from each other in controlled tasks such as reading-aloud when the vocabulary and grammatical structures are constrained.

When it comes to the specific dimensions of pronunciation, the distinctive effect of these two different task types is not supported by sufficient empirical evidence. Up to now, very limited empirical research has targeted the area, and the findings are not congruent. In terms of segmental accuracy, Rau, Change and Tarone's (2009) study seems to provide empirical support for the task effect. They found that L2 segments produced by Chinese speakers of English, such as /θ/, were more accurate when elicited from reading-aloud tasks than spontaneous tasks such as storytelling and interviews. However, Saito and Brajot (2013) reported that such task effect only took place on more experienced Japanese learners when they produced /r/, while not on inexperienced Japanese learners.

With regard to fluency, L2 speakers were perceived more fluent in monologue- or dialogue-based tasks than in a picture narrative (Derwing et al., 2004; Ejzenberg, 2000), because picture narratives are more cognitive demanding, requiring a search for vocabulary that learners might be unfamiliar with (Hilton, 2008). However, no difference was found in terms of speaking rate for Chinese speakers of English in a reading-aloud task and in a spontaneous picture narrative (Munro & Derwing,

1994). When it comes to the perception of accentedness, Munro and Derwing (1994) also found that the controlled reading-aloud task and the spontaneous picture description task did not present any difference. Therefore, they suggested that reading-aloud tasks can be valid as a means of assessing pronunciation when the speakers are familiar with the vocabulary and grammatical structures in the reading material.

In China, English pronunciation has been assessed in both controlled and spontaneous tasks. Spontaneous tasks are more often used for college students, since college English education is largely academic and communication oriented. For example, in TEM-4 Oral test, pronunciation is evaluated in spontaneous tasks such as note-taking and retelling, conversation, and improvised individual presentation. Conversely, controlled tasks take a dominant position in pronunciation assessment before college, and continue to play an important role in the assessment for college students. The reading-aloud task in particular has been used in various EFL formative assessments from primary schools to colleges, and in high-stakes provincial and national tests as well, such as high-school admission tests, college entrance exams, and nationwide CET-SET. This is not only because the reading-aloud task has a long history in language teaching and assessment (Cole, Dunston, & Butler, 2017), but also because most pronunciation assessment before college aims at examining the effect of pronunciation instruction, which to a large extent conforms to a Standard English norm, namely the Received Pronunciation or the general American accent. According to Chen and Li (2017), the reading-aloud task was accepted as an effective task for pronunciation assessment by half of the investigated Chinese college EFL teachers who were also raters for TEM Oral tests and CET-SET, ranking second after the task of situational conversation (60%).

The advantage of using reading-aloud material in pronunciation assessment is obvious. It controls the variation in vocabulary and grammatical structure, so as to ensure that the read speech samples cover the segmental and prosodic features of interest (Chen & Li, 2017; Munro & Derwing, 1994). Besides, it is confirmed by research as an effective task type in measuring the effect of pronunciation instruction (Saito & Plonsky, 2019) and provide diagnostic information for L2 learners (Gao, Zhu, & Yang, 2006). However, it needs to be noted that the holistic pronunciation rating in the reading-aloud task might be different from that in the spontaneous task. When the reading-aloud task takes the form of imitation (as in the National Matriculation English Test, Guangdong version, Xu & Zeng, 2017), and when the meaning of the read material is presented repeatedly and becomes transparent, the listeners' attention might turn to form to a greater extent (Munro & Derwing, 1994). This means in assessing pronunciation elicited from the reading-aloud task, intelligibility (in the broad sense) is less likely the sole or a sufficient criterion. With the wide application of the reading-aloud task in the pronunciation assessment in China, it is worthwhile to investigate the relationship between the criterial features and the pronunciation ratings for the L2 read speech.

2.2.2.4 Test takers

Fulcher (2003) proposed such test-taker variables as personability, capacities on the rating constructs, real-time processing ability, and the task-specific knowledge or skills. However, research on test taker variability in pronunciation assessment has mainly centered around the L1 background of the test takers.

Cross-linguistic variability seems evident and may cause difficulty in rating scale development (Isaacs et al., 2018). This is because speakers from different L1s tend to be different in their perception and production of segments (Munro & Derwing, 2006) and prosody (Li & Post, 2014), making it difficult to generate diagnostically oriented pronunciation descriptors that differentiate between different levels and applicable to different L1 groups. For example, Crowther, Trofimovich, Saito, and Isaacs (2015) found that segmental errors impeded the comprehensibility of the English speech produced by L1 Chinese speakers, whereas it was not the case for L1 Hindi-Urdu speakers. Therefore, compared with constructing a pronunciation scale that is universally applicable, it was suggested that a start with speakers of a single L1 background might be more practical (Isaacs et al., 2018).

In the current study, all the speech samples were produced by Chinese EFL learners. The phonology of Mandarin is different from that of English in many ways (Chen, 1999; Hua & Dodd, 2000). Mandarin has a narrower segment inventory than English, including 6 monophthongal vowels[①], 9 diphthongs, and 23 consonants. English, in contrast, has 12 monophthongs, 8 diphthongs, and 24 consonants. The

---

① The six standard Mandarin vowels are /i, ə, y, u, o, ɑ/; there might be more variations in the vowel production in conversations according to Flege, Bohn and Jang (1997).

descriptions of the vowel systems also differ in that the vocal tract vowel space for English is quadrilateral, with /i/ (high-front), /æ/ (low-front), /u/ (high-back) and /ɑ/ (low-back) at each corner (Chen, Robb, Gilbert, & Lerman, 2001b), while that for Mandarin is triangular with three corner vowels /i/, /u/ and /ɑ/ (Wu, 1964). With regard to prosody, the syllable structure of Mandarin is more restricted than English, with primarily a CV structure. Mandarin allows no clusters in initial or final position, whereas English allows both, and the final-position cluster could include as many as four segments (Cao, 2010). Besides, Mandarin is a tone language, with the tone choice altering the lexical identity of the word, while English is an intonational language, with the tone choice conveying only non-lexical meaning (Wells, 2006). The rhythmic structures of Mandarin and English are also different, representing syllable-timed and stress-timed languages, respectively (Dauer, 1983).

Considering the great effect of L1 interference on language learning, these differences in the phonological systems are likely to cause various production and perception difficulties for Chinese EFL learners, as interpreted by either the traditional contrastive analysis (Nilsen & Nilsen, 1973)[①] or Flege's (1995)

[①] Contrastive Analysis (Nilsen & Nilsen, 1973; Swan & Smith, 2001) is an approach to compare the sounds already found in a speakers' first language and the sounds would be acquired in the target language. The view is that if a sound is shared by or similar in both languages, it would be relatively easy to acquire; however, if the L2 sound does not exist or is produced differently in the L1, difficulties are predicted.

Speech Learning Model (SLM)[①]. These difficulties will be discussed in detail later in this chapter. However, one thing uncertain is to what extent these pronunciation problems identified in Chinese EFL learners' spoken English influence the raters' judgments on their pronunciation quality.

2.2.3 Automated scoring

The reliability of the subjective scoring has been a core concern in L2 spoken assessment (Chen, Wu, & Li, 2019; Luoma, 2004), and certainly in pronunciation assessment as well. Previous research has shown the effect of rater variability which often leads to differences in consistency and severity (See 2.2.3.1). The development of automated speech recognition (ASR) technology has made it possible for machine scoring to be an alternative rater in speaking and pronunciation assessment. (Bernstein, 1999; Cucchiarini, Strik, & Boves, 2000; Neumeyer, Franco, Digalakis, & Weintraub, 2000; Li et al., 2008; Chen et al., 2019). A number of automated scoring systems have been developed and employed in large-scale, high-stakes spoken tests, such as the Pearon's Versant™ tests (previously Phonepass), the SpeechRater™ system for the

---

① SLM generally posits that the L1 and L2 phonetic subsystems co-exist in a bilingual's phonological space, and interact with each other. Phonetic category assimilation occurs when L2 learners fail to establish a new phonetic category of an L2 sound so as to produce a nonnative-like L2 sound, either because the L2 sound is "too similar to an L1 sound" or because it is "perceptually subsumed by a fully-developed L1 category"; phonetic category dissimilation occurs when L2 learners can set up a new phonetic category for an L2 sound, probably because the L2 sound is distinctive enough to perceive (Flege, 2007, pp. 366 – 367).

TOEFL iBT, and the iFLYTEK automated scoring system in China.

The advantage of using automated scoring is evident. Beyond efficiency, automated scoring can average out rater variations, since the system is usually trained on pooled ratings across a large cross-section of human raters, thus helping increase test validity.

However, machine scoring is far from perfection. The text-dependent scoring is much more reliable than the text-independent scoring in terms of the correlation between machine scores and human ratings. The correlations of machine scores in various systems with human ratings vary from 0.7 to 0.829 (Franco, Neumeyer, Digalakis, & Ronen, 2000; Jiang, 2011; Li & Yan, 2012; Sangwan & Hansen, 2012). Generally, the pronunciation score given by the machine is based on how closely the test-taker is able to approximate the articulation of native speakers or highly proficient nonnative speakers according to a statistical model (Bernstein, 1999; Bernstein, Van Moere, & Cheng, 2010). This means that the features analyzed in the automated scoring system are often drawn from the deviations of a learner's speech from the properties of a reference set of speech, which is mostly made up of native-speaker speech. This approach not only raises the issue of nativeness norm in the assessment, but also lowers the discriminative power between different proficiency levels. To make a difference, Chen et al. (2019) reported increased discrimination by introducing the learners' interlanguage speech into the reference set in the iFLYTEK automated scoring system, which seems to suggest that a combination of native-speaker norms and nonnative-speaker norms might be a better choice in calibrating the machine scores.

Besides, the current ASR relies on segmental (spectral) and fluency (durational) measures more than other phonological features (Chen et al., 2019; Cincarek, Gruhn, Hacker, Nöth, & Nakamura, 2009; Pearson, 2011; Li & Yan, 2012). This means that the machine can evaluate the segmental and fluency aspects well. For example, when rating fluency, the correlation between a machine score and a human rating can be as high as 0.92 (Cucchiarini, Strik, & Boves, 2002). However, pronunciation proficiency covers prosodic aspects as well, such as intonation, stress and rhythm, and research has demonstrated the important role the prosodic features play in determining oral proficiency levels (Anderson-Hsieh et al., 1992; Kang, 2012; Kang, Rubin, & Pickering, 2010). Chen et al. (2019) reported the cooperation between pronunciation researchers and automated scoring program developers in training the machine to do analytic scoring for different pronunciation aspects. More research into the specific features that discriminate among pronunciation proficiency levels would bring more insights for the future development of automated scoring systems.

2.3 Criterial features in L2 pronunciation assessment

Although there has been a growing body of research on phonological features over the past decade, still not enough is known about how these features influence raters' perceptions of L2 pronunciation proficiency. This section first describes the mixed-method approach used to identify and validate the criterial features in assessing pronunciation. Then it reviews the phonological categories and features in the pronunciation theories, rating scales, and related empirical studies. At last, a summary of the phonological features to be analyzed in this study is presented, and the relative contribution of these features to the pronunciation ratings is reviewed.

2.3.1 The Mixed-method approach to identify criterial features

The identification of criterial features is closely related to the empirical construction and validation of rating scales in L2 speaking assessment; therefore, the scale construction methods can serve to guide the methodology in the identification of criterial features in pronunciation assessment.

Generally, the scale design methods fall into two main categories, intuitive and empirical approaches (Fulcher, 2003). The intuitive approach involves the judgment of an expert or a committee of experts, or may be an experiential one which often starts with expert judgment and evolves to adapt to a new context over time by experts. The Foreign Service Institute (FSI) rating scales were developed in this way (Fulcher, 2003). However, the intuitive-based approach has been criticized for the lack of a theoretical basis and of empirical data on the features of learner performance (Fulcher, 1996; Knoch, 2017). Researchers have been questioning the reliance on pooling descriptors at different levels from the perspective of second language acquisition, as well as the use of relativistic wording such as "some," "fairly frequent," and "very frequent" to differentiate between levels instead of providing detailed descriptions of salient features for different levels (Galaczi,

Ffrench, Hubbard, & Green, 2011). The empirically-based method, however, is usually believed to avoid subjectivity in the intuitive method, and has gained much recognition in the past two decades. It is data-driven, based on observable learner performance, in this case, the learner speech.

Literature seems to recognize the best method for rating scale development as a combination of intuition-based and empirically-based approaches, because expert intuition and expertise can be valuable too. Therefore, more and more rating scales have been developed through this complementary, multi-method process, such as the scales in the CEFR (2001, 2007), the Cambridge ESOL (Hawkey & Barker, 2004), the revised IELTS (Falvey & Shaw, 2006) and the revised Cambridge MS/BEC examination (Galaczi et al., 2011). Moreover, linguistic theories have also been incorporated into the scale construction process. When developing a diagnostic writing scale, Knoch (2007) combined several theories and writing models as the basis for the identification of the rating criteria.

The mixed methods have also been adopted to identify or validate criterial features used in rating L2 English speaking performance. In Brown et al.'s (2005) study, they applied two empirical methods to investigate the factors affecting TOEFL iBT raters' perception, namely a qualitative analysis of raters' verbal reports and a quantitative analysis of the relationship between raters' perception and candidates' performance in terms of the linguistic features drawn from the raters' report. By such combined methods of verbal reports and discourse analysis, they found six features (grammatical accuracy, grammatical complexity, vocabulary, pronunciation, fluency, and content) make significant differences across proficiency levels.

Similarly, Isaacs and Trofimovich (2012) applied the mixed-method approach to better the understanding of listeners' L2 comprehensibility ratings. They first analyzed 19 speech measures in the L2 English speech samples of 40 French learners, and correlated these measures with native English listeners' comprehensibility ratings. Then they collected three ESL teachers' introspective reports on the linguistic aspects of speech that affected their judgments. The combined analysis finally identified five speech measures that could distinguish between L2 learners at different levels of comprehensibility.

Following these studies, the present research applied such a mixed-method approach to identify and validate the criterial features in pronunciation assessment. As shown in Figure 2.2, phonological features were first identified in an intuition/theory-based approach; then they are validated in an empirically data-based approach by analyzing the relationship between these features and the holistic/analytic pronunciation ratings. The following three sections in this chapter describe the identification of the phonological features to be analyzed based on pronunciation theories, existing pronunciation scales and previous empirical studies, respectively. The pronunciation theories provided theoretical frameworks to identify the phonological categories, whose role in assessing pronunciation was then confirmed by an examination of the existing pronunciation rating scales. The confirmed categories helped guide the detection of phonological features in previous empirical studies. The validation of these features is to be introduced in detail in Chapter three.

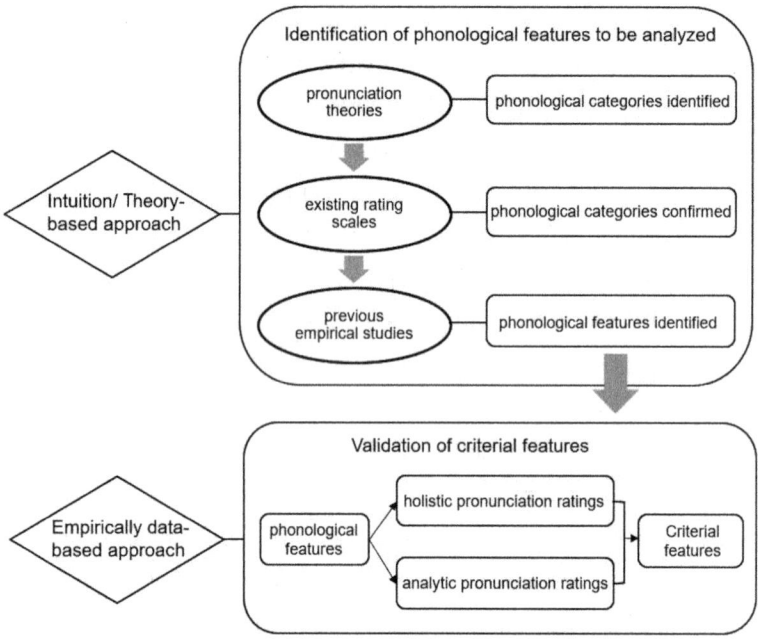

Figure 2. 2 The mixed-method approach in this study to identify criterial features in pronunciation assessment

2.3.2 Phonological categories derived from theories

Since there is an absence of a unified theoretical framework for L2 phonetics and phonology (Gut, 2009), a number of pronunciation theories related to different dimensions of pronunciation are applied in this study for the identification of phonological categories. As defined in Section 2.1, pronunciation encompasses both segmentals and suprasegmentals. Compared with the relatively clear categorization of segmentals into vowels and consonants, the suprasegmental aspects are more complex. Therefore, four theories are to be discussed to guide the categorization of the suprasegmental features, namely the

Three-Ts framework of intonation, the metrical theory of stress, the rhythmic typology and the framework of utterance fluency.

2.3.2.1 The Three-Ts framework of intonation

Halliday (1967) proposed the Three-Ts framework of intonation, which includes three distinct components: tonality, tonicity, and tone. Tonality refers to the intonation phrasing, i.e., the division of an utterance into intonation phrases (IP)[①] or information units, each with its own intonation pattern or tune. Tonicity is the placement of the tonic syllable (nucleus) or the most important accent[②] in the IP, indicating the focused part of the material, usually with a change in pitch. Tone is defined as the choice of pitch movement starting from where the nucleus is.

2.3.2.1.1 Tonality

As defined, tonality is the chunking of IP, which to a large extent, corresponds to the grammatical structure. The alignment of intonation structure and grammatical structure varies with the speech type, ranging from about 50% in spontaneous speech (Crystal, 1969), to 80% in monologues (Tench, 1996), to 95% in reading-alouds (Chen, 2006). This is mainly because whether the speaker breaks the utterance into separate IPs depends on not only grammatical structure, but also vocabulary, pronunciation, content planning, speaking

---

[①] Different authors use different names for the IP, including chunk, word group, tone group, tone unit, and intonation group.

[②] The term *accent* has been used by various authors to refer to different kinds of stress at the utterance level. Here it refers to the stressed syllable of the highlighted words in the IP.

rate, and cognition capacity. Therefore, the alignment ratio is high in the reading-aloud task, when vocabular, grammar, and content are controlled and the online processing load is low (Chen & Bi, 2015).

Wells (2006) describes some exceptions of where the intonation structure does not align with the grammatical structure. Those that do not usually form separate IPs, even though they stand apart from the basic clause structure and sometimes accompanied with punctuations, are summarized below.

(a) When vocatives are at the end of the sentence, they are usually attached to what precedes, forming part of the tail of the IP, because they are not the essential part of the sentence (p. 195);

(b) When the reporting phrase (such as *he said*, *she asked*) follow quoted words, there might be a rhythmic break in between, but the reporting phrase does not have its own nuclear tones since it is usually out of focus, hence not forming the IP of its own (p. 155).

(c) The defining relative clause does not have its own IP, as the non-defining one does. There is no intonation break before the defining relative clause in conversations because a break tends to make the meaning ambiguous[①] (p. 202).

(d) When the object clause follows a short introductory phrase such as *I think*, *I mean*, *I suppose*, *you know*, the so-

---

① Note the different between the defining relative clause "*He bought a camera which was strange*" and the non-defining relative clause "*He bought a camera, | which was strange*". The former clause means that the camera was strange, and the latter means his buying the camera was strange.

called main clause does not form its own IP, unless for example, the subject *I* is used for a contrastive or emphatic purpose (p. 191).

2.3.2.1.2　Tonicity

Tonicity is the most prominent accent (nucleus) in an IP. A syllable bearing the nucleus is often called a tonic syllable. The main function of the nucleus is to emphasize the information focus, in other words, to "express what the speaker decides to make the main point or burden of the message" (Halliday, 1970, p. 40).

According to Crystal and Davy's (1975, cited from Chen, 2006) theory of Tonicity's Conditions, unmarked tonicity normally falls on the stressed syllable of the last lexical item (content word) towards the end of an IP. However, the placement of the nucleus is also strongly influenced by the principles of information status and the contrastive focus (Wells, 2006), hence forming marked tonicity on the final functional item or non-final items. According to the information status principle, new information is to be accented, but old information is not. In other words, any repeated items or synonyms for the old information are not accented. Example (1) was given by Wells (2006, p. 111):

(1) *Shall we wash the clothes? Oh, I HATE doing the laundry.*

Though *laundry* is the last stressed content word in the IP, *doing the laundry* shares the same meaning as *wash the clothes*, hence the given information. The nucleus then falls on the new information *hate*.

The contrastive focus principle is associated with any contrast the speaker makes. In this sense, any word can be accented, including a function word. Here's an example (2) given by Chen and Bi (2015, p. 44):

(2) *No, no. Don't put them UNDER the table. Put them ON the table.*

What the speaker emphasizes and contrasts here is the location whether under or on the table; therefore, the nuclei fall on the prepositions. Example (3) is taken from the reading material of the present study.

(*Tell me a story about the clever monkey, mummy.*)
(3) ..., *there's a FOOLish monkey.*

The nucleus falls on *foolish* rather than the final content word *monkey* because it represents the contrast with the word *clever* in the previous sentence.

2.3.2.1.3 Tone

Tone refers to pitch movement, and is associated with a wide range of meanings (Tench, 1996). In the traditional British school, tone has been defined as the nuclear tone, which is the pitch movement starting from the nuclear stressed syllable (tonic syllable). The primary tones of English include the fall, the rise and the fall-rise, featuring grammatical or communicative functions. Secondary tones are high and low varieties of the falling and rising tones, expressing attitudes.

O'Connor and Arnold (1973) proposed seven nuclear tones according to the pitch level of the nucleus as compared to the head, namely High Fall, Low Fall, Rise Fall, High Rise, Low Rise, Fall Rise, and Level.

This study intends to examine the inappropriate choices of tones in learners' speech, hence focusing on the primary tones rather than secondary tones, because speakers' attitudes vary and it is not always easy to judge the right attitude from the wrong. Besides, this study focuses on identifying features that could distinguish learners across different pronunciation rating levels, and secondary tones were found to be deviated from the native production even for high-proficiency Chinese EFL learners (Chen, 2008a).

There are mainly two functions of primary tones[①], serving both communicative and discoursal purposes (Tench, 1996). With regard to the communicative function, a fall indicates knowing, authority and confidence; on the other hand, a rise suggests not knowing, uncertainty and doubt. EFL learners are commonly taught that a falling tone should be applied to declarative structures such as statements, exclamations and commands, while a rising tone to yes/no questions.

However, these are only the unmarked or default tones for different sentence types; it could be much more complex in the application of tone in the speech. More specifically, a rising tone can appear in declarative structures to signal concessions, contradictions and challenges (Tench, 1996; Wells, 2006). For

---

[①] To mark the tone choices, \ is used before the nucleus to signify a fall, / a rise, and V a fall-rise. Besides, | is used to mark the boundary of an IP, and syllables in caption are the nuclei.

example (4), the speaker implies a contrast or disagreement by a rise on *sorry*.

> (A: *I don't think Mary likes swimming.*)
> (4) B: *I'm /SORRy. | Mary DOES like swimming.*

As rises might be used in statements, falls can accompany polar interrogatives, i.e., yes/no questions. When speakers use a question not for inquiry, but rather to give opinions and encourage an agreement from the listener, they often use a falling tone. Therefore, tag questions serving for the purpose of inquiry are accompanied with a rise, and for a conducive agreement with a fall.

As to the discoursal function, falling tones are often associated with finality and closeness, and non-falling tones with incompleteness and openness. If there is a leading dependent element preceding the main clause (5), a non-falling tone, very often, a fall-rise tone is used on the leading element to indicate that there is more information to come, or in other words, non-finality (Wells, 2006).

> (5) *Once upon a \/ TIME, | ...*

This is particularly distinctive between the closed fall and the open non-fall in the listing structure, either in the form of a statement or an alternative question. The following are examples (6, 7) for both types.

> (6) *I want a pound of /MEAT, | a box of / CHOcolates, | and a loaf of \BREAD.*

(7) *Do you want to go to the cinema /toNIGHT,* | *or have you got to stay late at \WORK again?*

2.3.2.2 The metrical theory of stress

According to Liberman & Prince's (1977) metrical theory of stress, the perceived rhythm of an utterance depends on the combination of relative prominence of strong (s) and weak (w) syllables and the metrical grid assignment. As presented in their example, the phrase [[[law degree] requirement] changes], there is a rhythmic hierarchy with different metrical levels of prominence. The grid (Figure 2.3) shows that *law* is metrically the strongest syllable in the phrase, that *-gree*, *-quire*, *chang-* are metrically intermediate, and that *de-*, *re-*, *-ment*, *-es* are of weak metrical strength. One of the core ideas of this model is that there are different degrees of stress in an utterance rather than only one type in Bolinger's theory of pitch accent (1958)[1].

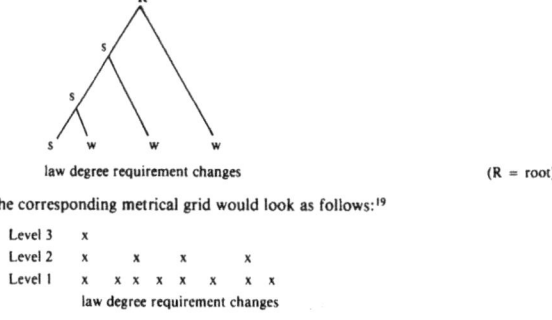

Figure 2.3 An example of the rhythmic hierarchy and metrical grid (Liberman & Prince, 1977, p. 324)

---

[1] Bolinger (1958) referred the utterance-level prominence as accent, signified by pitch prominence.

The metrical representation of stress describes three characteristics of stress (Hayes, 1995). First, stress is rhythmically distributed. Syllables are perceived stressed when they coincide with a rhythmic beat, and a relatively equal timing of stresses can be seen at the utterance level. Second, stress is hierarchical, with multiple degrees of stresses. In English, there are at least three levels of stress, primary stress, secondary stress, and no stress. Third, stress is "culminative." In other words, there might be different levels of prominence at the foot level or at the IP level, but there is only one strongest stressed syllable (tonic syllable), or nucleus, within each domain.

2.3.2.3 The rhythmic typology

Speech rhythm, commonly regarded as the temporal organization of language, refers to the phonological representation of isochrony or "the regular recurrence of some form of speech unit" (Low, 2006, p. 99). Based on the concept of the recurred regular intervals, languages were categorized as stressed-timed and syllable-timed (Abercrombie, 1967; Pike, 1945). A stress-timed language features a relatively equal interval between stresses. It is the feet comprising a stressed syllable up to the next stressed syllable that should be of more or less the same length. The stressed syllables are usually longer and more prominent, while the unstressed syllables between the two consecutive stressed syllables tend to be compressed or reduced. In contrast, in a syllable-time language, it is the syllables that recur at equal intervals, with no distinction between full and reduced vowels. However, this dichotomous categorization has rarely been supported by empirical studies which failed to find perfect isochrony in speech production. A continuum of rhythmic typology was then proposed by Dauer (1983) and Miller (1984), along which languages fall at a point between the stress-based end and the syllable-based end.

English is commonly considered to be an archetypal stress-timed language. According to Dauer (1983), the phonological properties of stress-based languages feature a complex syllable structure and a strong distinction between full and reduced vowels. This difference is often represented in the duration between stressed and unstressed syllables, "with stressed syllables significantly longer than unstressed ones and most vowels in unstressed syllables reducing to a schwa" (Bolinger, 1965, as cited in Trofimovich & Baker, 2006, p. 11). The complex syllable structure mainly refers to the presence of more consonantal clusters in the onset and coda positions.

As illustrated below (8), the utterance includes three feet, starting with a change of breath or an accented syllable (signified in capital letters), and containing a different number of syllables in each: three in the first, five in the second, and two in the third. However, the English rhythm would require the length of the feet to be more or less the same. The duration of the foot does not increase with the rise in the number of syllables in the foot. Instead, the durations of syllables are stretched or compressed according to the number of syllables within the foot.

(8) ^*The HANDsome* | *BOY who is on his* | *BIcycle.* ||
(Note: The symbol ^ marks the change of breath, | the foot boundary, and || the boundary of a tone group.)

To reach foot isochrony, and at the same time to maintain a larger proportion in duration for the stressed syllable, the foot with more syllables must be spoken faster than that with fewer syllables. In other words, the more unstressed syllables are in an interval, the more compressed they are in duration. In Example (8), consonants and vowels in the unstressed syllables of the second foot would be reduced, linked or omitted if spoken in an English rhythm.

Of course, perfect isochrony does not exist. There is only a tendency towards isochronous stresses in English speech, which leads to phonetic and phonological properties such as vowel reduction and a wide variation in syllable length.

2.3.2.4 The framework of utterance fluency

Utterance fluency was one of the three facets of narrowly defined fluency[①] (Segalowitz, 2010). It is the objective aspect, and can be measured by a number of temporal or non-temporal features of the speaker production. Skehan (2003, 2009) proposed an analytic framework for utterance fluency, which includes the following three aspects, breakdown fluency, speed fluency, and repair fluency.

(a) Breakdown fluency concerns the interruption of the continuous speech signals, indexed by pausing phenomena.

(b) Speed fluency is characterized as the rate of the speech delivery, often measured by syllables per minute.

[①] The other two facets of narrowly defined fluency are perceived fluency and cognitive fluency. Perceived fluency is the subjective judgement of listeners, usually in the form of human or machine rating; and cognitive fluency was defined as "the efficiency of operation of the underlying processes responsible for the production of utterance" (Segalowitz, 2010, p. 165).

(c) Repair fluency is related to the disfluencies such as repetition, false starts and self-correction in the speech.

This division approach is particularly helpful for this study, for it creates three theoretically unrelated clusters of features, helping to avoid the problem of multicollinearity in the further analysis (De Jong, 2018). The low inter-collinearity across the three measure clusters have been empirically supported by Bosker, Pinget, Quene, Sanders and De Jong (2013) and De Jong, Groenhout, Schoonen and Hulstijn (2015).

Some higher order indices such as mean-length-of-run and phonation time ratio have been proved to be good indicators of perceived fluency (e. g., Derwing et al., 2004; Kormos & Denes, 2004; Towell, Hawkins, & Bazergui, 1996), but they are not included in this framework, because they incorporate speed and pausing at the same time, and might cause serious problems in the regression analysis which led to an insignificant correlation between perceived fluency and pausing measures (De Jong, 2018).

2.3.2.5 Summary

The above-discussed theories shed light on the analysis of four suprasegmental aspects, intonation, stress, rhythm, and fluency. A list of categories can be drawn to guide the identification of more specific phonological features (Table 2.1). One thing that should be noted is that there is an overlapping of Halliday's (1967) Three-Ts framework and Liberman & Prince's (1977) metrical theory in terms of the nucleus. In this study, the nuclear features are to be analyzed only in the stress dimension.

Table 2.1 The categories of suprasegmental features derived from pronunciation theories

Category	Subcategory	Theories
Intonation	Tonality (intonation phrasing) —aligning/non-aligning with the grammatical structure	Halliday (1967)
	Tonicity (nucleus)	
	Tone —marked/ unmarked tone	
Stress	Sentence stress	Liberman & Prince's (1977)
	Nuclear stress	
Rhythm	Stress timing	Dauer (1983), Miller (1984)
Fluency	Breakdown	Skehan (2003, 2009)
	Speed	
	Repair	

2.3.3 Phonological categories derived from rating scales

To confirm the role of the theoretically-derived phonological categories in the pronunciation assessment, a number of phonological features are specified in the rating rubrics of seven scales in three high-stakes international English examinations and one framework of reference (Table 2.2). They are the Delivery scale in ISE (Trinity College London, 2015), the Delivery scale in TOEFL iBT (Educational Testing Service, 2014), the Pronunciation scale and Fluency-and-Coherence scale in IELTS (IELTS, 2018), the old and new Phonological scales in CEFR (Council of Europe, 2001; Piccardo, 2016) and the Spoken-Fluency scale in CEFR (Council of Europe, 2001).

Generally, the descriptors cover three categories of features:

Table 2.2 The categories of phonological features derived from rating scales and framework of reference

	ISE delivery (2015)	TOEFL delivery (2014)	IELTS pronunciation (2018)	IELTS fluency & coherence (2018)	CEFR phonological control (2001)	CEFR phonological control (2016)	CEFR spoken fluency (2001)
Sound/ phoneme	✓	✓	✓		✓	✓	
Prosody		✓				✓	
- Lexical stress	✓					✓	
- Sentence stress					✓	✓	
- Focal stress	✓						
- Intonation	✓	✓			✓	✓	
- Rhythm			✓				
Fluency	✓	✓		✓			✓
-Rate/pace	✓	✓					✓
-Pause/hesitation	✓	✓		✓			✓
-Repair				✓			✓

segmentals, prosody, and fluency. The prosody and fluency categories were further divided into subcategories, with stress, intonation and rhythm for the former, and rate, pausing and repairs for the latter. This generally suggests that the suprasegmental categories derived from theories (See Table 2.1) play a role in assessing pronunciation, hence reasonable to guide further identification of the phonological features.

It is worth noting that in the prosody aspect, the rating rubrics include more detailed descriptors with regards to stress than intonation or rhythm, covering three types of stress, lexical stress, sentence stress and focal stress (nuclear stress). This supplements the categories derived from the metrical theory of stress. In contrast, in the intonation aspect, the rating rubrics provide rather general descriptors, giving no hints for further classification in this respect. Therefore, the subcategories drawn from the theory serve to guide the identification of specific intonation features.

2.3.4 Phonological features derived from empirical studies

Guided by the categories reviewed previously in Section 2.3.2 and Section 2.3.3, this part describes the related empirical studies, with the purpose of identifying specific phonological features and their operationalizations that may represent pronunciation proficiency or if not, overall English proficiency.

2.3.4.1 Segmentals

English segmental features have been studied thoroughly, either acoustically by analyzing features such as vowel formants and space, vowel duration, VOT and stop closure duration (see Ghanem & Kang, 2018, for a review), or auditorily by identifying segmental errors such as segmental substitution, deletion and insertion at different positions in a word (e.g., Cheng & He, 2008; Munro & Derwing, 1995; Suenobu, Kanzaki, & Yamane, 1992; Zhou & Song, 2015). Since most literature relating segmental features to pronunciation constructs (particularly intelligibility) has targeted auditory features, this study focuses on the analysis of such features rather than the acoustic ones.

Previous studies seem to suggest that when segmental substitution, deletion, and insertion were grouped and calculated together as segmental errors, they had a rather weak relationship with pronunciation. Derwing and Munro (1997) examined such an overall segmental feature in L2 speakers' picture narratives, and correlated it with the intelligibility scores, comprehensibility and accentedness ratings by the native Canadian English listeners. They found that overall phonemic accuracy was significantly correlated with intelligibility for only 8% of the listeners, and with comprehensibility and accentedness for 15%. This finding indicated the inappropriateness of including phonemic substitution, deletion and insertion all in one feature, since not every kind of segment deletion would be errors, and not segment substitution at any word position would impair listeners' perception. A careful division of segmental features might be needed in the correlation analysis.

2.3.4.1.1 Phoneme substitution

Phoneme substitution in L2 speech is common, and often

attributed to the learners' difficulties in segment acquisition. For Mandarin speakers of English, they tended to produce more consonant errors than vowel errors, more coda-position errors than onset-position errors (Cheng & He, 2008; Zhou & Song, 2015) in either read or spontaneous speech. The coda-position errors were found to increase with the length of coda-position consonant clusters (Cao, 2010; Hansen, 2001). Also, researchers have specified a list of vowel and consonant difficulties for Chinese speakers of English. Table 2.3 presents such a list adapted from Zielinski's (2006, pp. 42-44) summary of the findings by a number of studies (Chang, 2001; Deterding, 2006; Flege et al., 1997; Munro, Derwing, & Thomson, 2015; Rogers, 1997; Rogers & Dalby, 2005).

From this pool of segmental difficulties, it is hard to draw a conclusion of specific types of vowels or consonants that feature Chinese EFL learners' segmental problems on the whole, for example, as discrete as the substitution of the Japanese flap /ɾ/ for English liquids /ɹ/ and /l/ (Riney et al., 2000). It seems that individual variability is considerable in terms of segmental acquisition, which has also been empirically supported by Munro and Derwing (2008) for vowel acquisition and Munro et al. (2015) for consonant acquisition. They found that the errors or the improvements were uniform in neither study. More importantly, how these difficulties might influence the raters' judgments of the speakers' pronunciation remains unclear.

Table 2.3 The segmental difficulties for Mandarin speakers of English

Vowels	/e/ and /æ/ /iː/ and /ɪ/ /uː/ and /ʊ/ /ʌ/ and /ɒ/ /ɑ/ and /aʊ/ English diphthongs produced "with not enough distinction between the two component vowels" (Chang, 2001, p. 311)
Consonants	/θ/ and /ð/ (/s/ produced in place of /θ/ and /z/ or /d/ in place of /ð/) /v/ (produced as /w/) /ʒ/ (produced as a retroflex approximant or /r/) /h/ (produced as a palatal fricative) /dʒ/, /tʃ/, and /ʃ/ /z/ (produced as /d/, /ð/, or /s/ in word-final position) /n/ and /ŋ/ (in word-final position) /b/, /d/, and /g/ (produced as /p/, /t/, and /k/ in word-final position) /st/ (in word-initial position); /ld/, /nd/ (in word-final position)

Note: Adapted from Zielinski (2006), pp. 42 – 44

Studies investigating the relationship between segmental features and holistic pronunciation ratings are rare (Anderson-Hsieh et al., 1992). In Anderson-Hsieh et al.'s (1992), they investigated the SPEAK Test raters' judgments of nonnative pronunciation and three phonological features, segmental errors, goodness of prosody and syllable structure (deletion or insertion of segments). They found prosody had the strongest effect in predicting the pronunciation rating, though all three features were significantly correlated with the rating. However, their study did not separate vowels from consonants, or specify specific segmental features.

Quite a few other studies examined the relationship

between specific segmental features and pronunciation in terms of intelligibility and accentedness, and have generally found a certain degree of relationship between them. Three studies (Bent, Bradlow, & Smith, 2007; Rogers & Dalby, 2005; Zielinski, 2006) are to be reviewed in detail because they offered useful information for the division of segmental features which provides insights for the speech analysis in this study.

Rogers & Dalby (2005) investigated the relationship between segments and intelligibility by relating the utterance intelligibility scores (based on the mean percentage of content words correctly transcribed by the native American listeners) of L2 learners' sentence reading-aloud with the intelligibility scores for a list of single words sensitive to different phonemic contrasts. This means that each word in the list bears a segment in a minimal pair. When the listeners heard the word spoken by the learner, they had to choose between two choices which was the one they heard, the target word or the foil word. The phonemic contrasts for consonants included voicing, place, manner, and number of segmental in the cluster; the phonemic contrasts for vowels are tenseness, height and diphthong.

They found that consonant scores did not significantly correlate with the utterance intelligibility, while vowel scores did, with those representing vowel tenseness contrast (e.g., /i/-/ɪ/) having the strongest correlation with utterance intelligibility. The minimal vowel tenseness pair /i/-/ɪ/ was found to be particularly problematic for Mandarin speakers of English in Munro and Derwing's (2008) study, with only 10% and 31% produced correctly. This difficulty seems to cause trouble for the listeners. Rogers & Dalby's (2005) study seems to suggest that vowel accuracy plays a more important role than consonants in intelligibility for Mandarin speakers of English, which provided counter-evidence to Jenkins' (2000) proposal of Lingua Franca Core which suggested the relative more importance of consonants.

Likewise, Bent et al. (2007) also focused on the relationship between segmental accuracy and intelligibility score (based on the number of key words correctly transcribed by native American listeners) in sentence reading-aloud, but they took a step further by investigating the impact of segmental errors at different word positions. They found that Mandarin speakers of English produced significantly more word-final consonant errors than word-initial consonant errors, but the word-initial consonant errors tended to be more detrimental to intelligibility than errors in word-final positions. They also found that intelligibility was significantly correlated with vowel accuracy, but not with overall consonant accuracy. The significant role of word-initial position was interpreted by Marslen-Wilson's (1989) activation-competition model of lexical access. According to this model, word-initial segments play a crucial role "in activating lexical items since segmental information is encoded sequentially and the encoding of initial segmentals activates possible completions" (p. 336). Therefore, an onset mistake will activate a wrong word in the listeners' perception, so as to incur a greater processing cost for the recovery of the intended lexical item than an error later in a word. This model seems to well justify Bent et al.'s (2007) findings and was supported by other studies as well. For example, in Suenobu et al.'s (1992), they found many inaccurately transcribed words in Japanese-accented English were caused by word-initial consonant errors, such as the substitution of /ɹ/ in the target word *runs* with /l/ leading to the inaccurate transcription of the word *lunch*.

The last study to be reviewed is Zielinski's (2006), which adopted a very different way to investigate the contribution of phonological features to intelligibility. He carried out several case studies involving three speakers from L1 Korean, L1 Chinese, and L1 Vietnamese and three native Australian listeners. The researcher observed and questioned the listeners about their difficulties when they transcribed the speakers' connected speech. The study focused on the relationship between phonological features and sites of reduced intelligibility, so as to connect the difficulties of the listener with specific non-standard phonological features in the speech.

The most important finding is that the listeners relied on an interaction between suprasegmental and segmental features to identify intended words, particularly the syllable stress pattern and the segments in the strong syllables within that pattern. The correct stress pattern did not guarantee intelligibility if the segments within the pattern was inaccurately produced; nor did the segmental accuracy necessarily guarantee intelligibility if the stress pattern was wrong. To put it another way, the listeners felt it difficult to understand the speech or failed to understand it correctly at sites where segments were produced inaccurately in the strong syllables. Furthermore, the vowel errors and syllable-initial consonant errors in the strong syllables were found to play a substantial role in reducing intelligibility. Zielinski's (2006) findings were consistent with Bent et al.'s (2007) and Rogers and Dalby's (2005) reports on the negative effect of vowel errors and word-initial consonant errors on intelligibility, and supported Bond and Small (1983) who also found the vowel errors in strong syllables impair intelligibility. According to Zielinski, the segments in strong syllables seemed to provide the listeners "with a trustworthy source of information to rely on" (p. 131). Vocabulary analyses also help to explain this phenomenon. It has been revealed that there is a highly significant tendency for stress in English words to fall on the initial syllable, especially high-frequency words (Cutler & Carter, 1987). From the listeners' perspective then, they tend to perceive the stressed syllable as the beginning of a new word.

2.3.4.1.2　Phoneme deletion and insertion

According to Cheng and He (2008), Chinese EFL learners tended to produce less segment deletion or insertion errors in either read or spontaneous speech, compared with segmental substitution. Besides, most segment deletion (89%) and insertion (78%) errors occurred at the word-final positions (Wu & Xiao, 2011).

Chen and He (2008) found that around 63% of the segment deletion errors were word-final plosives, such as /t/, /d/, and /k/, when they were followed by words starting with vowels. This kind of word-final plosive deletion is different from the cases of incomplete plosion of plosives, which were applied in intersyllabic consonant sequences when a stop was immediately followed by another stop, an affricate (Hieke & O'Connell, 1983), a nasal, a fricative or a liquid (Cruttenden, 2001) within or across morpheme boundaries. The incomplete plosion of plosives in connected speech has been acknowledged as elision, a kind of pronunciation skill (Cruttenden, 2001).

Other studies have also found that adding extraphonemes, most often /ə/, at the word-final positions was quite often for Mandarin speakers of English (Deterding, 2006; Hansen, 2001; Zielinski, 2006), probably due to the learners' difficulty in producing word-final consonants because Mandarin does not allow such a syllable structure. However, this might also be interpreted by proficiency levels. As Jenkins (2000) indicated, adding /ə/ to word-final consonants could be a feature of more proficient learners, and deleting the word-final consonants is a characteristic of less proficient learners.

2.3.4.1.3 Summary

Taken altogether, it can be assumed that vowels and onset-position consonants in the stressed syllables might play a more significant role in pronunciation evaluation, while the effect of segment addition or deletion, particularly of those at the word-final position, remains uncertain. The segmental features identified from previous literature are presented in Table 2.4.

Table 2.4 Segmental features identified in the literature

Category	Feature
Phoneme deletion	Phoneme deletion errors
	Incomplete plosion of plosives
Phoneme insertion	Overall phoneme insertion
	Vowel/ consonant insertion at the word-final position
Phoneme substitution	Overall phonemic substitution in stressed syllables
	Vowel/ consonant substitution in stressed syllables
	Consonant substitution at the onset/ coda position in stressed syllables

2.3.4.2 Prosody

L2 prosody has been empirically studied in terms of intonation, stress, and rhythm.

2.3.4.2.1 Intonation

Previous studies suggested that L2 learners differed from native speakers in all three aspects of Halliday's Three-Ts framework (1967), i.e., tonality, tone, and tonicity[①].

Tonality

Tonality refers to intonation phrasing. Chen (2008a) investigated the intonation patterns in the reading-aloud speech by Chinese EFL learners, and found that learners tended to produce more intonation phrases (IPs). This might be attributed to the negative L1 transfer, since the Chinese rhythm features the chunking of two-syllable feet (Wu & Zhu, 2001). Different from native speakers who could use various ways including pauses, lengthening and pitch reset to chunk IPs, Chinese EFL learners mainly separated IPs by pauses. For this reason, the present study does not include the number of IPs as an intonation feature since it might be highly correlated with the feature of pause frequency.

Chen (2008a) also found that when chunking intonation phrases (IPs), Chinese EFL learners tended to be greatly influenced by punctuations, and break the sentence into different IPs at syntactic boundaries. For example, the sentence-final adjunct (vocative or reporting clause), defining relative clause and simple object clause were often separated

---

① Studies related to tonicity in L2 learners' oral production are to be reviewed in Section 2.3.4.2.2.

from the main clause in Chinese learners' speech. This reflected a good command of English syntactic structures, but might cause confusion of information focus when the appropriate intonation phrasing does not align with grammatical boundaries (Chen & Bi, 2015). Besides, Chen (2008a) failed to find significant difference between the high- and low- level groups in their intonation phrasing patterns, suggesting less important role tonality plays, compared with tonicity and tone, in conveying information and affecting pronunciation ratings. It is, however, still in need of verification.

Tone

Tone refers to pitch movement, and is often measured by tone choice and pitch range. With regard to the tone choice, the use of rising tones seemed to pose great challenges for L2 learners. Wennerstrom (1994) found that Japanese, Thai and Chinese speakers were likely to use falling tones at boundaries between related constituents where rising or midlevel tones were expected. Similar preference for the use of falling tones were reported in other studies at positions where native English speakers would use non-falling tones to indicate respect, continuity and reservation, such as sentence-final vocative, non-final listing items (Chen & Bi, 2015) and places contradicting a previous speaker (Hewings, 1995). Pickering (2001, p. 250) also pointed out the ITAs' inability to use the rising tones to indicate shared context so as to reach "a state of informational and social convergence" with their students, which led to a communication failure between ITAs and their students.

There is only one study (Kang et al., 2010) linking L2 learners' tone choice to pronunciation rating, to the researcher's knowledge. In this study, 29 suprasegmental features were examined in relation to comprehensibility and oral proficiency, among which 9 tone choices were included (High/Mid/Low-Falling, High/Mid/Low-Rising and High/Mid/Low-Level). They found suprasegmental fluency cluster (a number of speech rate measures, a stress measure and mid-falling tone choices) and high-rising tones were the strongest predictors for comprehensibility, followed by mid-rising tones and boundary markers (number of silent pauses and low termination tones). Their findings suggest the positive role of the mid- and high-rising tones in comprehensibility judgments, which was attributed to the function of rising tones as conveying "shared background between speaker and listener" (p. 562). Conversely, what was indicated is that overuse of falling tones might convey "negative impressions of speaker arrogance or over assertiveness as well as erode comprehensibility" (p. 562).

Although Kang et al.'s (2010) found a strong correlation between tone choices and comprehensibility, an important variable they did not consider is the actual locations for these tone choices. After all, what matters is the appropriate use of tone choices at certain locations, rather than the number of some types of tone choices. As studies have revealed, L2 learners did not conform with native speakers in the tone choice in certain sentence structures, especially the use of non-default tone choices, for example, declarative sentence with a sentence-final vocative, the parallel structure, the quotation clause followed by the reporting clause, alternative questions, etc (Chen & Bi, 2015). However, whether the deviated tone choices at certain locations affect the pronunciation rating has not been investigated.

As to pitch range, literature has shown that nonnative English speech often features an overall narrower pitch range (Chen, 2008a; Wennerstrom, 1994), compared with the native English speakers. Wennerstrom (1994) measured the contrast between the high and low pitch in the information structure and boundary structure in the speech production of L2 speakers from Thai, Spanish and Japanese, and did not find significant contrast. The restricted pitch ranges were also found in learners' English speech from different L1 backgrounds, such as Japanese (Taniguchi, 2001), Finnish (Toivanen, 2004), Arabic (Binghadeer, 2008), and Chinese (Chen, 2002; Chen, 2008a; Dou, 2003; Hincks & Edlund, 2009; Pickering, 2001; Wennerstrom, 1998).

The compressed pitch range in learner speech was found to make the speech sound more foreign-accented. Kang (2010) studies the relative contribution of five suprasegmental features, overall pitch range included, to the judgments of accentedness and comprehensibility of the ITA speech. He found that the overall pitch range and word stress were the best predictors of accent ratings, with the overall pitch range alone explaining 24% of the variance; however, the comprehensibility rating was not associated with the pitch range, but with speaking rate measures only.

In Chen's (2008a) research on English intonation patterns in the sentence reading-aloud task, she found a connection between the pitch range in Chinese EFL learners' sentence reading-alouds and their pronunciation ratings. Students rated high tended to have a wider pitch range (11 semitones) than those rated low (8 semitones), though still lower than native English speakers' pitch range of 14 semitones. An explanation was that a monotonous intonation lacked expressiveness, so that listeners might easily "lose concentration or misunderstand the speakers' intent" (Kang, 2010, p. 304).

Taken together, Table 2.5 presents a summary of the intonation features identified in the previous studies.

Table 2.5　Intonation features identified in the literature

Category	Feature
Intonation phrasing	Intonation phrasing deviation
Tone	Overall falling/ rising tone deviation
	Falling/ rising tone deviation at default/ non-default locations
	Pitch range

2.3.4.2.2　Stress

The empirical studies on lexical stress, sentence stress and nuclear stress are reviewed in this section.

Lexical stress

English is a lexical stress language, which "means that in any English word with more than one syllable, the syllables will differ in their relative salience" (Cutler, 2005). Much work on lexical stress has proposed four acoustic factors influencing the perception of stress in English, namely duration, intensity, fundamental frequency (f0) and vowel quality (e.g., Beckman, 1986; Fry, 1958). Generally, stressed syllables are found to be longer, louder and higher in pitch or contain more pitch movement than unstressed syllables. Literature also suggested that these correlates were of different degrees of importance, generally with duration and pitch as the most important cues of perceptual stress, and intensity and vowel quality of lesser importance (e.g., Fry, 1958; Sluijter, 1995; Van Katwijk,

1974).

With regard to the studies on lexical stress production by L2 learners, ample evidence has been found to support the L1 negative transfer (Chen & Guo, 2017; Zhang, Nissen, & Francis, 2008). For learners whose native phonology has no distinctions of stress, to produce an English native-like lexical stress can be challenging, particularly how to reduce the vowel in the unstressed syllable in a word (Cutler, 2005). Two studies are found to directly relate to the acoustic correlates of English lexical stress by Mandarin speakers of English.

One is Zhang et al.'s (2008), in which they compared the English stress contrasts by native speakers of English and Mandarin speakers of English (with three to four years' residence in the U.S.) by manipulating the f0, duration, intensity and vowel quality of paired disyllabic words (as *reCORD* and *REcord*). Their finding showed that though both speaker groups were similar in the use of amplitude and duration for stressed and unstressed syllables, they differed in f0 on stressed syllables and vowel reduction. Mandarin speakers tended to produce a higher f0 than English speakers on stressed syllables, and were unable to reduce vowels in certain unstressed syllables in an English-like way. Their study suggested the impact of the Mandarin lexical tones and the contrasts between Mandarin and English vowel inventories on the acquisition of English lexical stress.

Chen and Guo's (2017) study moved a step further, by not only comparing Chinese EFL learners' production of lexical stress pairs with native American English speakers', but also comparing the production of two different English proficiency levels. Also, they examined the ratio of stressed to unstressed syllables in terms of the three acoustic correlates of lexical stress (duration, f0 and intensity), as well as the value of these correlates on stressed and unstressed syllable. They found that beginners were significantly different from native speakers in all three correlates, and advanced learners were comparable with the native speakers in terms of f0, but produced shorter duration and lower intensity than native speakers. Also, beginners and advanced learners differed significantly from each other in terms of f0 and intensity, but not duration. This finding seems to suggest a more robust role intensity and pitch may play as the stress cue, which is inconsistent with the early studies on L1. However, one major contribution of their study is to reveal the influence of L2 proficiency on the production of English lexical stress, but whether this difference affects the rating of pronunciation quality remains unknown.

Very little research on pronunciation assessment involved specific acoustic correlates of lexical stress. One study found is Shah's (2004), in which he used stressed-unstressed (S/U) vowel duration as a measure of lexical stress, and examined its correlation with the accentedness rating of Spanish-accented English. The result showed that among the eight high-frequency multisyllabic target words, only one word, *economic*, was significantly correlated with the perception of accentedness in terms of S/U vowel duration. This study seems to suggest a less important role suprasegmental realization of lexical stress might play in the judgment of pronunciation.

In contrast, the segmental property seems to have a greater effect than suprasegmental features, when it comes to the correlation between misplacement of lexical stress and word recognition or intelligibility. A number of studies have found that a pure shift of stress without the change of vowel quality (full versus reduced), as in *STAMpede* for *stamPEDE*, did not affect listeners' correct recognition of the words (Fear, Cutler, & Butterfield, 1995; Field, 2005; Slowiaczek, 1991). Field (2005) further suggested that a loss of intelligibility might occur when a weak-quality vowel was produced in a stressed syllable, but less marked when "the stress shift was accompanied by a change of vowel quality (from weak to full)" (p. 415). Despite the important role of the vowel quality in examining the relationship between lexical stress and pronunciation, this feature cannot be analyzed in the present study for the lack of paired disyllabic words in the read dialogues.

Sentence stress

Sentence stress is generally researched in terms of its placement and acoustic realization. Since the research on the acoustic realization of sentence stress often analyzed stress as a representation of English rhythm, their studies will be reviewed in Section 2.3.4.2.3 where rhythm is discussed. This part only focuses on the placement of sentence stress.

The placement of sentence stress was first associated with word categories by Pike (1945), and was described in more details by Kingdon (1958). Both categorized words into two groups, content words and function words. Content words "carry the major semantic weight of the sentence" (Pike, 1945, p. 118), and were usually stressed; function words, however, serve to mark grammatical relationships and have little semantic content, hence unstressed in normal circumstances. Table 2.6 and 2.7 give summaries of the word categories typically stressed and unstressed, based on Kingdon's (1958).

Table 2.6 A summary of word categories typically stressed (adapted from Kingdon, 1958)

Word categories	Instances
Nouns	The *noise* of the *train* was **deaf**ening.
Main verbs	He is *painting* the **wall**.
Adjectives	It's a *famous* **tragedy**.
Adverbs	I can **do** that *easily*.
Determiners	
Demonstrative	*That* **coat** is **nice**.
Negative	There's *no* **doubt** about **that**.
Quantifying	There are a *few* **small** ones.
Pronouns	
Demonstrative	*That's* what I **told** you.
Possessive	I **didn't know** *his* was **miss**ing.
Indefinite (as subject)	*Somebody* has **told** him.
Interjections	*Oh*!
Interrogatives	*Who's* **com**ing?

Note: Illustrative words are set in italics, and bold type marks the location of sentence stress.

Of course, the location of sentence stress is also affected by the rhythmic principle of alternation (Couper-Kuhen, 1986). For example, in a sentence with a succession of words belonging to the unstressed word category, like *they might have been there for years*, the stresses may be added to ensure the rhythm (*they might have **been** there for **years***). There might also be a stress shift if two stresses are adjacent to each other, as in *thirteen men*, in which the stress of the word thirteen would move forward (***thir**teen **men***) to create an alternating rhythm.

Table 2.7 A summary of word categories typically unstressed (adapted from Kingdon, 1958)

Word categories	Instances
Pronouns	
Personal	*They* **didn't give** *me* **one**.
Indefinite (as object)	I've **seen** *someone* **look**ing for him.
Determiners	
Possessive	I **saw** *your* **daugh**ter and *her* **hus**band **yes**terday.
Partitive	Has she **bought** *any* **sugar**?
Articles	*The* **book** is on the **table**.
Prepositions	**Why** are they **star**ing *at* the **man**?
Auxiliaries (affirmative)	She *has* **fin**ished the **home**work.
Conjunctions	
Co-ordinating	**Tom** *and* **Jer**ry are **cute**.
Subordinating	I pro**pose** *that* we should **wait** for him.
Relative	**This** is the **girl** *who* **typed** the **letter**.

Note: Illustrative words are set in italics, and bold type marks the location of sentence stress.

Previous research concerning the distribution of sentence stress in nonnative speakers' production often examined the number of stressed words in the learners' speech (Kang, 2010; Kormos & Denes, 2004), and found low-proficiency learners tended to produce more stressed words than high-proficiency learners. However, only a few studies have focused on the appropriateness of sentence stress placement, even less related to those produced by Chinese EFL learners. These studies (Chen, 2008b; Chen & Bi, 2015; Yang, 2010) have revealed not only a cumulative accentuation (Kettemann & Wieden, 1993) in Chinese EFL learners' stress production, but also pointed out that compared with the native English speakers, Chinese EFL learners tended to position sentence stresses on a greater amount of function words (45%–54%) (Yang, 2010) which do not typically belong to stressed word categories according to literature (Kingdon, 1958; Pike, 1945; Wells, 2006). How this kind of inappropriate placement of sentence stresses affects the judgment of learners' pronunciation remains unknown, and is worth further examination.

Nuclear stress

The empirical studies on nuclear stress usually focus on either the placement or the acoustic correlates of nuclear stress. With regard to the placement of nuclei, Hahn (2004) found the speech with no focus and with misplaced focus significantly impaired listeners' ability to recall information. This misplacement of nucleus or the monotone, however, has been found to feature the interlanguage speech of Asian L1 speakers (Wennerstrom, 1994). Chen (2006) investigated the nuclei position in the reading-aloud speech by eight native English speakers and 45 Chinese EFL learners from two proficiency groups. She found that native speakers used function words as unmarked nuclei mostly for emphatic or contrastive focus, while nearly half of the nuclei on function words in Chinese EFL learners' speech were inappropriate, particularly the location of nuclei on personal pronouns. A series of studies in Chen and Bi's (2015) further examined Chinese EFL learners' nucleus placement (tonicity), together with tonality and tone, in different sentence patterns. They found that compared with native English speakers, Chinese EFL learners tended to place nuclei regardless of their function and semantic importance. Besides personal pronouns, they were also likely to place nuclei on connectives and sentence-final vocatives in complex declarative sentences. What is promising is that Yang (2010) revealed the effectiveness of repeated exercises of imitation in improving the accuracy in both marked and unmarked nucleus distribution.

The studies on the acoustic correlates of nuclear stresses include either features like pitch level (f0), intensity and duration of the tonic (nuclei) and non-tonic (non-nuclei) syllables (Chen et al., 2001a; Hua, 2003), or the ratio of the tonic to non-tonic syllables (Yang, 2010). All of the three studies compared native English speakers' and L1 Mandarin speakers' production of English nuclear stress, with only Hua's (2003) involving proficiency groups (EFL and ESL) of the learners.

Both Chen et al. (2001a) and Hua (2003) involved all three acoustic correlates in their studies, and both found that Chinese Mandarin speakers were able to differentiate stressed and unstressed counterparts by features of pitch, intensity and duration, though the realization of stress was different from the native English speakers. Generally, Mandarin speakers differed from native English speakers in a significantly higher f0 on either stressed or unstressed words, shorter duration on stressed words and greater intensity on unstressed words (Chen et al., 2001a). Hua's (2003) findings, however, showed that Mandarin speakers generally produced "relatively shorter, softer, and lower-pitched strong syllables, and relatively longer, louder, and higher-itched weak syllables" than native English speakers (p. 291). She suggested that Chinese EFL learners did not realize as many levels of stress (main-stressed, weakly stressed, unstressed) as native English speakers, proposing a "binary division" or a "flatter" hierarchy of stress (p. 292) in Chinese learners' production. She also indicated that all the three acoustic correlates mattered in telling the difference in realizing stress patterns between different proficiency groups and between L1 Mandarin speakers and native English speakers, though the difference lay mainly in a particular rhythmic type featuring a long stretch of weak syllables between strong ones.

Another study, Yang (2010), followed Hua's (2003) three-level division of stress, and identified tonic syllables (nucleus), weakly stressed syllables (sentence stress), and unstressed syllables. Instead of measuring the level of pitch, duration and intensity on each syllable type, she measured the pitch and duration ratio of tonic to stressed syllables, and of stressed to weak syllables. Her finding supported Hua's (2003) claim of a "flatter" stress hierarchy in Chinese EFL learners' production by a much lower tonic/stressed duration ratio (pretest: 1.11), stressed/weak duration ratio (pretest: 1.15), tonic/stressed pitch ratio (pretest: 0.96), and stressed/weak pitch ratio (pretest: 1.05), compared to those of native English speakers (1.56, 1.73, 1.30, 1.33, respectively). More interestingly, she found that repeated exercises could help to improve the duration ratios to be more native-like, but not the pitch ratios.

To recap, for the category of stress, features of three aspects will be investigated in the present study, lexical stress, sentence stress and nuclear stress (Table 2.8). For lexical stress, though literature has shown some effect of lexical stress mistakes on intelligibility and comprehensibility, it must involve a certain number of bi- or multi-syllabic words, which were in short supply in the stimuli of this study. Therefore, only the acoustic feature, lexical stressed-unstressed vowel duration ratio, will be analyzed. For sentence stress, the auditory feature, sentence stress errors, will be analyzed in the stress category, and its acoustic feature will be analyzed in the following category of rhythm. Nuclear stress will be analyzed in terms of both placement errors and the three acoustic correlates (the duration, intensity and pitch ratio of tonic to weak syllables). Only tonic syllables (nuclei) and weak syllables (unstressed) are compared because literature has suggested a flatter hierarchy of stress in Chinese EFL learners' production.

Table 2.8 Stress features identified in the literature

Category	Feature
Lexical stress	Lexical stressed-unstressed vowel duration ratio
Sentence stress	Sentence stress placement error
Nuclear stress	Nuclear stress placement errors
	Tonic-weak syllable duration/f0/intensity ratio

2.3.4.2.3 Rhythm

Speech rhythm can be quantified by a number of rhythmic metrics, but previous studies appear to show that they do not yield similar results (Gut, 2012). Generally, there are three sets of rhythmic features, the overall stress-timing, the CV-interval features, and the syllable variability features.

Overall stress timing

In quantifying rhythm, Trofimovich and Baker (2006) proposed the overall stress timing (OST), calculated as a single ratio of unstressed to stressed syllable durations across the utterance. In their study, they examined suprasegmental features (rhythm, intonation, pause, and speech rate) in the low-pass filtered speech[①] of native English speakers and Korean learners of English. The OST was used as a feature to measure rhythm. They found that for native English speakers, the OST was lower, closer to 0.5, because unstressed syllables are shorter than stressed syllables in a stress-timed language like English; the OST for Korean learners in the inexperienced and moderately experienced groups was significantly higher, but not for the more experienced learners. The finding showed the L1 effect on the rhythmic patterning, since Korean is, like Chinese, a syllable-timed language, and is expected to have a higher OST closer to 1. At the same time, it indicated that the target language rhythm can be acquired with a longer time of exposure to the target language. However, when this feature was correlated with the rating of accentedness, only a significantly weak correlation was found; when it was examined together with fluency-based features, the OST was not found to be as effective as features such as pauses and speech rate in predicting the accentedness rating.

Another study using a similar feature is Yang's (2010), which studied the development of Chinese EFL students' stress patterns in the conditions of listen-and-repeat. One of the findings of this study is that by listen-and-repeat exercises, students could acquire a more native-like stress pattern in terms of the duration ratio of stressed to unstressed syllables. This

---

① Low-pass filtering is a technical manipulation of speech, by which all energy components of the speech signals above 450 Hz are removed, thus preserving suprasegmentals while removing most of the segmental content.

ratio is just the opposite of the above-mentioned OST value. She found that this duration ratio of students' speech increased from 1.15 (0.87 if converted to the OST value) in the pretest to 1.37 (0.73 if converted to the OST value) in the third posttest, indicating a greater duration contrast acquired between stressed and unstressed syllables, although still low compared with the ratio for native speakers (1.73, and 0.58 if converted to the OST value).

CV-interval variability

The interval metrics can be traced back to Ramus, Nespor and Mehler's (1999, p. 272) three interval measures, "the proportion of vocalic interval within the sentence" (%V), "the standard deviation of the duration of consonantal intervals" (ΔC), and "the standard deviation of the duration of vocalic intervals" (ΔV). This approach is easy to apply, for it does not require to consider the phonological makeup of the syllable. The researcher just needs to divide the speech into vocalic and consonantal intervals[①].

The rational of these measures is that in a stressed-based language such as English, %V should be lower than that in a syllable-based language such as Chinese, because of vowel reduction in the unstressed syllables and the presence of consonant clusters. For the same reason, ΔV and ΔC should be larger in the stress-based language than in the syllable-based language. Ramus et al. (1999) applied the three variables to

---

① Here is an example given by Ramus et al. (1999, pp. 271 – 272). The phrase "next Tuesday on" is phonetically transcribed as /nɛkstjuzdeiɔn/. It has the following vocalic and consonantal intervals: /n/ /ɛ/ /kstj/ /u/ /zd/ /eiɔ/ /n/.

analyze the read speech (sentence reading) by speakers of eight languages, and resulted in a classification of three types of rhythmic patterns, stress-based (Polish, Dutch and English), mora-based (Japanese) and syllable-based (Catalan, Spanish, Italian and French). Their finding confirmed %V and ΔC as effective measures to indicate different rhythmic patterns, but failed to show significant effect with ΔV. Since Ramus et al.'s (1999) metrics were later found to be inversely related to speech rate, Dellow (2006) and White and Mattys (2007) normalized the ΔC and ΔV values by the mean duration of the consonantal or vocalic intervals, hence deriving metrics VarcoC and VarcoV, respectively. Their studies suggested that VarcoC and VarcoV were more robust than ΔC and ΔV in capturing the differences between stressed-timed and syllable-timed languages.

A few studies are related to the development or acquisition of rhythmic properties in L2 speech by examining CV-interval features. Though some yielded no significant difference between proficiency levels when measuring with either %V, ΔC, ΔV, VarcoC or VarcoV (Jang, 2008), others did provide some evidence for the effectiveness of these features in differentiating between levels. Three studies are to be discussed below.

Chen (2008b) studied the rhythmic pattern of the read speech (passage reading) by 45 Chinese EFL learners' and 8 English native speakers, in terms of %V and ΔC. She found that for English native speakers, the %V-ΔC projections were relatively convergent, with a small proportion of vocalic intervals within the sentence and great variability of consonantal intervals; for the Chinese EFL learners, the %V-ΔC projections were divergent. The low-proficiency group presented a large proportion of vocalic intervals and small variability of consonantal intervals, while most of the high-proficiency group shared the similar rhythmic patterning with the English native speakers. This showed that Chinese EFL learners had major difficulties in vowel reduction in unstressed syllables and in producing durational contrast between stressed and unstressed syllables; however, it was possible for learners to acquire the English stress-timing as proficiency increased.

Li (2014) applied %V, VarcoC and VarcoV, together with other metrics, to examine the rhythm acquisition by L1 Mandarin learners and L1 German learners, and compared their production to native English speech. Her study showed that all the three interval metrics could differentiate between the rhythm of native English speech and two learner speeches, but only vocalic interval features (%V and VarcoV) best discriminated between L2 proficiency levels for learners of both L1s. For vocalic variability (VarcoV), learners started with relatively low values, and progressed toward the high native English value with the increase of proficiency levels. For the proportion of vocalic duration (%V), L1 Mandarin learners gradually reduced their vocalic proportion, and L1 German learners followed an opposite direction with the development of proficiency, both with a trajectory towards the target native English rhythm, since Mandarin has a much higher %V value while German has a slightly lower %V than native English.

Partly different from Li's (2014) finding, Galaczi, Post, Li, Barker and Schmidt (2017) found %V and VarcoC to be discriminative for CEFR levels when they studied Spanish learners of English. There was a steady progression in consonantal variability along with the improving levels of proficiency, except for the lowest A1 level. With regard to %V, however, it only presented difference between B1 and B2 levels.

Syllable variability

Syllable variability features are among a variety of pairwise variability metrics. The earliest version was the pairwise variability index (PVI), developed by Low, Grabe and Nolan (2000). Compared with the interval measures, it depicts rhythm more locally, focusing on the durational difference between adjacent intervals. The pairwise variability metric measures the mean of the duration difference between neighboring temporal intervals in an intonation phrase. The temporal intervals are most commonly adjacent vowels or consonants, but it can also be syllables (Deterding, 2001; Lee & Kim, 2005). Since speech rate was found to have great effect on the PVI values, a normalization has often been carried out by the mean duration of the adjacent intervals (Grabe & Low, 2002; Low et al., 2000).

Low et al. (2000) confirmed that a stress-timed language tends to have high PVI values, and a syllable-timed language low PVI values in their study, where they measured the normalized PVI for vowels (nPVI-V) for British English (BE) and Singapore English (SE), and found British English speakers presented a greater variability in duration of successive vowels than the Singapore English speakers. In the context of L2 English rhythmic development, learners whose L1s are syllable-based are expected to produce speech with lower PVI values. The limited research in this respect has shown different effect of the various PVI metrics.

Li (2014) found that the normalized pairwise vowel

variability (nPVI-V) was able to discriminate between proficiency levels for L1 Mandarin speakers of English, with a significant increase with proficiency levels. However, this measure was not confirmed effective in Galaczi et al.'s (2017) study for L1 Spanish speakers of English. Instead, they found nPVI-C could differentiate between all CEFR levels, except the lowest A1 level.

While inconsistent results were found with the PVI values measured on adjacent vowels and consonants, some researchers have measured the pairwise variability in consecutive syllables. A study relevant is Lee and Kim's (2005), in which they compared the pairwise variability (PWV) in American English and Korean-accented learner English, by calculating the durational difference between the stressed syllable and its unstressed counterparts within a foot and then normalized it by the mean duration of the two syllables. They confirmed the effectiveness of their index PWV in differentiating between the American English (0.81) and Korean-accented learner English, with a significantly lower PWV for Korean-accented English (0.46 for learners before instruction, and 0.51 after instruction). They also found that classroom instruction was effective in helping learners achieve more stressed-timed rhythm. Compared with the PVI values measured on adjacent vowels and consonants, the PWV value seems to better represent the core property of stress-timing: the stress alteration between the successive feet.

Finally, one study focusing on the acquisition of different types of stress-timing by Chinese ESL and EFL learner is worth noting (Hua, 2003). She did not measure the various rhythmic metrics mentioned above; instead, she compared three groups of speakers, native English speakers, Mandarin Taiwan ESL learners and Mandarin Taiwan EFL learners, in terms of duration, intensity and pitch of stressed and unstressed syllables in their read speech. The most insightful of her study is the identification of two different types of rhythmic patterns in the measurement. One (Type-A) features a regular alteration between strong and weak syllables (e.g., SwSwSw), while the other (Type-B) features two widely spaced strong syllables with a long stretch of weak syllables in between, or one strong syllable with a long stretch of weak syllables hanging after (e.g., SwwwwwS, Swwwww). She found that learners experienced more difficulties with the Type-B timing than with Type-A timing. Although for both Type-A and Type-B sentences, ESL learners produced a larger durational contrast between the strong and weak syllables than did EFL learners, and a small durational contrast than did native English speakers, the difference between native speakers and learners were much more distinctive for Type-B sentences than for Type-A sentences. Therefore, she suggested that it is necessary to take the foot structure into consideration when analyzing rhythmic parameters.

In sum, previous literature has shown inconsistent findings with the effectiveness of rhythm features in discriminating between different languages, between L1 and L2, and between different levels of L2 proficiency. Various reasons have been discussed for this inconsistency, such as the acoustic segmentation procedure, the choice of speakers, speech rate and task type (Gut, 2012). However, research seems to show some progression in learners' English speech towards the native English rhythm with the improving proficiency levels, and at least some rhythmic features are able to present the trajectory. Therefore, the present study is to include all three sets of rhythmic features in the investigation (Table 2.9), the overall stress-timing, the CV-interval features (%V, Varco-C, Varco-V), and the syllable variability feature PWV, together with its measurement in the above-mentioned Type-A and Type-B structures.

Table 2.9 Rhythmic features identified in the literature

Category	Feature
Overall stress timing	Overall unstressed to stressed syllable duration ratio
CV- interval variability	%V, VarcoC, VarcoV
Syllable variability	Pairwise variability
	Pairwise variability in Type-A and Type-B feet

2.3.4.3 Fluency

Utterance fluency can be measured in terms of speed, breakdown (pausing) and repair (Skehan, 2003, 2009). Previous literature constantly found that speed and pausing measures, though measured differently, were significant predictors of perceived fluency (e.g., Bosker et al., 2013; Cucchiarini et al., 2002; Derwing et al., 2004; Rossiter, 2009), and overall L2 proficiency (De Jong et al., 2015; Kahng, 2014; Razatseva, 2001; Revesz, Ekiert, & Torgersen, 2016). Repair measures, however, were found to contribute little to fluency ratings (Bosker et al., 2013; De Jong et al., 2015).

When related to pronunciation, a number of studies have

found that perceived fluency is strongly correlated with comprehensibility (Derwing et al., 2004; Derwing et al., 2008), but not so much with accentedness or intelligibility. However, very limited research has focused on the contribution of specific fluency measures to pronunciation constructs, and their findings were not always congruent. While Trofimovich and Isaacs (2012) reported a moderate correlation between mean length of run and accentedness, Kang (2010) found speed measures could best predict comprehensibility. One study (Cucciarini et al., 2002) deals with the task type effect on the relationship between temporal measures and perceived fluency. They found that in both read speech and spontaneous speech, speed measures were most strongly correlated with the perceived fluency and frequency of filler pauses and disfluencies were not significantly correlated.

The following parts describe the discrete features measured in previous studies, in terms of the three aspects, breakdown, speed and repair (Skehan, 2003, 2009).

2.3.4.3.1 Breakdown fluency

Breakdown fluency is often represented by the frequency of silent and filler pauses (such as *uhm* and *er*) and the average length of silent pauses, among which silent pauses seem to play a more important role than filler pauses in affecting the fluency rating (Bosker et al., 2013; De Jong et al., 2015).

The frequency and duration of silent pauses have been associated with different global ratings of perceived fluency, overall proficiency and foreign accent. While most studies have confirmed that the silent pause frequency was closely associated with fluency ratings (Bosker et al., 2013; Cucchiarini et al., 2002), oral proficiency (Ginther, Dimova, & Yang, 2010), and foreign accentedness (Kang et al., 2010; Trofimovich & Baker, 2007), the duration of silent pauses has not yielded consistent findings. Some studies showed significant effect of pause duration on the fluency rating (Bosker et al., 2013; Ginther et al., 2010) or foreign accent (Kang, 2010), while others found no correlation of it to proficiency (De Jong et al., 2015; Towell et al., 1996).

In addition, scholars also pointed out the importance of taking the pause distribution into consideration when measuring pause frequency and duration (Skehan, 2009), suggesting that L1 and L2 speakers had different pausing patterns, with native speakers pausing mostly at an ASU[①] boundary for online processing, and L2 speakers pausing more within an ASU than L1 speakers (De Jong, 2016; Skehan, 2009). Other than ASUs, syntactic units have also been widely used in L2 fluency and pausing literature. Pauses at the syntactic boundaries (including sentence-, clause- and phrase-boundaries) are usually not considered to impair fluency (Towell et al., 1996). Pauses at non-boundary positions (within-phrase), however, are regarded as disfluent markers.

Studies concerning the pausing patterns of Chinese EFL learners found that students tended to produce more non-

---

[①] ASU is the short term of analysis of speech units, defined by Foster, Tonkyn, and Wigglesworth (2000, p. 365) as "a single speaker's utterance consisting of an independent clause, or a subclausal unit, together with any subordinate clause(s) associated with either".

juncture pauses in monologue tasks than native American speakers (Gao & Fan, 2011), due to the demand for more processing time for vocabulary retrieval and content organization. L2 proficiency level did have an effect on pause frequency and duration, with learners in higher levels producing less and shorter silent pauses than those in lower levels, but learners in different proficiency levels did not differ significantly in pause distribution in terms of the proportion of juncture and non-juncture pauses (Miao, 2009).

2.3.4.3.2 Speed fluency

In Skehan's approach, speed fluency is measured by articulation rate, instead of speech rate, because speech rate incorporates both the speed and pausing aspects of fluency, causing a high correlation to pausing measures, while articulation rate calculates the mean syllable duration by using articulation time (excluding the silence duration). This approach was followed by a number of researchers in the latest fluency literature to lower the inter-collinearity of the measures (Bosker et al., 2013; De John, 2016; De Jong, Steinel, Florijn, Schoonen, & Hulstijn, 2013; De Jong et al., 2015), hence adopted in this study. However, earlier research included both, with speech rate more often examined.

In either form, speed measures have been repeatedly confirmed to have great predicting power for perceived fluency (Bosker et al., 2013; Cucciarini et al., 2002; Derwing et al., 2004; Kormos & Denes, 2004), comprehensibility (Kang, 2010; Kang et al., 2010) and accentedness (Trofimovich & Baker, 2007). Moreover, the rate measures seem to be closely related to intonation, and regarded by some researchers as "an intonational phenomenon as well as a temporal one" (Kang et al., 2010, p. 562), since articulation rate was found to be grouped with mid-falling tone in the same feature cluster (Kang et al., 2010).

Studies comparing L1 and L2 speech have yielded a common result that L2 learners often speak at a slower rate than native speakers (Munro & Derwing, 1998), probably due to difficulties in the encoding and retrieval of phonological information, or in the articulation of L2 sounds, or both (Munro & Derwing, 2001). Either a too slow or too fast speech rate (Munro & Derwing, 2001) might impede comprehensibility, and signal nonnativeness (Anderson-Hsieh & Koehler, 1988). As proposed by Munro and Derwing (2001), there might be an optimal speed to enhance comprehensibility. The estimated optimal rates, as they suggested, "were somewhat faster than those actually used by the L2 speakers and somewhat slower than rates typical of native speakers of English" (p. 466).

2.3.4.3.3 Repair fluency

Repair fluency is represented by the frequency and length of disfluencies such as self-correction, repetition, and false starts. Except for De Jong et al.'s (2015), literature has not seen much evidence for a close connection between repair features and fluency ratings, though speech repairs can be perceived easily by raters (Bosker et al., 2013; Cucciarini et al., 2002; Derwing et al., 2004). In read speech, this might be attributed to the small number of disfluencies (Cucciarini et al., 2002); in spontaneous speech, on the other hand, repair phenomena were sometimes interpreted as a speech strategy used by the speaker to buy time for online planning (Guillot, 1999).

A conclusion could be drawn with caution that the more fluent speakers were found to speak faster, with fewer and shorter pauses than the less fluent speakers. The fluency features identified in previous studies are listed in Table 2.10.

Table 2.10 Fluency features identified in the literature

Category		Feature
Speed		Articulation rate
Breakdown	frequency	Overall silent pause frequency
		Clause-boundary silent pause frequency
		Phrase-boundary silent pause frequency
		Within-phrase silent pause frequency
	duration	Overall silent pause length
		Clause-boundary silent pause length
		Phrase-boundary silent pause length
		Within-phrase silent pause length
Repair	frequency	Frequency of disfluencies
	duration	Length of disfluencies

2.3.5 Summary of the phonological features identified in the literature

Table 2.11 presents the 42 phonological features identified in pronunciation theories, rating scales and empirical studies. They constitute the potential features to be analyzed in the present study.

Table 2.11 Phonological features identified in the literature

Dimension	Category	Feature		
Segmental	Phoneme deletion	Phoneme deletion errors		
	Phoneme insertion	Overall phoneme insertion	Word-final vowel insertion	Word-final consonant insertion
	Phonemic substitution	Overall phonemic substitution	Vowel substitution	Consonant substitution
		Word-final consonant substitution		Word-initial consonant substitution
Prosody	Intonation phrasing	Overall intonation phrasing deviation		
	Tone deviation	Falling tone deviation		Rising tone deviation
		Falling tone deviation at default locations		Falling tone deviation at non-default locations
		Rising tone deviation at default locations		Rising tone deviation at non-default locations
	Pitch range	Overall pitch range		
	Lexical stress	Lexical stressed/unstressed vowel duration ratio		
	Sentence stress	Sentence stress errors		
	Nuclear stress	Nuclear stress placement		Tonic/weak syllable duration ratio
		Tonic/weak syllable f0 ratio		Tonic/weak syllable intensity ratio
	Overall stress timing	Overall unstressed/stressed syllables duration ratio		
Rhythm	CV-interval variability	%V	VarcoC	VarcoV
	Syllable variability	PWV	PWV-A	PWV-B

Continued

Dimension	Category	Feature	
Fluency	Speed	Articulation rate	
	Breakdown	Overall silent pause frequency	Overall silent pause length
		Clause-boundary silent pause frequency	Clause-boundary silent pause length
		Phrase-boundary silent pause frequency	Phrase-boundary silent pause length
		Within-phrase silent pause frequency	Within-phrase silent pause length
	Repair	Frequency of disfluencies	Length of disfluencies

2.3.6　Relative contribution of the phonological features

Literature has seen a growing tendency to establish a link between listeners' perceptive scores and the speech discourse, and various phonological features have been shown to predict L2 speakers' pronunciation proficiency in the form of either a holistic score, or the comprehensibility/accentedness rating. This section gives a glimpse of their relative contribution to the pronunciation ratings.

2.3.6.1　Phonological features correlated with comprehensibility and accentedness

As previously introduced in this chapter, there are two competing conceptualizations in the research of L2 pronunciation, the nativeness and intelligibility principles (Levis, 2005). In line with this, most of the research on phonological features focused on their relative importance to the interrelated but partially separate constructs of pronunciation, comprehensibility, and accentedness.

A few studies combined a number of suprasegmental features (Kang, 2010; Kang et al., 2010; Trofimovich & Baker, 2006), and confirmed the important role suprasegmentals play in the perception of comprehensibility and accentedness. Of the suprasegmental features, fluency-related measures (Kang et al., 2010), particularly speaking rate (Kang, 2010), were detected to better predict comprehensibility than intonation or stress related measures. Trofimovich and Baker (2006) also suggested that fluency-related measures such as pause duration, pause frequency and speech rate outperformed other features such as stress timing and peak alignment in their contributions to foreign accent.

Later research included more features into investigation, encompassing not only phonological (segmental and suprasegmental) but also lexical, grammatical and discourse structural features (Isaacs & Trofimovich, 2012; Trofimovich & Isaacs, 2012). In their studies, 19 speech measures in the oral picture narrative of 40 native French speakers of English were examined in relation to comprehensibility and accent rated by native listeners. The findings first suggested that comprehensibility and accentedness were truly strongly correlated constructs ($r = 0.9$), and the phonological features significantly related to them were common, namely word stress and rhythm. However, the studies also disentangled comprehensibility from accentedness by revealing that comprehensibility was not only predicted by phonological features (word stress), but also by lexico-grammatical measures (grammatical accuracy and lexical type frequency), while accentedness was solely associated with aspects of phonology, including both segmental and suprasegmental features. Saito et al. (2015) studied the same set of speech data, but used a more subjective method to analyze the features. Instead of correlating the instrumentally analyzed measures with comprehensibility and accentedness, they established validity of associating 11 listener-rated variables to the global judgments of two constructs. Similarly, their findings confirmed the overlapping phonological features underlying both comprehensibility and accentedness, such as segmental accuracy and word stress, and supported comprehensibility as a construct beyond pronunciation. While accentedness judgments depended chiefly on pronunciation, raters relied on both pronunciation and the lexicogrammar for comprehensibility.

More recent research expanded the work to examine the roles of learners' L1 status (Crowther et al., 2015), listeners' L1 background (Crowther et al., 2016), task type (Crowther et al., 2018) and rating scales (Saito et al., 2016) in determining the relationship between different linguistic dimensions and the two constructs. Generally, these studies were in line with previous work, showing that comprehensibility and accentedness were closely related but partially independent constructs. Comprehensibility was associated with both pronunciation and lexicogrammar features, while accentedness was chiefly linked to phonological features, except when the task became more cognitively demanding. Crowther et al. (2018) compared three spontaneous tasks with increasing task demands, picture narrative (describing ordered pictures), IELTS long-turn task (giving individual speech on a given topic) and TOEFL iBT integrated task (giving response to both reading and listening stimuli), and found that the linguistic correlates of accentedness became more aligned with comprehensibility with the increased task complexity.

In terms of phonological features, these studies also suggested large overlapping between comprehensibility and accentedness, though the relative strength of different features to the two constructs may vary. For example, for both comprehensibility and accentedness, segmental accuracy was found to have a strong impact in Crowther et al.'s (2015), but word stress and rhythm were important predictors in Crowther et al.'s (2016). Also, Crowther et al. (2015) suggested a significant effect of speakers' L1 background on the feature-construct association when studying speakers from three L1 backgrounds (Chinese, Hindi, Farsi). They found that the association kept consistent across different speakers' L1 groups for accentedness, with segmental accuracy as the most salient feature; however, it varied as a function of the speakers' L1 for comprehensibility, with Chinese speakers influenced primarily by pronunciation features (segmental accuracy), Hindi speakers by non-pronunciation features (lexicogrammar), and Farsi speakers showing no strong connection with any linguistic variables. What's more, Saito et al. (2016) indicated that phonological features played different roles in differentiating between three rating levels. For accentedness, segmentals, word stress, intonation and speech rate were equally important in discriminating between all levels. For comprehensibility, when word stress and intonation were able to differentiate between all levels, speech rate was relatively more important at the beginner levels, and segmental accuracy characterized the higher level.

The above-mentioned empirical studies relating phonological features to comprehensibility and accentedness have shown a strong correlation between the two constructs, and the overlapping phonological features representing them. What separates the two constructs seems to lie in the broader linguistic domains comprehensibility may cover. Therefore, it is reasonable to assume that the two constructs of pronunciation might not distinguish from each other in assessing an oral reading task where the lexicogrammar aspects are controlled.

However, to the knowledge of the researcher, only two studies were found to be on the phonological features related to overall pronunciation quality in an oral reading task, and they drew inconsistent findings. One is Anderson-Hsieh et al. 's

(1992), in which prosodic errors was found to have a stronger effect on pronunciation judgment than do segmentals or syllable structure errors. The other is Cucchiarini et al.'s (2000), in which segmental quality had the highest correlation with overall pronunciation rated by human judges, but was predicted most poorly on the basis of the automated scores. The inconsistent findings from these two studies might be attributed to the effect of speakers' L1 background (Crowther et al., 2015). Cucchiarini et al. (2000) employed a single L1 speaking group, the native Dutch speakers, while Anderson-Hsieh et al.'s (1992) used speakers from 11 different L1s.

2.3.6.2 Debate over segmental and suprasegmental features

The phonological features under investigation were generally categorized as either segmental (individual sounds) or suprasegmental (fluency, stress, intonation, and rhythm). A long-standing debate is whether segmental or suprasegmental features play more important roles in contributing to more intelligible pronunciation.

On the one hand, it has been proposed that segmental features are more important to promote intelligibility, and should be given the highest priority in pronunciation teaching (Jenkins, 2000; 2002). Jenkins (2000) suggested that in the context of World Englishes when nonnative speakers of English are communicating with each other, segmental features are more important than suprasegmental features. She proposed a set of phonological features as Lingua Franca Core, which were considered crucial to intelligibility (Jenkins, 2002). In her set of core phonological features, there were five categories, four out of which concerned segmental features. They were the production of specific consonants, "phonetic requirements" involving voiced and voiceless consonants, "consonant clusters" and specific "vowel sounds" such as long and short vowel pairs and /ɜː/ (pp. 96-97). The only category related to suprasegmentals was the "production and placement of tonic (nuclear) stress" (p. 97), particularly the use of contrastive stress to signal meaning.

While Jenkins suggested the relative importance of consonants in the Lingual Franca Core, some researchers argued the great impact of vowel accuracy on intelligibility (Bent et al., 2007; Rogers & Dalby, 2005). Bent et al. (2007) also found that segmental errors in the word-initial position were more detrimental to intelligibility than those in other positions. Furthermore, Munro and Derwing (2006) argued that it might be the nature rather than the number of segmental errors that were more important; in other words, the vowels and consonants with a high functional load[1] determined the impact on listeners' perception of comprehensibility to a greater extent than those with a low functional load.

On the other hand, suprasegmental features have gained more and more attention in pronunciation literature (See Tian & Jin, 2015, for a review), and have shown a great impact on comprehensibility and accentedness. While Field (2005) and Hahn (2004) targeted on a single feature, word stress and

---

[1] Functional load is a rank of segmental contrasts based on "factors such as frequency of minimal pairs, the neutralization of phonemic distinctions in regional varieties, segmental position within a word, and the probability of occurrence of individual members of a minimal pair" (Munro & Derwing, 2006, p. 522).

nuclear stress, respectively. Kang (2010) and Trofimovich and Baker (2006) investigated a range of suprasegmental features, and resulted in inconsistent findings. Kang (2010) found variance of comprehensibility ratings were mainly explained by speaking rate measures with mean length of run best correlated with the score, while the variance of accent rating by a wide range of features including pitch range, pauses, articulation rate and stress. However, Trofimovich and Baker (2006) suggested that fluency-related features such as pauses and speech rate have a greater predicting power than stress-timing and intonation measures in accentedness rating. Besides, Chela-Flores (2001) proposed a model for teaching pronunciation in meaningful units, with a clear emphasis on suprasegmentals. In this model, he placed rhythmic pattern at the central position as a starting point in the instruction, and highlighted the lengthening and shortening of stressed syllables in meaningful units. He argued that having a certain control of rhythmic patterns could make it easier to teach segments and intonation.

Various other studies which included both segmental and suprasegmental features into investigation drew different conclusions (See 2.3.1.1). There is little empirical evidence to support one over the other (See Ziehinski, 2015, for a review). In fact, literature has been moving towards a more balanced view that both are important. Instead of treating segmental and suprasegmental features as separate entities, it is more suitable to view them as part of "an integrated system where one might interact with the other to influence intelligibility" (Ziehinski, 2015, p. 402). As Weismer and Martin (1992) described,

In running speech, segmental and suprasegmental

events are executed simultaneously. Modifications of segmental elements ... may influence not only the perception of those particular segments but also the perception of the rhythmic structure of the utterances as a whole. In this sense, the segmental event may contribute to a modification of the prosodic structure. (p. 83)

Similarly, the rhythmic structure of a speaker determines the stress pattern, and in turn, influences the articulation of segments. Compared with the unstressed syllables, the stressed syllables are usually more prominent, with a longer duration, a stronger intensity and a higher/lower pitch. Ziehinski (2008) found that segmental errors in strong syllables had the greatest influence on intelligibility, regardless of the speakers' L1 background. This finding empirically supports the view of interactive features, and paves the way for the present study to analyze segmental features in a more integrated way, which is to target the segmental errors in the strong syllables of the prominent words in a sentence.

To sum up, previous literature has yielded inconsistent findings of the relative contribution of the various phonological features to the pronunciation ratings. More studies are needed to better understand the relationship between the two.

Chapter Three
METHODOLOGY

This part reports the methodology of the present study, including research questions, speech corpus, speech coding, and data analysis. The coding and analysis work comprised two phases. In Phase Ⅰ, a general coding of 30 speech samples was carried out in terms of the phonological features identified in the literature review. The aim of Phase Ⅰ was to validate the criterial features, and choose the most distinguishing ones for the more in-depth analysis in Phase Ⅱ. In Phase Ⅱ, the total 89 speech samples were coded in terms of the criterial features validated in Phase Ⅰ. A series of statistical analyses were carried out to examine their role in differentiating between holistic rating levels and predicting the analytic ratings.

3.1 Research questions

The present study intends to identify and validate the criterial features in assessing Chinese EFL students' pronunciation in the reading-aloud task. To be more specific, the study aims at answering the following questions:

1. What phonological features identified in previous literature contribute to the ratings of the Chinese EFL learners' pronunciation?

(a) What phonological features contribute to the holistic

ratings of the Chinese EFL learners' pronunciation?

(b) What phonological features contribute to the analytic ratings of the Chinese EFL learners' pronunciation?

2. What role do the phonological features play in distinguishing the holistic rating levels of Chinese EFL learners' pronunciation?

(a) Are there any phonological features that can successfully distinguish all the holistic rating levels? If yes, what are they?

(b) What phonological features can differentiate the lower and higher holistic rating levels?

3. What are the differential contributions of the phonological features to the analytic ratings of Chinese EFL learners' pronunciation?

(a) What are the differential contributions of the segmental features to the segmental ratings?

(b) What are the differential contributions of the prosodic features to the prosodic ratings?

(c) What are the differential contributions of the fluency features to the fluency ratings?

3.2 Speech corpus

The oral reading speech samples used in this study were taken from ReadEnglish Speech Corpus of Chinese Learners (RESCCL), which is a sub-corpus of English Speech Corpus of Chinese Learners (ESCCL) (Chen, Wen, & Li, 2010). This section first introduces the speech samples, the existing phonetic annotations, and the pronunciation ratings in RESCCL. Next, the selection of the speech samples for this study is described, followed by a brief introduction to a referential corpus of Native American Speakers' read speech.

3.2.1 RESCCL

3.2.1.1 The speech samples in RESCCL

RESCCL contains the dialogue reading-alouds by Chinese EFL learners. The speakers came from 10 different major dialectal areas of China (North China, Wu, Xiang, Gan, Hakka, Yue, Min, Jin, Ping and Hui), and from 4 educational levels (junior-high schoolers, senior-high schoolers, college English majors, and postgraduate English majors). Only the speech samples by college English majors were chosen for this study because they were phonetically annotated, and rated for pronunciation proficiency.

Table 3.1 Sentence types and syntactic structures in the read speech

Sentence types & syntactic structures	Examples
Simple declarative sentence	Something's wrong with my computer.
Object clause	I've heard that that film ...
Attributive clause	... to the shop where you bought it.
Alternative question	Do you want to ..., or have you ...?
Yes-no question	Do you know that boy?
Wh-question	What do you want to buy?
Tag question	..., didn't they?
Imperative sentence	Tell me the story ...
Exclamatory sentence	Oh yes!
Parallel	... spring, summer, autumn and winter.
Sentence-final vocative	..., mummy.
Sentence-final reporting clause	"..." Betty asked.

	Continued
Sentence types & syntactic structures	Examples
Contrast	... clever ... foolish ...
Emphatic structure	Mary does like swimming.
Compound noun	New York
Negative structure	... don't ...
Modifier & the modified	... a famous tragedy ...

Note: Adapted from Figure 3 in Chen et al. (2010).

The oral reading task includes ten short dialogues. The vocabulary in the reading text is simple, most of which are monosyllabic words. Such a design is to impose no difficulty on speakers, junior-high schoolers included, when they read aloud the dialogues. The sentences in the reading text not only cover such major English sentence types as declarative, interrogative, imperative and exclamatory sentences, but also include a variety of syntactic structures, for example, parallel and vocative structures (Table 3.1). Therefore, such a text would require different intonation patterns when read aloud.

3.2.1.2 The phonetic annotations in RESCCL

Of all the speech samples by college English majors in RESCCL, 390 were phonetically annotated and double checked by experienced annotators in Praat. The annotation includes six tiers (Figure 3.1): orthographic tier, segmental tier, break index tier, accent tier, intonation tier, and ToBI tier (Chen et al., 2010).

The orthographic tier (Tier 1) and the segmental tier (Tier 2) present students' actual reading, by words and syllables respectively. The syllabification in Tier 2 follows Wells'

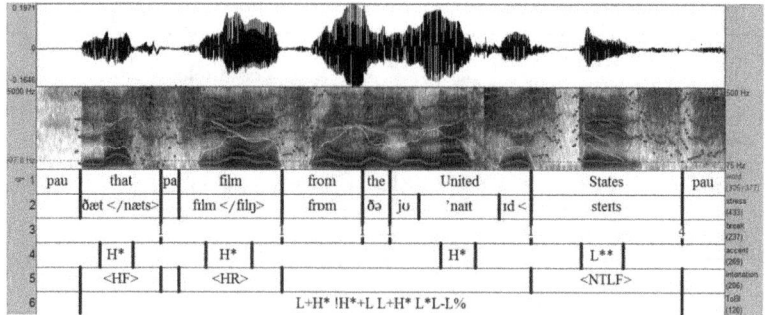

Figure 3.1 The existing annotation of the utterance *that film from the United States* taken from a student sample in RESCCL. The numbers on the left side of the figure indicate the six Tiers of the annotation.

principle (1990), which assumes that the consonants belong with whichever of the syllables is more heavily stressed, so long as this does not break the phonotactic constraints of syllable onsets and codas. For example, *united* is syllabified as /ju • naɪt • ɪd/, and *monkey* as /mʌŋk • ɪ/. The VOT of a word-initial plosive was not included in the consonant, but marked separately as a pause. In Tier 2, students' actual pronunciation is phonemically transcribed by syllables, together with marks (</) signifying phonemic deviations, if there are any, from the citation form of the British pronunciation in *Longman English pronunciation dictionary* (Wells, 2005).

The other four tiers provide suprasegmental annotations. Tier 3 is the break index tier, in which the number four marks the intonation phrase boundary, three the intermediate phrase boundary, one the prosodic word boundary, and 0 the clitic group[①]. Tier 4 is the accent tier, marking the stressed vowels

---

① In ToBI, there are 5 indexes signifying the degrees of connection between words. Level 2 is not adopted in the annotation of RESCCL.

with H* and L*, according to their relative pitch positions in the pitch range of the intonation group. The pitch accent of an intonation group receives double asterisks. Tier 5 and 6 are tone tiers, corresponding to the British intonation system and American ToBI system, respectively.

The existing annotations in RESCCL served as a basis for the speech coding in this study (See Section 3.3.2 for details).

3.2.1.3 The ratings of the read speech in RESCCL

Of all the speech samples by college English majors in RESCCL, 570 were both holistically and analytically rated for their pronunciation proficiency.

The holistic ratings required the raters to evaluate the speakers' overall pronunciation proficiency on a 100-point scale, based on their intuition. No detailed instruction was given for their global judgment. The raters included four native English-speaking (NS) raters and three Chinese raters. The NS raters came from different English-speaking countries, with two from the U.S., one from the U.K., and one from Australia, while all had EFL teaching experience in Chinese colleges for more than two years and were familiar with the Chinese-accented English. Besides, two of the native English-speaking raters reported having IELTS examiner qualifications. The three Chinese raters were college EFL teachers who had at least 15 years' EFL teaching experience and were phonetically trained.

In contrast, the analytic ratings were given only by the three Chinese raters described above, after they finished the holistic ratings. Each sentence in the read speech was rated analytically on four 10-point scales, namely segmentals, intonation, stress, and fluency. There was a training session for the raters prior to their analytic ratings, in which rating criteria were provided. The intonation and stress ratings were conflated into a prosodic rating in the present study, and this will be explained later in Section 3.2.2.3.

3.2.1.4 Rater interview

The three Chinese raters were interviewed individually by the researcher after they completed all the ratings[①]. The recording of one student's reading-aloud was randomly selected and used in the interview. The raters listened to and rated the read speech first holistically and then analytically. They were also asked to clarify their ratings. More specifically, they were encouraged to talk about which phonological features influenced their holistic ratings most, and what constituted their judgments of segmental quality, intonation, stress, and fluency.

The interview data were transcribed and analyzed qualitatively. The following were the major findings. First, the three raters put different weight on different pronunciation dimensions when rating the read speech holistically, with English rhythm, fluency, and segmental quality as the most important factors, respectively. Second, the raters were similar in terms of the phonological features they put into consideration when rating the read speech analytically. All the raters attached great importance to vowel/consonant accuracy in their evaluation of segmental quality. All reported to consider the appropriateness of boundary tone choices when rating

---

① The NS raters were not interviewed, because they left China after they finished the ratings for RESCCL and were not accessible by the researcher.

intonation, and word/sentence/nuclear stress placement errors when rating stress. They also described fluency in a similar way, pointing out features such as speaking rate, frequency/length of silent pauses, self-repair and liaison. Third, though rhythm was not specified in the interview questions or required to be rated, all three raters mentioned rhythm in the rating process, and described it as an important feature affecting both the overall judgment of pronunciation and of the prosodic dimension in particular.

The findings of the rater interview were used when discussing the research findings of the present study.

3.2.2 The speech samples for this study

3.2.2.1 The selection of the read speech samples for this study

The selection of the read speeches for this study involved the following three steps.

First, the speech samples were chosen from the 390 samples with the existing annotations to guarantee the expertise in the speech coding.

Second, a balance between different levels of pronunciation quality was taken into consideration, since the study was to investigate the relationship between pronunciation ratings and various phonological features. In order to ensure a higher inter-rater reliability and minimize the disagreement between the Chinese and NS raters, the 390 speech samples were classified into five groups according to the average holistic ratings by the Chinese rater group and the NS rater group respectively, and only those which were grouped by both rater groups into Levels one, three and five (signaling the high, medium and low

Levels) were chosen. More specifically, there were 93 speech samples sharing the high agreement between both rater groups, with 36 in the high-level group, 20 in the medium-level group, and 37 in the low-level group. After a further examination of the 93 audio samples and their annotations, one from the high-level group and three from the medium-level group were removed, due to either damaged audio files, or incompletion in the annotations. Therefore, a total of 89 speech samples were finally selected for the study.

Third, the read speech examined in this study only employed the first nine dialogues (Appendix A) read by each of the chosen speakers because the 10th dialogue in the RESCCL differed. These nine dialogues covered all the sentence types and syntactic structures described in Section 3.2.1.1. They included 32 sentences, 220 words, 272 syllables in each sample, and 89 samples formed a speech corpus of about 143 minutes.

3.2.2.2 The speakers

The speakers of the 89 chosen speech samples included both males and females, coming from both the north (Beijing, Tianjin, Henan, Shandong, Xuzhou) and the south (Shanghai, Hangzhou, Suzhou, Fujian, Jiangxi) of China (Table 3.2).

Table 3.2 The speakers of the 89 speech samples in this study

Rating level	Gender		Hometown		Total
	Male	Female	North	South	
High	17	18	17	18	35
Mid	6	11	10	7	17
Low	22	15	11	26	37
Total	48	45	39	54	89

3.2.2.3 The ratings and rater reliability

The existing holistic and analytic ratings in RESCCL were used in this study. The holistic score of each speech sample was calculated as the average holistic scores by seven NS and Chinese raters on a 100-point scale. As to the analytic scores, the existing analytic ratings of the 32 sentences were first summed up in each pronunciation dimension (segmentals, intonation, stress, fluency), and then converted to 100-point scales, respectively. Considering that pronunciation has been widely researched from three dimensions, segmental, prosody and fluency (See Section 2.1.1), this study conflated the existing intonation and stress ratings, and calculated their average as the prosodic ratings. As a result, for each speech sample under investigation, there was a holistic rating and three analytic ratings in terms of segmentals, prosody, and fluency.

Table 3.3 The holistic and analytic ratings of the 89 speech samples in this study

	Maximum	Minimum	Mean	SD
Holistic rating	86.43	65	76.72	6.15
Segmental rating	81.67	56.35	71.82	6.12
Prosody rating	79.95	63.23	71.44	4.65
Fluency rating	81.67	62.40	72.16	5.40

As is shown in Table 3.3, the mean holistic score for the 89 speech samples ranged from 65 to 86.43, with a mean of 76.72; the mean analytic scores were 71.82, 71.44, and 72.16 for segmental quality, prosody and fluency, respectively.

The inter-rater reliability was featured by intra-class correlation coefficient (ICC). ICC might be a better way than

Pearson's *r* to feature inter-rater reliability because what is checked is the agreement between different raters on their judgment of the same set of student speech samples. As described by Yu, Luo, Sa and Ai (2011), Pearson's *r* features the bivariate relation between variables of different measurement classes, with each variable centered and scaled by its own mean and standard deviation. In contrast, ICC is used to look at the consistency between variables in a single measurement class, with the data centered and scaled using a pooled mean and standard deviation. Field (2005) claimed that when the contestant's performance is assessed by a panel of judges, it is a perfect scenario for an intra-class correlation. The stepped-up consistency version of the ICC is equal to Cronbach's alpha, which can be obtained by running the reliability analysis in SPSS.

For the holistic ratings of the 89 speech samples, the ICC of the seven raters was 0.84; for the analytic ratings, the ICC of the three raters was 0.80, 0.82 and 0.87 for the segmental, prosody and fluency ratings, respectively. All reached a good rater reliability according to Cicchetti's description (1994).

3.2.3 Read English Speech Corpus of Native American Speakers

A read English speech corpus of 10 native American speakers (RESCNAS) was taken from the native read speech corpus in Chen and Bi's research (2015). It was employed for reference when annotating the tone deviations and nuclei deviations in the students' speech samples.

The ten native American speakers were three female and

seven male college students from Washington State University. RESCNAS includes the reading-aloud of the nine dialogues in the 89 selected speech samples from RESCCL, with minor changes in Dialogue 2 and 9. Table 3.4 shows the differences.

Table 3.4　The differences in the read speech between RESCCL and RESCNAS

Dialogue	RESCCL	RESCNAS
2	I don't think Mary likes swimming.	I don't think Mary speaks French.
	Mary does like swimming.	Mary does speak French.
9	Somebody ... a famous tragedy.	Somebody ... a famous one.
	Well, let's have a look at ...	Let's go.

The native speech was annotated for the boundary of intonation phrases, the location of nuclei, the pitch accent and boundary tones. The annotation was based on the researcher's perception together with the spectrographic cues.

3.3　Phase-Ⅰ study

Phase Ⅰ was undertaken to validate the intuitively and theoretically identified criterial features in the literature review, and to reduce the number of features for further analysis in the Phase-Ⅱ study.

3.3.1　Speech samples in Phase Ⅰ

Due to the complexity of speech coding and the large number of phonological features identified in the literature review, the Phase-Ⅰ study only involved 30 of the 89 speech samples described in Section 3.2.2.1. The 30 speech samples were selected according to their average holistic score by the raters. They included the top ten samples in the high-level group, the last 10 in the low-level group, and the 10 in the middle of the medium-level list.

Table 3.5 gives a detailed description of the speakers of these 30 speech samples. The speakers were almost evenly distributed in the gender and hometown groups. Their read speeches formed a speech corpus of about 48.5 minutes.

Table 3.5　The speakers of the 30 speech samples in the Phase-I study

Rating level	Gender		Hometown		Total
	Male	Female	North	South	
High	5	5	4	6	10
Mid	3	7	7	3	10
Low	6	4	4	6	10
Total	14	16	15	15	30

3.3.2　Speech coding in Phase Ⅰ

Based on the literature review, 42 phonological features (See Table 2.11) were coded, in terms of the three pronunciation dimensions: segmentals, prosody, and fluency. The existing speech annotations were used, based on which further annotations were done by the researcher in Praat (version 6.0.36).

3.3.2.1　Segmentals

The segmental coding focused on ten features from three categories: phoneme deletion, insertion, and substitution. The existing segmental annotations of the speech samples in RESCCL were used (Tier 2), and further annotations were made by the researcher to mark the various types of phoneme deletion, insertion and substitution at different positions.

3.3.2.1.1 Phoneme deletion

This category included both the deletion of a consonant or a vowel, as an error (DE), in the articulation of a word in the original reading text, and the cases of incomplete plosion of plosives (ICP) as well, since they were coded as phoneme deletion in the existing annotations. Both features were calculated by counting the number of their occurrence (Table 3.6).

Table 3.6 Features of phoneme deletion and operationalizations

Category	Feature	Operational definition
Phoneme deletion	DE	Phoneme deletion errors, such as pronouncing *Mary* as /meər/, *let's* as /les/, and *asked* as /aːsk/ or /aːst/
	ICP	Incomplete plosion, such as pronouncing *back to* as /bæ • tə/, and *last night* as /laː s • naɪt/

3.3.2.1.2 Phoneme insertion

Phoneme insertion referred to the insertion of a phoneme (PI), a consonant or a vowel, in the articulation of a word in the original reading text. The words or syllables inserted due to disfluency, such as the wrong start, repetition, self-repair, or filled pauses, were not counted as phoneme insertion. The word-final position was singled out for cases of both consonant and vowel insertion (CIF, VIF), for it is where most segment insertion occurs based on previous literature and the speech data in this study as well.

Table 3.7 Features of phoneme insertion and operationalizations

Category	Feature	Operational definition
Phoneme insertion	PI	Phoneme insertion
	CIF	Consonant insertion at the word-final position, such as pronouncing *that* as /ðæts/, and *know* as /nəʊn/
	VIF	Vowel or syllable insertion at the word-final position, such as pronouncing *that* as /ðætə/, *late* as /leɪtə/

In total, there were three features of phoneme insertion, which were also calculated as the number of their occurrence (Table 3.7).

3.3.2.1.3 Phoneme substitution

Phoneme substitution referred to the deviated phonemes from the citation form, as marked in the segmental annotations. However, only those in the stressed syllables of the stressed words in the students' speech were analyzed. This was done for three reasons. First, the annotated phonemic deviations include all the weak forms which are common in native speakers' actual speech; second, the unstressed parts of the speech usually do not carry important information, and the phonemic substitutions in the unstressed syllables would not be easily perceived; third, previous literature (Zielinski, 2006) suggested the important role of segments in strong syllables in listeners' judgment of intelligibility.

Besides, three types of phoneme substitutions were excluded from the analysis for the following reasons.

First, in the existing segmental annotation, American

pronunciation was marked as a phonemic deviation because the citation form was based on the pronunciation of British English in *Longman English pronunciation dictionary* (Wells, 2005). In this study, however, both British and American pronunciations were considered as standard English accents when students' read speeches were rated. Therefore, the deviations marked due to American pronunciation were not counted in this study, for example, /æ/ in the first syllable of *answer*, and /ɑ/ in *shop*.

Second, some marked deviations were caused by sound assimilation. For example, /s/ in *newspaper* was marked as a deviation from its citation form /z/. However, this kind of sound assimilation was very common in the ten native speakers' reading-aloud of the same text, and often regarded as a pronunciation skill to achieve fluency. Such deviations were excluded from the analysis.

Third, those signifying phonetic rather than phonemic deviations, such as /p^h/ in *spring*, were not included.

There were altogether five features of phoneme substitutions (Table 3.8). The substitutions of vowels and consonants were separated, and the consonant substitutions at onset and coda positions were specified. The consonant substitutions occurring within the onset- or coda-position consonant clusters were also counted as cases of onset- or coda-position substitutions. The number of types of phoneme substitutions was counted in each subcategory (SVT, SCT, SCTonset, SCTcoda) and all together (ST).

Table 3.8 Features of phoneme substitution and operationalizations

Category	Feature	Operational definition
Phoneme substitution	ST	Phoneme substitution types in stressed syllables
	SVT	Vowel substitution types in stressed syllables
	SCT	Consonant substitution types in stressed syllables
	SCTonset	Consonant substitution types at the onset position in stressed syllables
	SCTcoda	Consonant substitution types at the coda position in stressed syllables

3.3.2.2 Prosody

The coding of prosodic features included three categories: intonation, stress and rhythm, with 21 features examined in total. The existing prosodic annotations of the speech samples in RESCCL (See Section 3.2.1.2) were used to identify the intonation phrasing (Tier 3), the sentence/ nuclear stress (Tier 4), and the boundary tone choices (Tier 6). Further annotations were carried out by the researcher and are to be described in detail in this section.

3.3.2.2.1 Intonation

Intonation was coded in terms of three aspects—overall pitch range, intonation phrasing deviation (IP deviation), and tone deviation, with eight features in total (Table 3.9).

Table 3.9 Intonation features and operationalizations

Aspect	Feature	Operational definition
Overall pitch range	OPR	Distance in semitone between f0 maximum and f0 minimum on the vowels of stressed syllables over the read speech
IP deviation	IPD	Intonation phrasing deviation

Continued

Aspect	Feature	Operational definition
Tone deviation	TRD	Failure to use the rising or level tone as expected
	TRD1	Failure to use rising or level tones at non-default boundaries (including five non-final listing items, a simple statement with a contrastive focus and a sentence-initial time adverbial phrase)
	TRD2	Failure to use rising or level tones at default boundaries (including a yes/no question, a tag question and the non-final choice in an alternative question)
	TFD	Failure to use the falling tone as expected
	TFD1	Failure to use falling tones at default boundaries (including four simple statements at the final position of an utterance)
	TFD2	Failure to use falling tones at non-default boundaries (including four wh-questions and the final choice in an alternative question)

Overall pitch range

Overall pitch range (OPR) referred to the distance between the highest and the lowest point of f0 value (Pierrehumbert & Hirschberg, 1990) over the read speech. Following Kang (2010), it calculated such a distance only on the stressed vowels, which were marked in Tier 4 of the existing annotation. The f0 values were obtained as the average pitch in the span of these stressed vowels, and were described in semitone rather than in Herz. According to Li (2005), semitone is more commonly applied when human perception is involved, for it helps eliminate physiological variation, hence making it possible to compare the pitch variation among different speakers (Hincks & Edlund, 2009).

Intonation phrasing deviation

Intonation phrasing, known as tonality, referred to the breaking up of speech into chunks, or intonation phrases, in which the utterance "has its own intonation pattern" (Wells, 2006, p. 6).

Table 3.10 Cases of intonation phrasing deviation

Structure	Cases
Sentence-final vocative	Tell me the story about the clever monkey, *mummy*.
Sentence-final reporting clause	"Will they come tomorrow?" *Betty asked*.
	"No, they will come two days later," *Bob answered cheerfully*.
Restrictive attributive clause	Take it back to the shop *where you bought it*.
	The handsome boy *who is on his bicycle*.
Object clause	I don't think *Mary likes swimming*.
	I don't know *what I can do with it*.
	I've heard *that film from the United States is really good*.
	* I think *it's called Gone with the Wind*.
	Somebody told me *that it's a famous tragedy*.

Note: The sentence with the asterisk is not included in the coding of deviated intonation phrasing.

The boundary of an intonation phrase (IP) generally corresponds to a syntactic boundary; however, there are exceptions. According to Wells (2006), simple object clauses, defining relative clauses, sentence-final adjuncts such as vocatives, and reporting clauses do not usually form separate

IPs of their own. These rules were confirmed by the analysis of the ten native read speeches in RESCNAS. In the read speech, there was one case of sentence-final vocative, two cases of sentence-final reporting clauses, two cases of defining relative clauses, and five cases of object clauses (Table 3.10). None of the ten native speakers broke these sentences into different IPs, except the one with the asterisk in Table 3.10; in two native speakers' reading-aloud, *Gone with the Wind* formed a separate IP for emphasis. In contrast, Chen and Bi (2015) found that Chinese EFL learners tended to break the sentences at the boundaries between the main clause and sentence-final vocatives/ reporting clauses/ defining relative clauses. Therefore, the sentences in Table 3.10, excluding the one with the asterisk, were identified for the examination of students' intonation phrasing patterns.

The break index tier (Tier 3) in the existing annotation of RESCCL was used to mark the intonation phrasing of the above-mentioned nine sentences in students' read speech. If students broke these sentences to form different IPs, it was counted as a deviation from the norm. The number of all the deviations (IPD) in the nine examined sentences (Table 3.10) was calculated.

Tone deviation

There were two steps in the measurement of tone deviation. First, based on previous literature (Bartels, 1999; Chen & Bi, 2015) and concordant tone choices by the native speakers in RESCNAS, locations for tone examination were specified. Second, learners' boundary tone choices at these locations were retrieved from Tier 6 in the existing annotation in RESCCL and checked by the researcher. No disagreement was found. Deviations from the native speaker norm were then counted.

At least nine out of ten native speakers agreed on the application of rising tone or level tone in 13 IPs, and falling tone in 22 IPs (See Appendix C).

Of the 13 IPs whose tone choices were expected to be the rising or level tones, those with the sentence-final vocative and sentence-final reporting clauses were not coded for tone deviation. This is because almost all learners had a deviated intonation phrasing pattern from the native's, and formed the sentence-final adjuncts into separate IPs, hence making it difficult to compare the tone choices with the norm. The remaining 10 IPs were then examined in the learners' speech for tone deviation. If learners failed to use a non-falling boundary tone in these IPs, a deviation was counted (TRD). Furthermore, the deviation was analyzed in two subcategories, those used in the statements (TRD1), and those in the questions (TRD2).

Of the 22 IPs whose tone choices were expected to be falling tone, one was the final choice or the second clause in an alternative question, four were wh-questions, and 17 were statements. Considering that learners often separated a subordinate clause from the main clause, only simple statements were analyzed to ensure that learners phrased them in the same way as by natives. Also, the statements which were in the middle of a speaker's utterance in a dialogue were usually followed by further clarifications. Such statements may not signify finality, hence possible to have a non-falling tone, such as a fall-rise tone to indicate continuation dependence (Bartels, 1999). To avoid such possibilities, only the statement at the end of a speaker's utterance in a dialogue was analyzed for tone deviation. Consequently, four simple declarative sentences at the utterance-final positions remained. If learners failed to adopt a falling tone in these four statements (TFD1) and five questions (TFD2), a deviation was counted (TFD).

3.3.2.2.2 Stress

Stress was investigated in terms of three aspects, lexical stress, sentence stress, and nuclear stress, with six features in total (Table 3.11).

Lexical stress

The number of lexical-stress errors was not counted, since over 80% of the words in the reading text were monosyllabic, and there were too few lexical-stress errors in students' read speech. Therefore, lexical stress was only analyzed acoustically. Following Shah (2004), the temporal measurement (S/U) was an average ratio of stressed to unstressed vowel duration in the sampled bi-syllabic words.

In the reading text, there were 27 bi-syllabic words. In selecting the bi-syllabic words for the acoustic analysis, five steps were followed. First, only the words bearing the sentence stress were taken into consideration, hence crossing out *many* in *how many* and the determiner *something*. Second, those located at the sentence-final positions or before punctuations were deleted from the list to avoid the effect of final lengthening which has been considered a common phenomenon in speech production and an important mark of boundary (Duez, 1993). Third, the words with any vowel following /r/ were not selected because of the difficulty in discriminating between the semi-vowel /r/ and vowel sounds in the spectrograph, such as *story* and *really*. Fourth, if the word ending up with a vowel which tended to be linked to the beginning vowel of the following word, this word was crossed out, for example, *only* in the phrase *only if*. Last, if the unstressed vowel in the word was often reduced to null and not pronounced, this word was not analyzed, such as *season*. In the end, only four bi-syllabic words were left for further analysis. They were *clever*, *handsome*, *foolish* and *famous*. The unstressed vowels in them are either /ɪ/ or the schwa /ə/. The stressed vowels in them include the mid front vowel /e/, the low front vowel /æ/, the high back vowel /u/ and the diphthong /eɪ/.

In actual coding, if students did not pronounce the unstressed vowels in the bi-syllabic word, the ratio of stressed to unstressed vowel duration of this word was not calculated. There were five such cases in the students' speech samples. Two students pronounced *clever* as /klev/ and /klevm/; two reduced the second syllable in *handsome* as /sm/; and one pronounced *foolish* as /fulʃ/.

Sentence stress

Sentence stress was coded as the number of sentence stress errors (SE). SEs were identified as the stressed syllables in the students' speech which were not included in the list of the syllables possible to be stressed in the reading text. The syllables in this list were generally the unmarked stressed syllables in content words, namely nouns, verbs, adjectives, adverbs, numerals, negatives, demonstratives, interjections, and interrogatives. The list also included a contrastive modal word *must* and an emphatic auxiliary verb *does*. Of the 272 syllables in the reading text, 117 were identified according to phonetic rules as the syllables possible to be stressed (Appendix D). The stressed vowels in the students' speech were marked with asterisks in Tier 4 in the existing annotation of RESCCL. Their corresponding syllables were then annotated by the researcher as the actually stressed syllables. By comparing the actually stressed syllables in the students' speech with those in the should-be list, the sentence stress errors were singled out.

Nuclear stress

Nuclear stress was analyzed both perceptually and acoustically. First, nuclei placement errors (NE) were identified. NEs were the deviations from the phonetic rules and the accented syllables identified in the native speech. According to the annotation of nuclei locations in the RESCNAS, any accented syllable in the native speech, even if there was only one occurrence, was considered as possible nuclei positions. This resulted in 57 locations for possible nuclei (Appendix E), among which 45% were marked nuclei (non-final lexical items). In the annotation of the nuclei in the students' speech, the researcher followed the existing annotation of RESCCL. The syllables in which the vowels were marked with double asterisks in Tier 4 were annotated as nuclei in the students' speech. If they did not fall on the possible locations described above, they were counted as nuclei errors, whether or not they formed separate intonation phrases.

Then, acoustic features (T/W dur, T/W f0, T/W int) concerning the contrast between tonic and weak syllables were analyzed in terms of duration, intensity and pitch. There were 23 tonic syllables sampled for analysis, mostly the nuclei found in all the native speeches, usually occurring before a clause or sentence boundary, or bearing contrastive or emphatic meaning. The sampled weak syllables were in 24 unstressed monosyllabic function words, with reduced vowels in all native speeches, occurring at non-final positions, including articles, prepositions, personal pronouns, relative pronouns/adverbs, connectives, possessive adjectives, auxiliary verbs, the infinite *to*, and the contraction of *there be* (Appendix E). These two types of syllables represented extremes in duration, intensity and pitch in the English sentence stress.

Since the features calculated the duration ratio of sampled tonic to weak syllables, the syllable duration was not normalized. The intensity was featured as the peak intensity of the syllable (Hua, 2003), and the pitch as the mean f0 value of the syllable in semitone.

Table 3.11 Stress features and operationalizations

Aspect	Feature	Operational definition
Lexical stress	Lexical S/U	Average ratio of the stressed to unstressed vowel duration in sampled bi-syllabic words (*handsome*, *foolish*, *clever*, *famous*)
Sentence stress	SE	Sentence stress errors
Nuclear stress	NE	Nuclear stress errors
	T/W dur	Duration ratio of sampled tonic to weak syllables
	T/W f0	F0 ratio of sampled tonic to weak syllables
	T/W int	Intensity ratio of sampled tonic to weak syllables

3.3.2.2.3 Rhythm

The rhythmic features were analyzed acoustically on three levels—the overall utterance level, the CV-interval level, and the syllable level. There were seven features in total (Table 3.12).

In the measurement, the stressed or unstressed syllables did not refer to the actually stressed or unstressed syllables in the students' speech. The division between stressed and unstressed syllables was based on phonological rules, as described in Section 3.3.2.2.2. The stressed syllables were the bold syllables shown in Appendix D, and the unstressed syllables were the rest.

Table 3.12 Rhythmic features and operationalizations

Aspect	Feature	Operational definition
Overall stress-timing	OST	Duration ratio of unstressed to stressed syllables over the whole speech
Syllable variability	PWV	Pairwise variability calculated as average duration difference between stressed and unstressed syllables in each foot of the four sampled sentences
	PWV-A	Average duration difference between stressed and unstressed syllables in each Type-A foot (with short stretches of weak syllables) of the four sampled sentences
	PWV-B	Average duration difference between stressed and unstressed syllables in each Type-B foot (with long stretches of weak syllables) of the four sampled sentences
CV-interval variability	VarcoC	Standard deviation of consonantal intervals normalized by the mean duration of all consonantal intervals in the four sampled sentences
	VarcoV	Standard deviations of vocalic intervals normalized by the mean duration of all vocalic intervals in the four sampled sentences
	%V	Average proportion of the duration of vocalic intervals in the four sampled sentences

Only the measurement of overall stress timing (OST) was computed over the whole speech; the other measurements, due to the complexity in annotation, were conducted locally in four sampled sentences (Table 3.13). The four sentences were deliberately selected, for each of them embraces two types of foot structures—Type-A with a short stretch of weak syllables (one or two weak syllables) and Type-B with a long stretch of weak syllables (more than two weak syllables) in a foot. In other words, these sentences do not have a regular rhythmic pattern of alternating strong and weak syllables, and the number of weak syllables between the stressed syllables varies from one to four. According to Hua (2003), the Type-B pattern was more difficult for L2 learners to acquire. As shown in Table 3.13, of the four sampled sentences, there are four Type-B feet, the fifth foot in S2 and the second foot in S1, S3 and S4; the other feet are Type-A feet.

Table 3.13 The four sentences sampled for rhythmic analysis

S1	||Tell me the | story about the | clever | monkey |, mummy.||
S2	||I want a | pound of | meat, a | box of | chocolates, and a | loaf of |bread.||
S3	||The handsome | boy who is on his | bicycle.||
S4	||Somebody| told me that it's a | famous | tragedy.||

Note: The symbol \| marks the foot boundary, and \|\| the boundary of a tone group.

Overall stress-timing

The overall stress timing (OST) referred to a duration ratio of unstressed to stressed syllables over the whole speech (Trofimovich & Baker, 2006). The raw duration was not normalized by the speaking rate because it was the duration ratio that was counted.

Syllable variability

There were three features for syllable variability, PWV, PWV-A, PWV-B.

PWV referred to the average duration difference between

the stressed and unstressed syllables in each foot of the four sampled sentences. When calculating PWV, the last syllable in each of the utterance was excluded from analysis because final-syllable lengthening is a common feature of stress-timed languages and would interfere with the measurement of syllable-timing (Deterding, 2001). The raw duration values were normalized by the mean duration of the pair, as shown in equation (1).

Equation (1)

$$PWV = \sum_{k=1}^{m} \left| \frac{d_k^s - d_k^w}{(d_k^s + d_k^w)/2} \right| /m$$

Note: m is the number of feet; d_k^s is the duration of the stressed syllable in the kth foot; and d_k^w is the duration of the unstressed syllable in the kth foot.

According to Lee and Kim (2005), this feature "has been widely used in studies of nonnative speech rhythm" (p. 102), and the algorithm is the simplest among various methods. The normalization was not applied in absolute value because the negative value of the cases could be detected "when the learners pronounced the stressed and unstressed counterparts in the reversed way" (Lee & Lee, 2005, p. 102).

PWV was also calculated in Type-A and Type-B feet respectively, resulting in the other two features, PWV-A and PWV-B.

CV-interval variability

The three CV-interval features (VarcoC, VarcoV, %V) were analyzed in the four sampled sentences. Their operationalizations are presented in Table 3.12.

The segmentation of consonantal and vocalic intervals was

labeled by the researcher in Praat (the bottom tier in Figure 3.2), based on the previously annotated segmentation of syllables in Tier 2 of the corpus, the visual inspection of speech waveforms and wideband spectrograms following White and Mattys' (2007) standard criteria. Vowel-consonant boundaries were placed at the end of the pitch period preceding a break in formant structure, usually associated with a significant drop in waveform amplitude; consonant-vowel boundaries were primarily determined by the onset of vocalic formant structure at the beginning of the pitch period, particularly the second formant. The consonantal or vocalic intervals refer to the duration of the sequences of consecutive consonants or vowels. Pauses longer than 100ms were marked separately; however, if the consonant following the pause was a plosive, 60 milliseconds of the pause was segmented with the plosive as the VOT of an English plosive is approximately of the length. When the pause was shorter than 100ms, it was not marked if it appeared within a consonantal or vocalic interval.

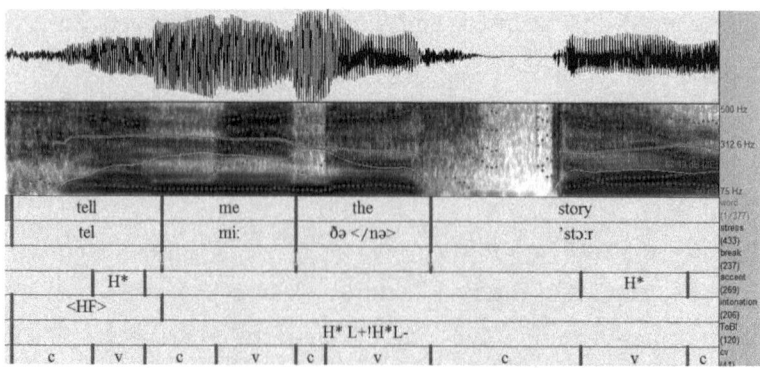

Figure 3.2 The segmentation of vocalic and consonantal intervals, presented in the bottom tier.

3.3.2.3 Fluency

Fluency measurement involved information from three aspects: breakdown fluency, repair fluency, and speed fluency. Altogether, 11 features were analyzed.

3.3.2.3.1 Breakdown fluency

Breakdown fluency was represented by pausing. The pauses measured in this aspect were silent within-sentence pauses longer than 100 milliseconds. Duez (1982) defined silent pause as "any interval of the oscillographic trace where the amplitude is indistinguishable from that of the background noise" (p. 13). Silent pauses within each dialogue and between dialogues were marked as *pau* and *sil* in the orthographic tier (Tier 1) in the existing annotations. The researcher checked the annotation of these pauses, and then sorted out the within-sentence pauses for further analysis. Pauses between sentences and dialogues were not included, for they are usually natural pauses that do not disrupt the smooth flow of speech in perception.

The threshold value of a pause adopted in fluency and pausological research varies, mostly ranging from 100 milliseconds to 400 milliseconds. Many studies on L2 spontaneous speech (Bosker, Quene, Sanders, & De Jong, 2014; Gao & Fan, 2011; Kormos & Denes, 2004; Ma, 2014; Miao, 2009; Towell et al., 1996; Zhang & Wu, 2001) followed the conventional cut-off point of 250 – 300 milliseconds, as Goldman-Eisler (1968) claimed that pauses shorter than 250 milliseconds were articulatory pauses, not caused by hesitation. This threshold was later proved optimal for studies investigating the relationship between pause frequency and L2 proficiency (De Jong & Bosker, 2013). However, studies on L2 read speech

(Anderson-Hsieh, 1994; Chen, Liang, & House, 2004; Chen, 2008a) usually adopted a shorter threshold of 100 milliseconds since read speech requires less cognitive load and less planning time. A shorter threshold in read speech was supported by Hieke, Kowal and O'Connell (1983) who found the majority of pauses of 130 – 250 milliseconds in reading were psychological rather than articulatory. Cheng (2020) further confirmed the minimum cut-off point of 130 milliseconds by associating unnatural pauses longer than 130 milliseconds in the L2 read speech with a significantly higher perception rate. Therefore, considering that this study used the read speech by L2 learners, and the reading material was relatively simple for the speakers, the threshold of silent pauses was set to 100 milliseconds.

The pauses in this study were then marked according to their syntactic location within a sentence. The categorization was mainly based on Hawkins (1971). He developed four general categories for the syntactic location of the pauses on a data-driven basis: a) at clause-boundaries, b) before the predicator, but following the subject or other initial items, c) at group-boundaries elsewhere within the clause, d) at word-boundaries, within the group. This study followed his division generally, but combined the pauses in category b and category c together into a more general category, phrase-boundary pauses. The term "phrase" refers to an immediate "constituent consisting either of one word or of more than one word" (Quirk et al., 1985, p. 40). Consequently, the within-sentence pauses were grouped into three general categories: A) clause-boundary pauses, B) phrase-boundary pauses, and C) within-phrase pauses. Specific locations of these pauses were shown in Appendix B.

Table 3.14 Features of breakdown fluency and operationalizations

Aspect	Feature	Operational definition
Breakdown fluency	PF	Total number of pauses per minute
	ALP	Average length (in milliseconds) of pauses normalized by the ratio of the speech time to the average speech time of all the sample speeches
	PFA	Number of clause-boundary pauses per minute
	ALPA	Average length (in milliseconds) of clause-boundary pauses normalized by the ratio of the speech time to the average speech time of all the sample speeches
	PFB	Number of phrase-boundary pauses per minute
	ALPB	Average length (in milliseconds) of phrase-boundary pauses normalized by the ratio of the speech time to the average speech time of all the sample speeches
	PFC	Number of within-phrase pauses per minute
	ALPC	Average length (in milliseconds) of within-phrase pauses normalized by the ratio of the speech time to the average speech time of all the sample speeches

The pausing pattern was analyzed in terms of overall pause frequency (PF) and average length of pauses (ALP), as well as the PF and ALP in each of the three location groups. Consequently, there are eight pause features (Table 3.14). In the calculation of ALP, the raw length (in milliseconds) of pauses was normalized by the ratio of the speech time to the average speech time of all the sample speeches.

3.3.2.3.2 Repair fluency

Repair fluency was analyzed as disfluencies, including repetition, repair (such as *how many rea-seasons* ...) and filled pauses (such as *Uhm*). Filled pauses were usually considered a kind of pausing phenomenon, included in the aspect of breakdown fluency. In this study, however, since the number of filler pauses were too small in the read speech, they were coded together with other disfluency markers as a feature of repair fluency.

Table 3.15 Features of disfluencies and operationalizations

Aspect	Feature	Operational definition
Repair fluency	DN	Number of syllables repeated, repaired, or filled pauses
	DL	Total length (in milliseconds) of syllables repeated, repaired, or the filled pauses, normalized by the ratio of the speech time to the average speech time of all the sample speeches

As shown in Table 3.15, two features were analyzed, the number (DN) and length (DL) of all the syllables with respect to disfluencies. To minimize the impact of speech rate on the length of disfluencies, DL was normalized by the ratio of the speech time to the average speech time of all the sample speeches.

3.3.2.3.3 Speed fluency

Speed was measured as articulation rate (AR), i.e., the number of syllables produced per minute. Phonation time, or articulation time, was calculated to be the divisor, which refers to the amount of time excluding the length of all intra- and inter-sentence silent pauses (Table 3.16).

Table 3.16 The feature of speed and its operationalization

Aspect	Feature	Operational definition
Speed	AR	Number of syllables per minute in the time taken to produce them (i.e., excluding the length of all intra- and inter-sentence silent pauses)

3.3.3 Data analysis in Phase Ⅰ

Data were recorded into an SPSS (Statistical Package for the Social Sciences, 20.0) spreadsheet, including an ID number for each speech sample, an average holistic score, a holistic rating level, and three analytic scores given to each speech sample, together with the value of each of the 42 features coded in Phase Ⅰ.

To answer the first research question, each feature was subjected to a Pearson's correlation analysis in SPSS, first with the average holistic scores, and then with its corresponding analytic scores[①] of students' read speech. To validate the criterial features, a significant correlation at the 0.05 level of probability with the ratings was required. Also, to lower intercollinearity in the same category, the features with higher correlation coefficients with the ratings were favored.

---

① This means the segmental features are correlated with the segmental ratings, the prosodic features with the prosodic ratings, and the fluency features with the fluency ratings.

3.4 Phase-II study

The remaining 59 of the 89 speech samples, as described in Section 3.2.2 underwent the speech coding in Phase II, in terms of the validated features in Phase I.

3.4.1 Speech coding in Phase II

Since the method of speech coding has been described in great detail in Phase I (See 3.3.2), the definitions of the features validated in Phase I are therefore not repeated. The remaining 59 speech samples were coded by the researcher, based on the existing annotation of RESCCL by trained annotators, thus making up for the lack of a second coder.

3.4.2 Data analysis in Phase II

To answer the second and third research questions, two kinds of statistical analysis were carried out in SPSS. First, to explore the role of the phonological features in distinguishing the holistic rating levels, one-way ANOVA was conducted. Then, to investigate the predicting power of the phonological features to the analytic ratings, multiple linear regression was carried out. This section gives a detailed description on how these two analyses were carried out.

3.4.2.1 Distinguishing the holistic rating levels

The 89 speech samples were grouped into three rating levels as described in Section 3.2.2.1 and 3.2.2.2, with 35 samples in the high-level group (Level 1), 17 in the mid-level group (Level 2), and 37 in the low-level group (Level 3). To find out how the validated phonological features distinguish between different pronunciation rating levels of Chinese EFL students' read speech, each of the validated features in Phase I was subjected to a one-way Analysis of Variance (ANOVA). There are three assumptions for an ANOVA (Field, 2000; Wild & Seber, 2000). The first assumption is the independence of samples, which was met in this study, as no speech sample was repeated in the comparison between level groups. The second assumption relates to the normal distribution of the sample. This is not satisfied for every feature; however, Wild and Seber (2000) pointed out that ANOVA is robust enough to deal with data with departures from this assumption (p. 452). Most importantly, the third assumption requires homogeneity of variances when the groups are compared. This can be indicated by Levene's Test of Homogeneity of Variances. In this study, if the variance differences were found significant in a Levene's Test, with an alpha level of 0.05, a Welch test was adopted instead. This test is more reliable in coping with unequal variances and unequal group sizes. A Games-Howell procedure was conducted as the post hoc test followed by either ANOVA or Welch's test to test the difference between all pairwise comparisons, since this test does not assume equal variance or equal group size (Field, 2000, p. 276).

3.4.2.2 Predicting the analytic ratings

To explore the relative saliency of the validated criterial features in predicting the analytic pronunciation ratings of Chinese EFL students' read speech, three stepwise multiple linear regression analyses were conducted. The dependent variable was the segmental ratings, prosody rating and fluency rating, respectively. The independent variables were the validated phonological features in each of the three categories.

What was also important to consider was whether the data satisfied the assumptions for a multiple linear regression. According to Stevens (2009), there are five key assumptions. First, the relationship between the independent and dependent variables needs to be linear. The linearity assumption was met since the independent variables to be analyzed in the regression were those with significant correlations with the dependent variable. Second, the errors between observed and predicted values (i.e., the residuals of the regression) should be normally distributed. This may be checked by looking at a histogram or a Kolmogorov-Smirnov test on the residuals. Third, no multicollinearity should be found in the data, which means the independent variables are not highly featured with each other. Multicollinearity can be indicated by Variance Inflation Factor (VIF). Fourth, the observations should be independent, which can be tested by the Durbin-Watson statistics. The closer it is to 2, the more independent the observations are. The last assumption is homoscedasticity which stipulates a similar variance of error terms across the values of the independent variables. A scatterplot of residuals versus predicted values is a good way to check for homoscedasticity. The check of the latter three assumptions was conducted in the present analysis to ensure the validity of multiple linear regression.

A stepwise procedure was adopted in the regression analyses, for it produces an efficient model with minimal redundancy among predictors. It first includes in the model the independent variable that best features with the dependent variable, and then adds or removes the remaining independent variables one at a time using the variable's statistical significance until the addition of a remaining independent variable does not increase R-squared by a significant amount.

3.5 Summary

To conclude, in order to identify and validate the criterial features in assessing Chinese EFL learners' pronunciation in the reading-aloud task, the present study was divided into two phases. In Phase I, all the phonological features derived from the literature review were coded in 30 of the 89 speech samples, and their relationships with both the holistic and analytic pronunciation ratings were verified. In Phase II, the validated features were coded in all speech samples, and analyzed to explore their capability in distinguishing holistic pronunciation rating levels and their relative importance in predicting the analytic pronunciation ratings.

Chapter Four
RESULTS AND DISCUSSION I:
The Validation of Criterial Features

This chapter reports the results and discussion of the Phase-I study concerning the first research question, which addresses what phonological features identified in previous literature contribute to the ratings of the Chinese EFL learners' pronunciation.

The descriptive statistics of the 42 features are reported first, followed by their correlation results to the holistic and analytic ratings. The features with a significant correlation with the ratings, and representing a higher correlation with the ratings in the same category are validated as the criterial features.

4.1 Segmental features

There were ten segmental features divided into phoneme deletion, phoneme insertion, and phoneme substitution. They were first correlated with the holistic ratings, and then segmental ratings.

The descriptive statistics of the three groups of features can be found in Table 4.1. There seemed to be more cases of phoneme substitution (ST: 6.57) than those of phoneme deletion errors (DE: 2.9) or phoneme insertion errors (PI:

2.73). Also, ST varied to a greater extent in the speech samples than DE or PI, with a standard deviation of 4.49. There were more types of vowel substitution (SVT) than those of consonant substitution (SCT), but the types of consonant substitution at the onset positions (SCTonset) and those at the coda positions (SCTcoda) were similar. In addition, there were a large number of cases of incomplete plosion (ICP) in the speech samples, with a mean of 13.43, and a higher standard deviation (7.21) than other features.

Table 4.1 Descriptive statistics of segmental features (n=30)

Category	Feature	Mean	SD	Range
Phoneme deletion	DE	2.9	2.26	0—7
	ICP	13.43	7.21	1—29
Phoneme insertion	PI	2.73	3.83	0—19
	CIF	1.27	3.23	0—18
	VIF	1.03	1.75	0—6
Phoneme substitution	ST	6.57	4.49	1—17
	SCT	2.97	2.51	0—9
	SVT	3.60	2.74	0—11
	SCTonset	1.33	1.77	0—6
	SCTcoda	1.63	1.50	0—6

Note:
DE: Phoneme deletion errors
ICP: Incomplete plosion
PI: Phoneme insertion
CIF: Consonants inserted at the word-final position

VIF: Vowel or syllable insertion at the word-final position
ST: Phoneme substitution types in stressed syllables
SVT: Vowel substitution types in stressed syllables
SCT: Consonant substitution types in stressed syllables
SCTonset: Onset consonant substitution types in stressed syllables
SCTcoda: Coda consonant substitution types in stressed syllables

Table 4.2 presents the correlations of the segmental features with both the holistic pronunciation ratings and the segmental ratings. The contributions of segmental features to the two types of ratings were similar. While phoneme deletion errors (DE) did not feature significantly with either type of the ratings, incomplete plosion played a positive role, and presented a significantly moderate correlation with both the holistic ratings (Pearson's $r = 0.50$, $p < 0.01$) and the segmental ratings (Pearson's $r = 0.44$, $p < 0.01$). Moreover, all the phoneme substitution features, except SCTcoda, significantly correlated with the two types of ratings. The more phoneme substitution types there were, the lower rating was given to the read speech. The total number of phoneme substitution types in stressed syllables (ST) had the strongest correlation with the holistic ratings (Pearson's $r = -0.72$, $p < 0.01$) and the segmental ratings (Pearson's $r = -0.75$, $p < 0.01$), followed by vowel and consonant substitution types (SVT, SCT). The impact of consonant substitution seemed to be only prominent at the onset positions, with even a higher correlation coefficient of SCTonset than that of SCT for either the holistic ratings (SCTonset: Pearson's $r = -0.64$, $p < 0.01$; SCT: Pearson's $r = -0.57$, $p < 0.01$) or the segmental ratings (SCTonset: Pearson's $r = -0.69$, $p < 0.01$; SCT: Pearson's $r = -0.66$, $p < 0.01$); therefore, SCTonset might be more representative than SCT as a criterial feature.

Chapter Four RESULTS AND DISCUSSION I : The Validation of Criterial Features

Table 4.2 Pearson's correlation coefficients (two-tailed) between segmental features and pronunciation ratings (n=30)

	DE	ICP	PI	CIF	VIF	ST	SVT	SCT	SCT onset	SCT coda
Holistic rating	−0.04	0.50**	−0.28	−0.17	−0.25	−0.72**	−0.65**	−0.57**	−0.64**	−0.20
Segmental rating	−0.10	0.44**	−0.47*	−0.38*	−0.25	−0.75**	−0.63**	−0.66**	−0.69**	−0.30

Note:
** significant at the 0.01 level of probability
* significant at the 0.05 level of probability
DE: Phoneme deletion errors
ICP: Incomplete plosion
PI: Phoneme insertion
CIF: Consonants inserted at the word-final position
VIF: Vowel or syllable insertion at the word-final position
ST: Phoneme substitution types in stressed syllables
SVT: Vowel substitution types in stressed syllables
SCT: Consonant substitution types in stressed syllables
SCTonset: Onset consonant substitution types in stressed syllables
SCTcoda: Coda consonant substitution types in stressed syllables

The difference between the contributions of the segmental features to the holistic and the segmental ratings lay in the features of phoneme insertion (PI, CIF). While none of the phoneme insertion features (PI, CIF, VIF) showed significant correlations with the holistic ratings, PI presented a moderately significant correlation (Pearson's $r = -0.47$, $p < 0.01$), and CIF a weak correlation (Pearson's $r = -0.38$, $p < 0.05$) with the segmental ratings. Since PI had a higher correlation coefficient than CIF, PI was selected as a criterial feature, contributing negatively to the segmental ratings.

To sum up, of the ten segmental features, four were selected as the criterial features for the holistic pronunciation ratings, namely the number of incomplete plosions (ICP), the number of all phoneme substitution types in stressed syllables

(ST), the number of vowel substitution types in stressed syllables (SVT), and the number of onset consonant substitution types in stressed syllables (SCTonset). For the segmental ratings, one more feature, phoneme insertion (PI), was included together with the above-mentioned four.

4.2 Prosodic features

Altogether, 21 prosodic features were investigated, including eight intonation features, six stress features, and seven rhythmic features. They were first correlated with the holistic ratings, and then the prosodic ratings.

4.2.1 Intonation features

Table 4.3 presents the descriptive statistics of the eight intonation features in three groups, pitch range, intonation phrasing deviation (IP deviation), and tone deviation. The overall pitch range (OPR) was measured by the distance between the f0 maximum and f0 minimum, with a mean of 11.95 semitones. In contrast, IP deviation and tone deviation were measured by the number of deviations. Of the nine examined sentences (See Section 3.3.2.2.1), an average of 4.23 sentences were broken inappropriately into separate intonation phrases (IPD). As to tone deviations, it seemed that learners made fewer mistakes in using falling tones (with a mean TFD of 1.53) than those in using rising or level tones (with a mean TRD of 2.90). Most tone deviations occurred at non-default boundaries; that is to say, learners had more difficulties in using rising or level tones in the statements where needed (TRD1: 2.27) than in the questions (TRD2: 0.63), and in using falling tones in the questions as expected (TFD2: 1.20) than in the statements (TFD1: 0.33).

Table 4.3 Descriptive statistics of intonation features (n=30)

Category	Feature	Mean	SD	Range
Pitch range (st)	OPR	11.95	3.60	7.63—23.48
IP deviation	IPD	4.23	1.50	2—7
Tone deviation	TRD	2.90	2.26	0—9
	TRD1	2.27	2.10	0—7
	TRD2	0.63	0.85	0—3
	TFD	1.53	1.36	0—4
	TFD1	0.33	0.71	0—3
	TFD2	1.20	1.30	0—4

Note:
OPR: Overall pitch range
IPD: Intonation phrasing deviation
TRD: Failure to use the rising or level tone as expected
TRD1: Failure to use rising or level tones at non-default boundaries
TRD2: Failure to use rising or level tones at default boundaries
TFD: Failure to use the falling tone as expected
TFD1: Failure to use falling tones at default boundaries
TFD2: Failure to use falling tones at non-default boundaries

Table 4.4 Pearson's correlation coefficients (two-tailed) between intonation features and pronunciation ratings (n=30)

	OPR	IPD	TRD	TRD1	TRD2	TFD	TFD1	TFD2
Holistic rating	0.44*	-0.61**	-0.40*	-0.48**	0.10	-0.36	-0.12	-0.31
Prosodic rating	0.45*	-0.52**	-0.48*	-0.54**	0.07	-0.32	-0.11	-0.28

Note:
  ** significant at the 0.01 level of probability
  * significant at the 0.05 level of probability

OPR: Overall pitch range
IPD: Intonation phrasing deviation
TRD: Failure to use the rising or level tone as expected
TRD1: Failure to use rising or level tones at non-default boundaries
TRD2: Failure to use rising or level tones at default boundaries
TFD: Failure to use the falling tone as expected
TFD1: Failure to use falling tones at default boundaries
TFD2: Failure to use falling tones at non-default boundaries

The correlations between the intonation features and the holistic as well as the prosodic ratings are shown in Table 4.4. The intonation features which were significantly correlated with the two types of ratings were the same, though with different correlation coefficients. They were overall pitch range (OPR), intonation phrasing deviations (IPD), and the two features related to the failure in using the rising or level tones (TRD, TRD1). It seemed that the speech with a larger pitch range was likely to be rated higher both holistically (Pearson's $r = 0.44$, $p<0.01$) and analytically in prosody (Pearson's $r = 0.45$, $p<0.01$). In contrast, the deviations in intonation phrasing (IPD) negatively contributed to the ratings, with a Pearson's correlation coefficient of -0.61 with the holistic ratings ($p<0.01$), and -0.52 with the prosodic ratings ($p<0.01$).

As to the features of tone deviation, only TRD and TRD1 significantly correlated with the pronunciation ratings, particularly TRD1, which denoted learners' difficulty in using the rising or level tones at non-default boundaries, such as those in the statements to signify non-finality or contrast (with the holistic rating: Pearson's $r = -0.48$, $p<0.01$; with the prosodic rating: Pearson's $r = -0.54$, $p<0.01$). TRD2, the failure to use rising or level tones at default boundaries (e.g., in yes/no questions), and all the three features of falling tone deviation (TFD, TFD1, TFD2) did not significantly correlate with the pronunciation ratings. This was mainly attributed to the small number of cases of these tone deviations (Table 4.3), indicating the less difficulties of Chinese EFL learners in using falling tones or in using non-falling tones at default boundaries.

In a word, three intonation features were validated as the criterial features, namely overall pitch range (OPR), intonation phrasing deviations (IPD), and the failure to use rising or level tones at non-default boundaries (TRD1). TRD, though having a significantly moderate correlation with both types of the ratings, was not selected, for it was mainly represented by TRD1, and had a lower correlation coefficient than TRD1 with the ratings.

4.2.2 Stress features

There were six stress features divided into three groups, lexical stress, sentence stress, and nuclear stress. Table 4.5 gives the descriptive statistics of the six stress features. The lexical S/U examined the duration ratio of the stressed to unstress vowels in the sampled bi-syllabic words. It presented a mean ratio of 1.42, showing that speakers could pronounce stressed vowels longer than the unstressed vowels in the sampled words. It can also be seen clearly that Chinese EFL learners produced many sentences (SE) and nuclear stress errors (NE), with a mean of 18.47 and 16.97, respectively. The mean duration ratio of sampled tonic to weak syllables (T/W dur: 1.87) was higher than the mean f0 (T/W f0: 1.01) and intensity ratios (T/W int: 1.02), indicating a greater contrast that learners could produce in terms of duration rather than f0 or intensity between tonic and weak syllables. Also, the variations of T/W f0 and T/W int were very small, suggesting a common characteristic among the speakers.

Table 4.5 Descriptive statistics of stress features (n=30)

Category	Feature	Mean	SD	Range
Lexical stress	S/U	1.42	0.25	1.02—1.86
Sentence stress	SE	18.47	5.43	8—33
Nuclear stress	NE	16.97	2.55	12—22
	T/W dur	1.87	0.21	1.51—2.42
	T/W f0	1.01	0.01	0.98—1.03
	T/W int	1.02	0.02	0.98—1.06

Note:
S/U: Average ratio of the stressed to unstressed vowel duration in sample bi-syllabic words
SE: Sentence stress errors
NE: Nuclear stress errors
T/W dur: Duration ratio of sampled tonic to weak syllables
T/W f0: F0 ratio of sampled tonic to weak syllables
T/W int: Intensity ratio of sampled tonic to weak syllables

Table 4.6 presents the correlations of stress features with both the holistic and prosodic ratings. Three stress features, sentence stress errors (SE), nuclear stress errors (NE), and duration ratio of sampled tonic to weak syllables (T/W dur), significantly correlated with both types of ratings. NE had the highest correlation coefficients (with the holistic rating: Pearson's $r = -0.71$, $p < 0.01$; with the prosodic rating: Pearson's $r = -0.70$, $p < 0.01$), followed by SE (with the holistic rating: Pearson's $r = -0.66$, $p < 0.01$; with the prosodic rating: Pearson's $r = -0.60$, $p < 0.01$) and T/W dur (with the holistic rating: Pearson's $r = -0.54$, $p < 0.01$; with the prosodic rating: Pearson's $r = -0.57$, $p < 0.01$). The speech samples with less nuclear or sentence stress errors, and greater duration contrast between tonic and weak syllables tended to be rated higher. Other stress features, including the lexical S/U, T/W f0 and T/W int, did not show significant correlations with either type of the ratings.

Consequently, three features of sentence stress (SE, NE, T/W dur) were validated.

Table 4.6 Pearson's correlation coefficients (two-tailed) between stress features and pronunciation ratings (n=30)

	S/U	SE	NE	T/W dur	T/W f0	T/W int
Holistic rating	0.36	−0.66**	−0.71**	0.54**	0.07	0.17
Prosodic rating	0.25	−0.60**	−0.70**	0.57**	0.04	0.04

Note:
** significant at the 0.01 level of probability
S/U: Average ratio of the stressed to unstressed vowel duration in sample bi-syllabic words
SE: Sentence stress errors
NE: Nuclear stress errors
T/W dur: Duration ratio of sampled tonic to weak syllables
T/W f0: F0 ratio of sampled tonic to weak syllables
T/W int: Intensity ratio of sampled tonic to weak syllables

4.2.3 Rhythmic features

Table 4.7 presents the descriptive statistics of the seven rhythmic features in three categories, the overall stress-timing, syllable variability and CV-interval variability. It seemed that the Chinese EFL learners had difficulties in reducing the vowels in unstressed syllables and were incapable of producing a stress-timed rhythm in general, as is shown by a high OST value (0.77), and low values in PWV (0.36), VarcoC (0.5) and VarcoV (0.3). The only exception was PWV-A, the pairwise variability in type-A sentences with a regular alternation of stressed and unstressed syllables. The mean value of PWV-A was as high as 0.8, indicating a considerably large duration contrast between stressed and unstressed counterparts in the type-A sentences. In contrast, the value of PWV-B was negative (−0.74), showing that learners generally failed to reduce long stretches of weak syllables between strong syllables to the extent of meeting the native-like stress timing, leading to a longer duration of the stretch of weak syllables than that of the stressed counterpart. This difference between PWV-A and PWV-B suggests that Chinese EFL learners had better control of the stress-timed rhythm when producing sentences with type-A foot structure than those with the type-B foot structure.

Table 4.7 Descriptive statistics of rhythmic features (n=30)

Category	Feature	Mean	SD	Range
Overall stress-timing	OST	0.77	0.07	0.65—0.94
Syllable variability	PWV	0.36	0.16	−0.06—0.74
	PWV-A	0.80	0.18	0.32—1.14
	PWV-B	−0.74	0.18	−1.03—−0.04
CV-interval variability	VarcoC	0.50	0.51	0—1
	VarcoV	0.30	0.47	0—1
	%V	45.02	3.07	39.43—50.57

Note:
OST: Overall stress timing
PWV: Pairwise variability
PWV-A: Pairwise variability in type-A foot (with short stretches of weak syllables)
PWV-B: Pairwise variability in type-B foot (with long stretches of weak syllables)
VarcoC: Normalized standard deviation of consonantal intervals
VarcoV: Normalized standard deviation of vocalic intervals
%V: Average proportion of vocalic intervals in the sampled sentences

Table 4.8 Pearson's correlation coefficients (two-tailed) between rhythmic features and pronunciation ratings (n=30)

	OST	PWV	PWV-A	PWV-B	%V	Varco-C	Varco-V
Holistic rating	-0.55**	0.46*	0.45*	0.29	-0.05	0.02	0.13
Prosodic rating	-0.59**	0.50**	0.50**	0.30	-0.02	0.13	0.24

Note:
** significant at the 0.01 level of probability
* significant at the 0.05 level of probability
OST: Overall stress timing
PWV: Pairwise variability
PWV-A: Pairwise variability in type-A foot (with short stretches of weak syllables)
PWV-B: Pairwise variability in type-B foot (with long stretches of weak syllables)
VarcoC: Normalized standard deviation of consonantal intervals
VarcoV: Normalized standard deviation of vocalic intervals
%V: Average proportion of vocalic intervals in the sampled sentences

The correlations of the rhythmic features with the holistic and prosodic ratings were almost the same. As is shown in Table 4.8, three rhythmic features (OST, PWV, PWV-A) significantly correlated with both types of ratings, with OST having the highest correlation coefficients among the three (with the holistic rating: Pearson's $r = -0.55$, $p<0.01$; with the prosodic rating: Pearson's $r = -0.59$, $p<0.01$). The higher value of OST meant a smaller duration contrast between unstressed and stressed counterparts over the speech, hence contributing to a lower holistic and prosodic rating. With regard to pairwise syllable variability, the significant contribution of PWV to the ratings was mainly represented by PWV-A (pairwise variability in type-A feet with short stretches of weak syllables), rather than PWV-B (pairwise variability in type-B feet with long stretches of weak syllables), suggesting learners common difficulty in producing type-B stress timing. All the CV-interval features (VarcoC, Varco V, and % V) failed to feature with either type of the ratings.

Considering that both the overall stress-timing feature (OST) and the pairwise variability features (PWV, PWV-A) calculated the duration contrast between the stressed and unstressed counterparts, though one by ratio, and the other by distance, OST was chosen as a criterial rhythmic feature, as it had a stronger correlation with both types of the ratings.

4.3 Fluency features

Altogether, 11 fluency features were analyzed in terms of speed, repair, and breakdown. They were correlated with the holistic ratings first, and with the fluency ratings next.

The descriptive statistics of the three groups of features were shown in Table 4.9. The speed feature was calculated as articulation rate (AR), with a mean of 280.11 syllables per minute. Repair fluency was measured by the number (DN) and length (DL) of disfluencies (syllables repeated, repaired, or filled pauses). As is presented in Table 4.9, such disfluencies were rare, with a mean of 1.63 cases and an average length of 414.31 milliseconds. The breakdown fluency was analyzed in terms of the frequency (PF) and length (ALP) of within-sentence pauses, with a mean of 13.48 pauses per minute and an average length of 257.77 milliseconds. There seemed to be more phrase-boundary pauses (PFB: 5.92) than clause-boundary (PFA: 3.76) and within-phrase pauses (PFC: 3.73). As expected, the clause-boundary pauses were longer (ALPA:

334.66 milliseconds) than phrase-boundary pauses (ALPB: 246.93 milliseconds) and within-phrase pauses (ALPC: 180.31 milliseconds).

Table 4.9 Descriptive statistics of fluency features (n=30)

Category	Feature	Mean	SD	Range
Speed	AR	280.11	26.98	223.86—353.17
Repair fluency	DN	1.63	2.03	0—8
	DL	414.31	616.94	0—2300
Breakdown fluency	PF	13.48	4.36	5.54—24.78
	PFA	3.76	1.19	1.58—6.24
	PFB	5.92	2.28	0.79—9.78
	PFC	3.73	2.18	0—9.78
	ALP	257.77	67.48	150.28—404.26
	ALPA	334.66	110.48	171.83—556.31
	ALPB	246.93	81.60	141.41—430.26
	ALPC	180.31	85.74	0—485.23

Note:
AR: Articulation rate
DN: Number of disfluencies
DL: Average length of disfluencies
PF: Frequency of all silent pauses
PFA: Frequency of silent pauses at clause boundaries
PFB: Frequency of silent pauses at phrase boundaries
PFC: Frequency of silent pauses within phrases
ALP: Average length of all silent pauses
ALPA: Average length of silent pauses at clause boundaries
ALPB: Average length of silent pauses at phrase boundaries
ALPC: Average length of silent pauses within phrases

Table 4.10 presents the correlations between fluency features and both holistic and fluency ratings. The contributions of the fluency features to the two types of ratings were similar.

While features of repair fluency (DN, DL) and pause length (ALP, ALPA, ALPB, ALPC) did not correlate with either type of ratings, articulation rate (AR) and features of pause frequency (PF, PFA, PFB, PFC) showed significant correlations with both ratings. AR had the strongest association with both the holistic (Pearson's $r = 0.68$, $p<0.01$) and fluency ratings (Pearson's $r = 0.73$, $p<0.01$).

As to features of pause frequency, though they all significantly correlated with the ratings, their contributions varied, with the overall pause frequency (PF) ranking highest, followed by pause frequency between clauses (PFA), between phrases (PFB) and within phrases (PFC).

Therefore, for both types of the ratings, five fluency features (AR, PF, PFA, PFB and PFC) were validated as criterial features.

Table 4.10 Pearson's correlation coefficients (two-tailed) between fluency features and pronunciation ratings ($n=30$)

	AR	DN	DL	PF	PFA	PFB	PFC	ALP	ALPA	ALPB	ALPC
Holistic rating	0.68**	−0.23	−0.31	−0.59**	−0.54**	−0.44*	−0.42*	−0.27	−0.22	−0.28	−0.30
Fluency rating	0.73**	−0.13	−0.30	−0.53**	−0.51**	−0.38**	−0.37*	−0.25	−0.16	−0.28	−0.33

Note:
** significant at the 0.01 level of probability
* significant at the 0.05 level of probability
AR: Articulation rate
DN: Number of disfluencies
DL: Average length of disfluencies
PF: Frequency of all silent pauses
PFA: Frequency of silent pauses at clause boundaries
PFB: Frequency of silent pauses at phrase boundaries
PFC: Frequency of silent pauses within phrases
ALP: Average length of all silent pauses
ALPA: Average length of silent pauses at clause boundaries

ALPB: Average length of silent pauses at phrase boundaries
ALPC: Average length of silent pauses within pauses

4.4 Discussion

This part discusses in turn the phonological features that significantly contributed to the ratings of the Chinese EFL learners' pronunciation, and those that did not.

4.4.1 Features that significantly contributed to the pronunciation ratings

Of the 42 phonological features derived from previous literature, 16 were verified as the criterial features of the holistic pronunciation ratings. They covered all the three dimensions of pronunciation, including segmentals, prosody, and fluency. The verified features from each dimension also significantly contributed to their corresponding analytic ratings. Only one more feature, phoneme insertion, was found to correlate significantly to the segmental ratings but not to the holistic ratings. The large overlapping of the features correlated to the two types of ratings strengthens the validity of these criterial features in the pronunciation assessment. Table 4.11 presents a summary of these validated features.

4.4.1.1 Segmental features

Four segmental features significantly correlated to both holistic and analytic ratings. They were the features of phoneme substitution (ST, SVT, SCTonset) and that of incomplete plosion (ICP). One feature, phoneme insertion (PI), only significantly correlated to the segmental ratings, but not to the holistic ratings.

Table 4.11 The validated phonological features

Category	Feature		Operational Definition
Segmental	Phoneme deletion	ICP	Number of incomplete plosion
	Phoneme insertion	* PI	Number of phoneme insertion
	Phoneme substitution	ST	Number of phoneme substitution types in stressed syllables
		SVT	Number of vowel substitution types in stressed syllables
		SCTonset	Number of onset consonant substitution types in stressed syllables
Prosody	Intonation phrasing deviation	IPD	Number of intonation phrasing deviation
	Tone deviation	TRD1	Number of failures to use rising or level tones at non-default boundaries
	Overall pitch range	OPR	Distance in semitone between f0 maximum and f0 minimum on the vowels of stressed syllables over the read speech
	Sentence stress	SE	Number of sentence stress errors
		NE	Number of nuclear stress errors
		T/W dur	Duration ratio of sampled tonic to weak syllables
	Overall stress timing	OST	Duration ratio of unstressed to stressed syllables over the whole speech

	Category	Feature	Operational Definition
Fluency	Speed	AR	Number of syllables per minute in the time taken to produce them
	Pauses	PF	Total number of pauses per minute
		PFA	Number of clause-boundary pauses per minute
		PFB	Number of phrase-boundary pauses per minute
		PFC	Number of within-phrase pauses per minute

Note: * significantly contributing to the segmental ratings but not to the holistic ratings

4.4.1.1.1 Features of phoneme substitution

Compared with other segmental features, the features of phoneme substitution in stressed syllables played a more important role in raters' judgment of both overall pronunciation proficiency and segmental quality, which is probably owing to the fact that they tended to reduce intelligibility in a detrimental way (Zielinski, 2006). Also, when measured in stressed syllables, phoneme substitutions might possibly make the inaccurate segment production more prominent to raters as well. Two out of the three raters interviewed reported explicitly that they viewed more segment substitutions as a characteristic of lower pronunciation proficiency.

This study also suggests the important role of both vowel and consonant substitutions, and the position of consonant substitutions in the raters' judgment, so as to concord with Bent et al.'s (2007) and Rogers and Dalby's (2005) findings. The consonant substitutions at the onset positions correlated with the pronunciation ratings significantly, while those at the coda positions did not, as it is the onset consonant substitutions that impair intelligibility (Bent et al., 2007; Rogers & Dalby, 2005). It seems indeed true that the lexical access model (Marslen-Wilson, 1989) plays a role in the listeners' perception of not only word segmentation, but also pronunciation, since they are interrelated in terms of intelligibility. An error in initial segments might activate a wrong word and cause greater processing cost for a recovery of the intended content. For example, the substitution of /l/ for /n/ at the onset position in words such as *like* and *loaf* would impair intelligibility to a greater extent than the substitution of /l/ for /r/ at the coda position in the word *tell*; the substitution of /w/ for /v/ at the onset position of /wind/ affected the raters' perception more than the substitution of /d/ for /t/ at the coda position of /wind/.

4.4.1.1.2 Feature of incomplete plosion

Incomplete plosion also contributed significantly to the raters' perception of pronunciation, though not as greatly as phoneme substitutions did. It has long been one of the pronunciation skills taught in the classrooms and is also presented in the interpretation of the descriptor "range of pronunciation features" in the IELTS Pronunciation subscale (2018). According to Cruttenden (2001), one common feature of connected English is the elision of plosives, alveolar plosives in particular, when they are in consonant clusters prior to another stop, or an affricate, a nasal, a fricative and a liquid, within or across morpheme boundaries. Therefore, a high value of ICP presents an ability to apply plosive elision in the consonant sequences, and indicates a more fluent and stress-timing speech, according to the raters' comments. The less contribution it had to the perception of segmental quality than to the overall pronunciation might suggest its function in fluency and rhythm perception rather than in the perception of segmentals. The role incomplete plosion plays in the pronunciation ratings clearly deserves more attention in further research.

4.4.1.1.3 Feature of phoneme insertion

Phoneme insertion was the only feature that had a different contribution to the holistic and analytic ratings. It did not correlate significantly with the holistic ratings, but played a significant role in the segmental ratings.

Previous literature has revealed a common problem of adding extra syllables, most often /ə/, at the word-final positions for Chinese EFL learners, due to the difficulty caused by the difference between Chinese and English in syllable structure (Deterding, 2006; Hansen, 2001; Zielinski, 2006). This study is in line with them, and further found that besides /ə/, the fricative /s/ was also frequently added at the word-final positions, such as /miːts/ for *meat* and /wɒnts/ for *want*. This might be owing to an emphasis on English grammatical rules in the language classroom, since both the regular plural noun form and the third person singular verb form require the addition of an "s" at the end of the word.

However, either the insertion of vowel or consonant at the word-final position alone could significantly correlate with the pronunciation ratings. Only when calculated together, and with those at other positions could the overall phoneme insertion play a role in the judgment of the segmental quality, but not of the holistic pronunciation quality. For one thing, this suggests a less important role phoneme insertion played in the raters' perception when they had to judge the overall pronunciation from both segmental and suprasegmental dimensions. This is most probably attributed to the fact that phoneme insertion usually does not cause as much processing difficulty or intelligibility reduction as phoneme substitution does. For another, this finding also indicates that raters tended to take more aspects of pronunciation into consideration when rating analytically, so different descriptors or criteria should be included in the holistic and the segmental rating scales (if analytic rating scales are applied for pronunciation). This also empirically supports Weigle's (2002) that analytic scales could provide more diagnostic information for both raters and learners.

4.4.1.2 Prosodic features

Seven prosodic features were found to significantly contribute to both types of ratings, including three intonation features (OPR, IPD, TRD1), three stress features (SE, DE, T/W dur), and one rhythmic feature (OST). It seems that both types of pronunciation ratings were affected more by stress and rhythm than by intonation.

4.4.1.2.1 Stress and rhythmic features

The great contribution of stress and rhythmic features to the pronunciation perception suggests the importance of the communicative function of pronunciation. As pointed out by the intelligibility principle of pronunciation (Levis, 2005), a good pronunciation should be the one that facilitates understanding. English, as a stress-timed language, conveys meaning by stress. Therefore, listeners depend heavily on the stress pattern in the information decoding process (Cutler, 1984). That is to say, a correct stress pattern would help listeners grasp the semantic and pragmatic meanings of the speech more efficiently; if the stress is incorrectly placed, an error of interpretation will occur. This explains the high correlation between stress or rhythmic features and the pronunciation ratings.

The stress features involve both the placement of sentence and nuclear stress and the saliency of nuclear stress.

As discussed above, the misplacement of either sentence (SE) or nuclear stress (NE) could impair understanding in a detrimental way. As literature describes, sentence rhythmic stresses usually fall on the stressed syllables of content words in the utterance, unless for rhythmic reasons or speaker intentions. The inappropriate stress on function words rather than content words would result in a failure to convey information effectively. Consistent with findings in previous studies (Chen & Bi, 2015; Yang, 2010), a large majority of the sentence stress errors in the learners' speech are on function words, nearly half of which are personal pronouns (over 40%), such as *they*, *I* and *you*, particularly when they are located at sentence-initial or -final positions. The errors also include the connectives that link coordinate clauses and the subordinate clause to the main clause, as shown in Examples (9) and (10). Students were likely to break the compound and complex sentences before or sometimes after the connectives, and put a stress on the words at the boundaries. Other types of errors involve those on prepositions (as in the sentence *But only if there's something good on*), sentence initial *here/there* (as in **Here's** *another story*), sentence-initial adjunct *well*, infinite structure marker *to* at the sentence-final position (as in *I'd love to*), auxiliary/ model verbs (such as *do* and *can*), and non-subject indefinite *something*.

(9) *Do you want to go to the cinema tonight*, **or** *have you got to stay late at work again*?
(10) *Take it back to the shop* **where** *you bought it*.

Similarly, nuclear stress errors often appear on personal pronouns, particularly *they* at the end of the wh-question or tag-question [See Examples (11) and (12)], which concords with many previous studies (Chen, 2006; Chen & Bi, 2015; Ding, 2017; Makarova & Zhou, 2006; Yuan, 2010). The final-position nuclei errors may be attributed to the inappropriate break of intonational phrases. For example, when learners separated the main clause and the object clause, as in Example (13), the connective *that* becomes the last word in the former intonational phrase, hence bearing the nuclear stress. Another kind of final-position errors results from the negligence of contrastive or emphatic focus of the information, which plays an important role in forming marked tonicity (Wells, 2006) (See Example 3 in Section 2.3.2.1.2).

(11) *What are THEY?*
(12) *…, didn't THEY?*
(13) *I've heard THAT | …*

The saliency of nuclear stress was measured by the duration

contrast between the sampled tonic and weak syllables (T/W dur). This study is in line with Chen et al.'s (2001a) finding that Chinese EFL learners were able to distinguish tonic syllables and weak syllables by duration, as presented by a mean T/W dur higher than 1. The increasing value of T/W dur with the pronunciation ratings also supports Yang's (2010) to some extent that the duration contrast could be improved by repeated imitation exercises.

The rhythmic feature, OST, calculated the overall duration ratio of the intended unstressed to stressed syllables. According to Trofimovich and Baker's (2006), the OST in native speakers' speech was close to 0.5, and a high OST meant learners' inability to reduce the unstressed syllables. With a mean OST value of 0.77, the present study shows the Chinese EFL learners' difficulty in applying the stress-timing rhythm, which is consistent with a number of studies (Hua, 2003; Wang, 2001, as cited by Yang and Chen, 2005; Yang, 2010). The high OST value could also be a result of the misplacement of sentence stress, as OST calculated the intended stressed and unstressed syllables, not the actually stressed and unstressed counterparts. The downward tendency of the OST with the increased pronunciation ratings generally supports the previous studies that the stress-timing pattern can be improved with learner training and experience (Yang, 2010; Trofimovich & Baker, 2006).

4.4.1.2.2 Intonation features

Intonation features also significantly correlated with both types of pronunciation ratings, but their contributions were smaller, compared with the stress and rhythmic features, most probably owing to the less important role they play in the conveyance of semantic meanings. As suggested by this study, a higher pronunciation proficiency features less deviations in intonation phrasing (IPD) and non-default rising tone use (TRD1), and a wider overall pitch range (OPR).

Previous literature (Chen & Bi, 2015) has revealed Chinese EFL learners' difficulty in intonation phrasing where it does not align with grammatical boundaries (See Table 3.10 in Section 3.3.2.2.1), and in the use of rising tone to signify non-finality or contrast in the statements (See Example 4, 5 and 6 in Section 2.3.2.1.3). This study supports their findings and further confirms the negative correlation between these difficulties and the pronunciation ratings. A lower IPD or TRD1 indicated a higher ability to apply appropriate intonation phrasing patterns and rising tones to serve discoursal and attitudinal functions, hence enhancing comprehensibility (Pickering, 2001).

Besides, this study is also in line with a bunch of studies, which has found a narrower OPR for Chinese EFL learners, compared with native English speakers (e.g., Chen, 2002; Chen, 2008a; Hincks & edlund, 2009; Pickering, 2001). The upward trend of OPR with pronunciation proficiency is similar to that found in Chen's (2008a), although the mean OPR in this study was higher than that of the Chinese EFL learners' in her study. This is mainly caused by the learner sampling, with both middle school students and undergraduates/postgraduates in Chen's (2008a), and all college English majors in this study, who could reasonably be considered to have a higher English proficiency than the learners in Chen's. As suggested by Kang (2010), a compressed pitch range in learner speech might make the speech sound more foreign accented, and less expressive, which in turn would possibly lead to a loss of listeners' concentration and impair comprehensibility.

4.4.1.3 Fluency features

Five fluency features were found to significantly correlate with both types of the pronunciation ratings, including one speed feature (AR) and four breakdown features (PF, PFA, PFB, PFC), with AR demonstrating a stronger correlation than the breakdown features.

4.4.1.3.1 Speed feature

It is no surprise that AR functions well in contributing to the pronunciation ratings, as this feature has been repeatedly confirmed to significantly affect the perceived fluency (Bosker et al., 2013; Cucciarini et al., 2002; Derwing et al., 2004; Kormos & Denes, 2004), comprehensibility (Kang, 2010; Kang et al., 2010) and accentedness (Trofimovich & Baker, 2007). A slower rate in L2 speech has been considered as a result of difficulties in the encoding and retrieval of phonological information, or in the articulation of L2 sounds, or both (Munro & Derwing, 2001). A slower rate could also indicate the inability to use weak forms or apply pronunciation skills such as liaison and incomplete plosion to produce a stress-timing rhythm. As two of the three raters reported, a slow rate made the speech sound unnatural, with every word pronounced too clearly and popping out on its own.

4.4.1.3.2 Breakdown features

Breakdown fluency is another major factor influencing both overall pronunciation perception and fluency perception. This is generally in line with previous research, which constantly revealed that the L2 speech with less silent pauses would be perceived as more fluent (Bosker et al., 2013; Cucchiarini et al., 2002) and less accented (Kang et al., 2010; Trofimovich & Baker, 2007).

The breakdown fluency was measured by both the frequency and duration of intra-sentence silent pauses. The findings of this study seem to suggest a more important role of pause frequency than duration in the perception of pronunciation as a whole and of fluency in particular. While all the frequency features contributed significantly to both types of pronunciation ratings, all the duration features did not. This might be attributed to the task type and task difficulty. Since the speaking task was a dialogue reading-aloud task, and the reading material was easy with an average of 6.4 words per sentence, there was no need to pause within sentences, whether at the clause or phrase boundaries, whether to take a breath, or to prepare for ideas or vocabulary. Any intra-sentence pauses were considered inappropriate.

4.4.2 Features that failed to significantly contribute to the pronunciation ratings

The failure of some theoretically derived features to significantly contribute to the pronunciation ratings is attributed to two factors, the shared characteristics in learner production, and the less important role of these features in raters' perception.

4.4.2.1 Learner production

Some features presented the common difficulties in or good command of particular aspects of pronunciation among Chinese EFL learners, hence failing to significantly correlate with the pronunciation ratings.

With regard to the tone choices, the present study suggests that Chinese EFL learners had generally acquired the default tone choices in different sentence types; that is to say, learners were aware that falling tones are usually associated with the boundaries of statements, and non-falling tones with yes/no questions. Therefore, the deviated tone choices in default sentence types, such as TRD2 (failure to use rising tone at the boundaries of questions, wh-questions excluded) and TFD1 (failure to use falling tone at the boundaries of simple statements), were rare and did not contribute to the pronunciation ratings significantly. Besides, Chinese EFL learners had a good command of using the falling tone to signal finality not only in simple statements but also in questions. This can be seen by the insignificant role TFD2 (failure to use falling tone at the boundaries of questions) played in the pronunciation ratings. This good command of default tone choices is attributed to the English teaching tradition in China which has long adopted a narrow concept of English intonation and has emphasized the grammatical function of tone choices rather than their discoursal or attitudinal functions.

Another characteristic in Chinese EFL learners' pronunciation is the common difficulty in realizing nuclear stress by pitch level and intensity. Accented and unaccented counterparts could be differentiated by features of pitch, intensity and duration (Chen et al., 2001; Hua, 2003). Though Hua (2003) found that all the three features varied in how stress was realized by Mandarin speakers of different proficiency, realizing stress by pitch and intensity might be more difficult to acquire than by duration, as Yang (2010) reported the effect of repeated exercises on the improvement of the duration ratio, but not on the pitch ratio between the accented and unaccented counterparts. Consistent with Yang's (2010), this study found relatively stable f0 and intensity ratios of tonic to weak syllables (T/W f0, T/W int) in the speech samples, and the insignificant contribution they made to the pronunciation ratings.

Moreover, Chinese EFL learners were generally incapable of reducing vowels, particularly in a long stretch of weak syllables. This was reflected by a failed rhythmic feature, PWV-B, which indicated pairwise duration variability between adjacent stressed and unstressed syllable sequences in irregular feet (Type-B feet with a long stretch of weak syllables). Different from PWV-A, the pairwise variability in Type-A feet (regular feet with a short stretch of weak syllables), the mean value of PWV-B was negative, suggesting a longer duration of the long stretch of weak syllables than the stressed counterpart in the foot. This supports Hua's (2003) claim that Mandarin speakers of English had more difficulties producing Type-B (with a long stretch of weak syllables in a foot) than Type-A stress-timing (with a short stretch of weak syllables in a foot). The problem with Type-B timing is most probably attributed to the inability of Mandarin speakers to reduce vowels, apply linking and various types of coarticulation (Chen, 2008b; Hua, 2003; Li, 2014).

Similarly, all the CV-interval metrics (%V, Varco-C, Varco-V) did not show significant correlation with the pronunciation ratings, as they all represent the ability of vowel reduction to some degree. In previous literature, these features, together with their earlier versions (ΔC, ΔV), yielded inconsistent findings when relating them to proficiency levels

(Chen, 2008b; Jang, 2008; Li, 2014; Ramus et al., 1999). The present study supports Jang (2008) by showing the inability of these features to distinguish pronunciation ratings, with little variations among the speech samples. For one thing, this might indicate the shared difficulty for Chinese EFL learners in acquiring the stress timed rhythm, due to negative L1 transfer since Chinese is a syllable-timed language. For another, this might pose a challenge on the validity of these metrics in analyzing the rhythm in L2 English, because the greater variability of the consonantal intervals might not be a result of appropriate vowel reduction, but of vowel deletion errors. For example, when a speaker mispronounced /ˈbaɪsɪkl/ (*bicycle*) as /ˈbaɪskl/, the deleted /ɪ/ resulted in a longer consonantal interval of /skl/. Similarly, as a speaker omitted the article *a* in the sentence *It's a famous tragedy*, the word-final consonant cluster /ts/ in *it's* was then grouped with the following word-initial /f/ in *famous*, and formed a longer consonant cluster /tsf/. Such mispronunciations in Chinese EFL learners' speech were common, which might explain, to a certain extent, a higher Varco-C in speech samples with lower pronunciation ratings.

4.4.2.2 Rater perception

Rater perception is the other important factor leading to the failure of a few features to significantly contribute to the pronunciation ratings.

First, raters seemed to be more sensitive to the onset segments than the coda ones. As suggested by the lexical access model (Marslen-Wilson, 1989), the deviations at the coda positions might not impair intelligibility in a detrimental way as those at the onset positions (Bent et al., 2007). This view well explains why the segmental features concerning the coda positions did not significantly correlate with the pronunciation ratings, such as the coda consonant substitution (SCTcoda), the consonant and vowel insertion at the word-final positions (CIF, VIF) and the phoneme deletion errors (DE) since most deletion errors occurred at the word-final positions.

Second, rater perception could also be affected by the task type and task difficulty. As described in Section 4.4.1.3.2, the speech samples in the present study were elicited from the dialogue reading aloud task, with relatively easy reading material designed for average middle-school students. Such a task did not demand a high cognitive load for the speakers; therefore, intra-sentence pauses were not expected by the raters. This helps to explain why all the features of pause frequency significantly correlated with the pronunciation ratings, while all the features of pause length did not. It is evident that to the raters, pauses at any locations within a sentence were not welcomed in the read speech, whether they were short or long.

Third, raters' interpretation of some of the features in the speech samples might affect their perception of the speakers' pronunciation proficiency. In line with the previous studies (Bosker et al., 2013; Derwing et al., 2004), both features of repair fluency, the number of disfluencies (DN), and the length of disfluencies (DL), were not found to contribute to the pronunciation ratings significantly. This could be partly attributed to the attitude of the raters towards the disfluency phenomena, particularly self-pair. As rater-Y explained in the interview, some types of repair, such as self-correction, represented an ability of self-monitoring, showing that the speaker was able to correct his/her own mistakes. If the repair was correct, it would not negatively affect the rater's evaluation of the speaker's pronunciation proficiency.

Chapter Five
RESULTS AND DISCUSSION Ⅱ: Distinguishing the Holistic Rating Levels

This chapter presents the results and discussion of the Phase-Ⅱ study concerning the second research question, which addresses what role the phonological features play in distinguishing the holistic rating levels of Chinese EFL learners' pronunciation.

The 89 speech samples came from three holistic rating levels (High, Medium, Low) as described in Section 3.2.2.1, with 35 samples in the high-level group, 17 in the medium-level group, and 37 in the low-level group. The mean holistic ratings for the three groups are 83.35 (SD: 1.63), 77.08 (SD: 0.38) and, 70.28 (SD: 2.10), respectively. The 16 features validated in the Phase-I study were coded, and their abilities to distinguish the three holistic rating levels were examined by one-way ANOVA tests or Welch's tests[1].

Three pieces of information are to be presented for each feature under investigation, a table giving the descriptive statistics over the speech samples and across rating levels, a bar

---

[1] A Levene's Test was conducted for each variable. If the variance differences were found significant ($p > 0.05$), a Welch's test was adopted; otherwise, a one-way ANOVA test was run.

chart illustrating the mean values across the rating levels with a confidence interval of 0.95, and the result of a one-way ANOVA test or a Welch's test.

5.1 Segmental features

There were four segmental features under investigation, including three features of phoneme substitution and one feature of incomplete plosion.

Table 5.1 presents the descriptive statistics of phoneme substitution types in stressed syllables (ST), with a mean of 6.69. It is evident that more STs were identified in lower level groups (Table 5.1, Figure 5.1). Since Levene's test showed significant variance difference ($p < 0.001$), Welch's test was performed to reveal a significant difference between the different levels (Welch's F (2, 38.34) = 31.71, $p < 0.001$, est. $\omega^2 = 0.41$). The Games-Howell post hoc procedure showed statistically significant differences between the medium/high and low levels (medium-low: $p = 0.008$, Cohen's $d = 0.96$; high-low: $p < 0.001$, Cohen's $d = 1.88$), but not between the high and medium levels ($p = 0.131$).

Table 5.1 Descriptive statistics of ST across holistic rating levels and over the speech samples

Rating level	N	Mean	SD	Minimum	Maximum
High	35	3.86	2.51	0	12
Medium	17	6.18	4.39	0	20
Low	37	10.24	4.1	0	17
Total	89	6.96	4.61	0	20

Note: ST: Phoneme substitution types in stressed syllables

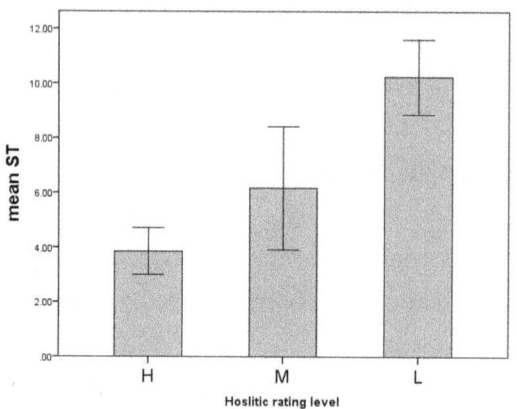

Figure 5.1 The mean ST across holistic rating levels

The other two features of phoneme substitution were the types of vowel (SVT) and onset consonant phoneme substitutions (SCTonset), as shown in Tables 5.2 and 5.3, with a mean of 3.49 and 1.56, respectively. Similar to ST, both features presented an increasing trend on average from the high to the low levels. The more types of vowel or onset consonant substitutions there were, the lower level the speaker was rated.

Table 5.2 Descriptive statistics of SVT across holistic rating levels and over the speech samples

Rating level	N	Mean	SD	Minimum	Maximum
High	35	1.8	1.45	0	6
Medium	17	2.82	3.05	0	13
Low	37	5.41	2.81	1	14
Total	89	3.49	2.92	0	14

Note: SVT: Vowel substitution types in stressed syllables

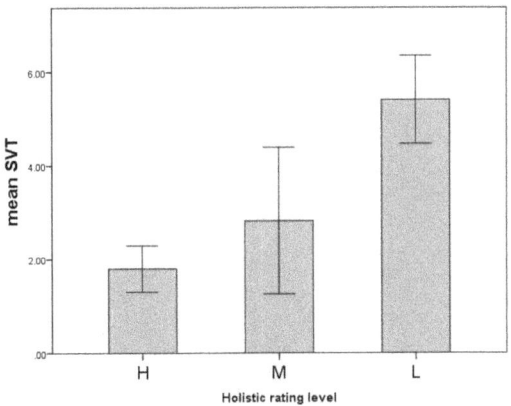

Figure 5.2 The mean SVT across holistic rating levels

For both SVT and SCTonset, there seemed a greater difference between the medium and low levels than between the medium and high levels (Figures 5.2 & 5.3). The Welch's tests revealed a significant difference between different levels (SVT: Welch's F (2, 36.53) = 23.33, $p < 0.001$, $est. \omega^2 = 0.33$; SCTonset: Welch's F (2, 45.99) = 11.92, $p < 0.001$, $est. \omega^2 = 0.20$). The Games-Howell post hoc procedure showed a significant difference between medium/high and low levels, but not between the high and medium levels for both SVT

Table 5.3 Descriptive statistics of SCTonset across holistic rating levels and over the speech samples

Rating level	N	Mean	SD	Minimum	Maximum
High	35	0.86	1.03	0	4
Medium	17	0.94	1.03	0	3
Low	37	2.51	1.82	0	7
Total	89	1.56	1.62	0	7

Note: SCTonset: Onset consonant substitution types in stressed syllables

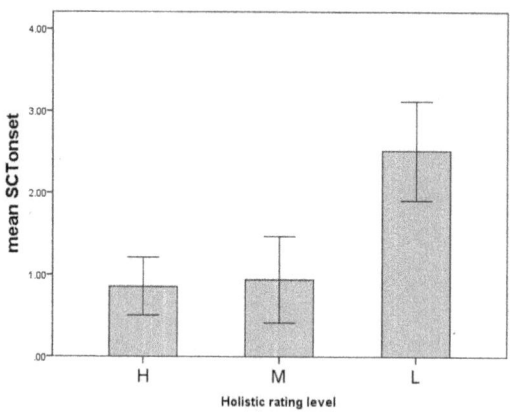

Figure 5.3 The mean SCTonset across holistic rating levels

(medium-low: $p=0.016$, Cohen's $d = 0.88$; high-low: $p<0.001$, Cohen's $d = 1.61$) and SCTonset (medium-low: $p = 0.001$, Cohen's $d = 0.88$; high-low: $p<0.001$, Cohen's $d = 1.13$).

Table 5.4 Descriptive statistics of ICP across holistic rating levels and over the speech samples

Rating level	N	Mean	SD	Minimum	Maximum
High	35	16.2	5.77	4	29
Medium	17	14.06	5.49	2	22
Low	37	9.32	5.35	0	24
Total	89	12.93	6.33	0	29

Note: ICP: Incomplete plosion

Table 5.4 depicts the feature of incomplete plosion (ICP) over the speech samples and across the three levels. The mean ICP over the speech samples was 12.93. It is clear that there was an upward trend of ICP with the rating levels, with more cases of ICP in the higher levels (Figure 5.4). Because the assumption of the equality of variance was not violated, a one-way ANOVA test was conducted. Significant differences were found between the different levels (F (2, 86) = 14.26, $p<0.001$, $\eta^2 = 0.25$). The Games-Howell post hoc procedure revealed statistically significant differences between the medium/high and low levels ($p = 0.016$, *Cohen's d* = 0.87; $p<0.001$, *Cohen's d* = 1.24), but not between the high and medium levels ($p = 0.407$).

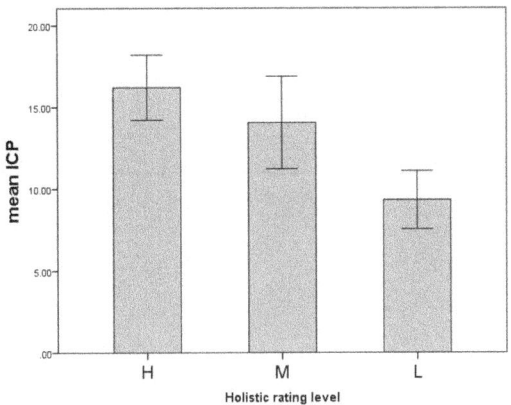

Figure 5.4 The mean ICP across holistic rating levels

5.2 Prosodic features

Seven prosodic features were analyzed, with three intonation features, three stress features, and one rhythmic feature.

5.2.1 Intonation features

Table 5.5 provides the descriptive statistics of intonation phrasing deviation (IPD), with a mean of 3.96 over the speech samples. As shown in Table 5.5 and Figure 5.5, IPD increased only slightly with rating levels going lower, from a mean of 3.57 in the high level to that of 4.38 in the low level. An ANOVA test did not find a significant effect on the rating levels ($p = 0.108$).

Table 5.5 Descriptive statistics of IPD across holistic rating levels and over the speech samples

Rating level	N	Mean	SD	Minimum	Maximum
High	35	3.57	1.75	0	8
Medium	17	3.82	1.29	2	6
Low	37	4.38	1.64	2	7
Total	89	3.96	1.65	0	8

Note: IPD: Intonation phrasing deviation

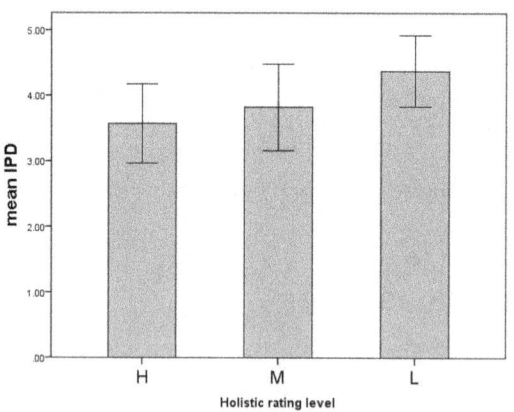

Figure 5.5 The mean IPD across holistic rating levels

The tonal feature, TRD1, was calculated as the number of failures to use rising or level tones to signify non-finality or contrast in the statements. According to Table 5.6 and Figure 5.6, though the mean TRD1 was small (2.22), a rising trend was still apparent, from a mean of 1.4 in the high-level group to that of 3.02 in the low-level group. An ANOVA test confirmed that there was a significant difference between rating levels (F

$(2, 86) = 7.27$, $p = 0.001$, $\eta^2 = 0.14$). However, the Games-Howell post hoc procedure did not find any statistical difference between adjacent levels. The only significant difference was between the high and low levels ($p = 0.001$, Cohen's $d = 0.91$).

Table 5.6　Descriptive statistics of TRD1 across holistic rating levels and over the speech samples

Rating level	N	Mean	SD	Minimum	Maximum
High	35	1.4	1.54	0	5
Medium	17	2.18	1.91	0	7
Low	37	3.02	1.99	0	7
Total	89	2.22	1.94	0	7

Note: TRD1: Failure to use rising or level tones at non-default boundaries

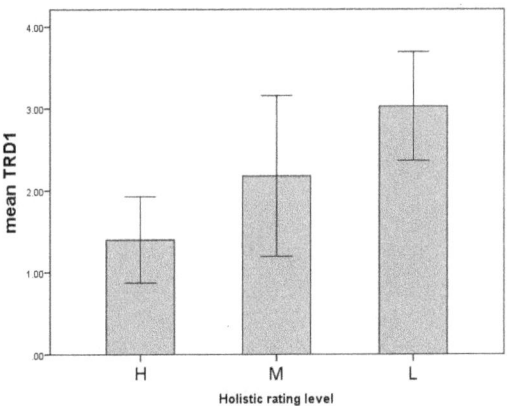

Figure 5.6　The mean TRD1 across holistic rating levels

Overall pitch range (OPR) was measured as the distance in semitone between f0 maximum and f0 minimum on the vowels of stressed syllables over the read speech. Table 5.7 presents the descriptive statistics of OPR, with a mean of 12.01 over the speech samples. There was a gradual decrease in OPR from the high (13.33) to the low rating levels (10.8) (Table 5.7 & Figure 5.7). The difference between rating levels was found to be significant by an ANOVA (F (2, 86) = 4.65, p = 0.012, η^2 = 0.10); however, as TRD1, the significant difference existed only between the high and low levels (p = 0.008, *Cohen's d* = 0.93), and no statistical difference was found between adjacent levels by the Games-Howell post hoc procedure.

Table 5.7 Descriptive statistics of OPR across holistic rating levels and over the speech samples

Rating level	N	Mean	SD	Minimum	Maximum
High	35	13.33	3.52	6.02	22.74
Medium	17	11.92	3.69	7.63	23.48
Low	37	10.80	3.44	6.2	22.17
Total	89	12.01	3.66	6.02	23.48

Note: OPR: Overall pitch range

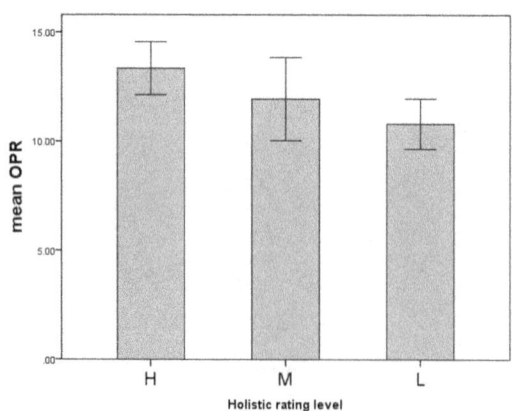

Figure 5.7 The mean OPR across holistic rating levels

5.2.2 Stress features

The distribution of sentence stress errors (SE) across the

rating levels is depicted in Table 5.8 and Figure 5.8, with a mean of 17.53 over all the speech samples. A clear increase in the number of sentence stress errors can be seen as the rating levels get lower. An ANOVA showed statistically significant differences between the levels (F (2, 86) = 18.79, $p<0.001$, $\eta^2 = 0.30$). The Games-Howell post hoc procedure revealed that besides the high and low levels ($p<0.001$, Cohen's d = 1.39), adjoining medium and low levels were statistically different from each other ($p = 0.01$, Cohen's d = 0.99).

Table 5.8 Descriptive statistics of SE across holistic rating levels and over the speech samples

Rating level	N	Mean	SD	Minimum	Maximum
High	35	13.97	5.20	6	27
Medium	17	16.71	4.36	11	25
Low	37	21.27	5.16	10	31
Total	89	17.53	6.00	6	31

Note: SE: Sentence stress errors

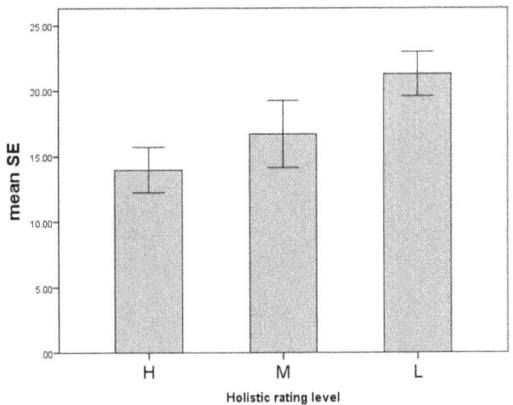

Figure 5.8 The mean SE across holistic rating levels

Nuclear stress was measured by both placement and duration contrast. As illustrated in Table 5.9 and Figure 5.9, the average number of NE was 16.38 over the samples, and there was an increasing number of NE in lower levels. Statistically significant differences were found by an ANOVA between the levels (F (2, 86) = 16.09, $p<0.001$, $\eta^2 = 0.27$). However, the Games-Howell post hoc procedure revealed a statistically significant difference between the high and medium/low levels (high-medium: $p = 0.001$, Cohen's $d = 1.09$; high-low: $p < 0.001$, Cohen's $d = 1.26$), instead of the medium and low levels.

Table 5.9   Descriptive statistics of NE across holistic rating levels and over the speech samples

Rating level	N	Mean	SD	Minimum	Maximum
High	35	14.46	2.43	8	21
Medium	17	16.88	2.00	13	20
Low	37	18.03	3.17	10	23
Total	89	16.38	3.09	8	23

Note: NE: Nuclear stress errors

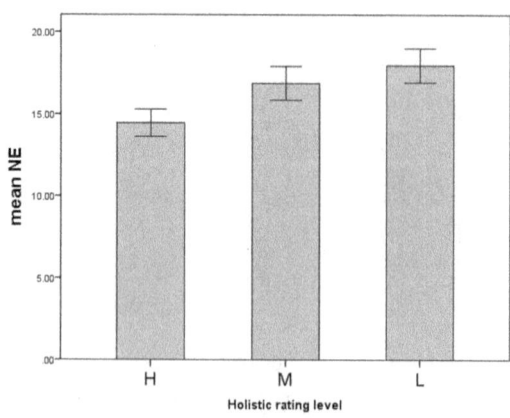

Figure 5.9   The mean NE across holistic rating levels

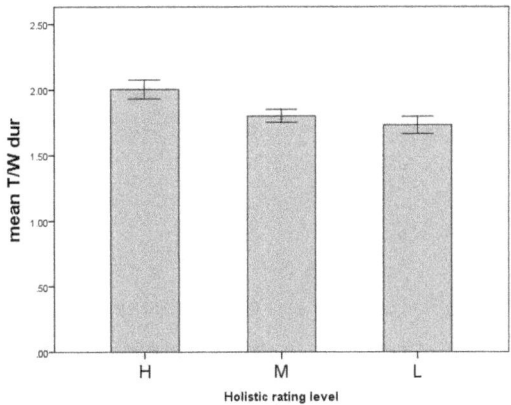

Figure 5.10 The mean T/W dur across holistic rating levels

Table 5.10 Descriptive statistics of T/W dur across holistic rating levels and over the speech samples

Rating level	N	Mean	SD	Minimum	Maximum
High	35	2.00	0.21	1.56	2.42
Medium	17	1.80	0.10	1.64	1.96
Low	37	1.73	0.20	1.33	2.16
Total	89	1.85	0.23	1.33	2.42

Note: T/W dur: Duration ratio of sampled tonic to weak syllables

An acoustic measure of nuclear stress, T/W dur, represented the duration contrast between the sampled tonic and weak syllables. As shown in Table 5.10, T/W dur had an average ratio at 1.85, which means that the duration of the sampled tonic syllables was longer than that of the sampled weak syllables. The ratio increased with the rating levels (Figure 5.10), though not drastically, with a mean of 1.73 in the low-level samples to 2 in the high-level samples. A Welch's test showed a significant difference between levels (Welch's F

(2, 55.81) = 16.99, $p<0.001$, $est. \omega^2 = 0.26$), and the Games-Howell post hoc procedure only suggested a statistically significant difference between the high and medium/low levels (high-medium: $p<0.001$, Cohen's d = 1.22; high-low: $p<0.001$, Cohen's d = 1.32).

5.2.3 Rhythmic feature

The rhythmic feature, overall stressing timing (OST), was measured as the duration ratio of unstressed to stressed syllables over the speech.

Table 5.11 presents the descriptive statistics of OST. The average OST was 0.76 over the speech samples, which means a shorter duration of all the unstressed syllables than that of stressed syllables. As illustrated in Table 5.11 and Figure 5.11, the OST value increased as the rating levels lowered, with the highest in the low-level group (0.81), down to 0.76 in the medium-level group, and 0.72 in the high-level group. A smaller duration ratio of unstressed to stressed syllables suggests the relative prominence of stressed to unstressed syllables in the utterance, hence the closeness to the stress-timed rhythmic pattern.

An ANOVA test showed significant differences between levels (F (2, 86) = 24.30, $p<0.001$, $\eta^2 = 0.36$), and the Games-Howell post hoc procedure revealed that OST could differentiate between all the three levels, the high and low levels ($p<0.001$, Cohen's d = 1.77), the high and medium levels ($p = 0.01$, Cohen's d = 0.88), as well as the medium and low levels ($p = 0.033$, Cohen's d = 0.91).

Table 5.11 Descriptive statistics of OST across holistic rating levels and over the speech samples

Rating level	N	Mean	SD	Minimum	Maximum
High	35	0.72	0.04	0.63	0.78
Medium	17	0.76	0.05	0.67	0.87
Low	37	0.81	0.06	0.70	1
Total	89	0.76	0.07	0.63	1

Note: OST: Overall stress timing

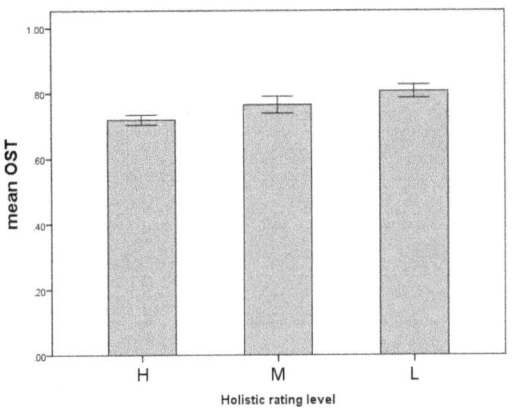

Figure 5.11 The mean OST across holistic rating levels

5.3 Fluency features

Fluency features included a speed feature, articulation rate (AR), and four breakdown features, which are overall pause frequency (PF), clause-boundary pause frequency (PFA), phrase-boundary pause frequency (PFB), and within-phrase pause frequency (PFC).

5.3.1 Speed

AR was calculated as the number of syllables per minute in the time taken to produce them (excluding all the pauses). As Table 5.12 depicts, the average AR of all the speech samples was 277.31 syllables produced per minute, with the highest mean of 297.70 in the high-level group, and the lowest of 255.78 in the low-level group. It is obvious that the faster one spoke, the higher level he/she was rated(Figure 5.12).

Table 5.12 Descriptive statistics of AR across holistic rating levels and over the speech samples

Rating level	N	Mean	SD	Minimum	Maximum
High	35	297.70	25.74	260.75	357.54
Medium	17	282.21	18.93	244.45	322.71
Low	37	255.78	21.44	208.86	303.80
Total	89	277.31	29.57	208.86	357.54

Note: AR: Articulation rate

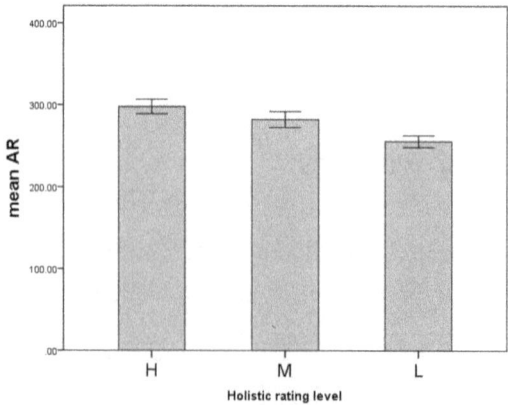

Figure 5.12 The mean AR across holistic rating levels

Because the assumption of homogeneity of variance was satisfied in this case, an ANOVA test was performed, resulting in a statistically significant difference found between rating levels (F (2, 86) = 30.81, $p<0.001$, η^2 = 0.42). The Games-Howell post hoc procedure revealed significant differences between all three levels, namely between the high and medium levels (p = 0.048, Cohen's d = 0.69), between the medium and low levels ($p<0.001$, Cohen's d = 1.31), and between the high and low levels ($p<0.001$, Cohen's d = 1.77).

5.3.2 Breakdown features

PF was measured as the total number of pauses per minute. According to Table 5.13 and Figure 5.13, the mean PF over the speech sample was 13.23 pauses per minute. The increase in the average pause frequency against the rating levels seemed to suggest that the more a speaker paused, the lower level he/she was rated.

An ANOVA supported this tendency (F (2, 86) = 14.41, $p<0.001$, η^2 = 0.25), and the Games-Howell post hoc test further found that the distinction between adjacent levels was only found statistically significant between the high and the medium/low pair (high-medium: p = 0.013, Cohen's d = 0.95; high-low: $p<0.001$, Cohen's d = 1.28).

Table 5.13 Descriptive statistics of PF across holistic rating levels and over the speech samples

Rating level	N	Mean	SD	Minimum	Maximum
High	35	10.52	3.40	3.43	19.56
Medium	17	14.26	4.42	4.21	24.78
Low	37	15.31	4.06	8.43	27.65
Total	89	13.23	4.44	3.43	27.65

Note: PF: Total number of pauses per minute

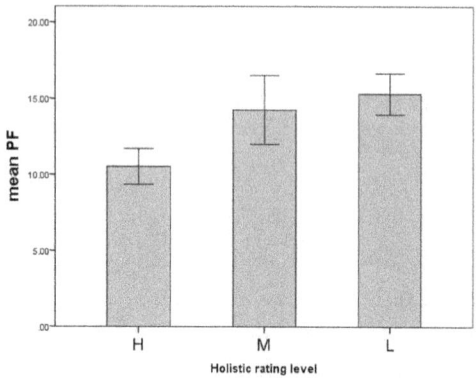

Figure 5.13　The mean PF across holistic rating levels

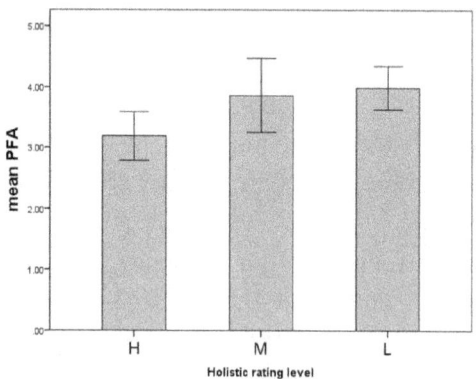

Figure 5.14　The mean PFA across holistic rating levels

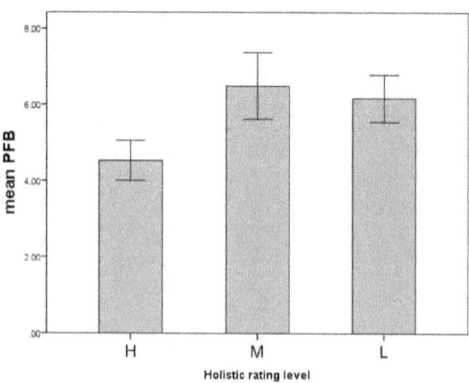

Figure 5.15　The mean PFB across holistic rating levels

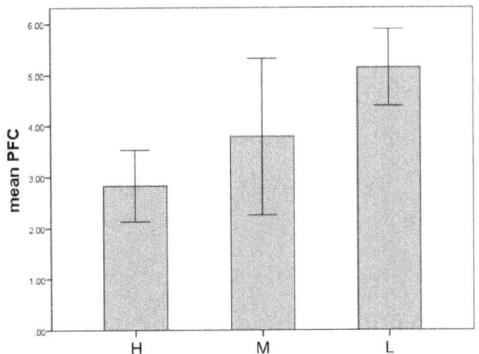

Figure 5.16 The mean PFC across holistic rating levels

PF was made up of the frequency of the pauses at the clause boundary (PFA), phrase boundary (PFB) and within phrases (PFC). Tables 5.14, 5.15 and 5.16 present their descriptive statistics, respectively.

PFA and PFC were similar in their means, with 3.65 and 3.97, respectively; however, there was a greater contrast between the high-level group and the low-level group in PFC than in PFA (Tables 5.14 & 5.16). Also, for both features, the pause frequency increased from the high to the low rating levels, suggesting that whether the pauses fell between the clause boundaries or within phrases, a higher pause frequency might signify a lower rating level (Figures 5.14 & 5.16). In contrast, PFB had a higher mean of 5.58 than PFA or PFC (Table 5.15). Though the high-level learners produced less phrase-boundary pauses than those on the low level, the medium-level learners paused most often at the phrase boundaries.

An ANOVA revealed significant differences between levels

for all the three features (PFA: F (2, 86) = 4.85, $p = 0.01$, $\eta^2 = 0.10$; PFB: F (2, 86) = 11.16, $p<0.001$, $\eta^2 = 0.21$; PFC: F (2, 86) = 8.97, $p<0.001$, $\eta^2 = 0.17$); however, for PFA ($p = 0.47$) and PFC ($p = 0.24$), a significant distinction was only found between the high and low levels by the Games-Howell post hoc test (PFA: $p = 0.01$, Cohen's d = 0.71; PFC: $p<0.001$, Cohen's d = 1.08), but no significant distinction was found between any adjacent levels. The only significant difference between adjacent levels was found for PFB between the high and medium levels ($p = 0.001$, Cohen's d = 1.21).

Table 5.14 Descriptive statistics of PFA across holistic rating levels and over the speech samples

Rating level	N	Mean	SD	Minimum	Maximum
High	35	3.19	1.17	0.71	5.38
Medium	17	3.86	1.19	1.40	5.58
Low	37	3.99	1.07	2.01	6.24
Total	89	3.65	1.18	0.71	6.24

Note: PFA: Number of clause-boundary pauses per minute

Table 5.15 Descriptive statistics of PFB across holistic rating levels and over the speech samples

Rating level	N	Mean	SD	Minimum	Maximum
High	35	4.53	1.53	0.79	7.68
Medium	17	6.49	1.70	2.81	9.78
Low	37	6.16	1.87	3.19	11.26
Total	89	5.58	1.90	0.79	11.26

Note: PFB: Number of phrase-boundary pauses per minute

Table 5.16 Descriptive statistics of PFC across holistic rating levels and over the speech samples

Rating level	N	Mean	SD	Minimum	Maximum
High	35	2.83	2.03	0	7.52
Medium	17	3.79	2.99	0	9.78
Low	37	5.14	2.25	1.15	10.75
Total	89	3.97	2.53	0	10.75

Note: PFC: Number of within-phrase pauses per minute

5.4 Discussion

The data analysis showed that most phonological features could successfully distinguish between the high and low pronunciation levels (H-L), with only one feature, intonation phrasing deviation (IPD), failing to differentiate between any of the levels. Table 5.17 gives an overview of how the 16 features are distinguished across the holistic rating levels.

It is clear that the phonological features played different roles. Two suprasegmental features, articulation rate (AR) and overall stress timing (OST), were able to differentiate between all the levels. While both segmental and suprasegmental features were found to differentiate between the lower levels (M-L), only the suprasegmental features could distinguish between the higher levels (H-M). More specifically, the suprasegmental features that differentiate the lower and higher levels differed, with sentence stress placement (SE) functioning between the lower levels, nuclear stress features (NE, T/W dur), and some pausing features (PF, PFB) between the higher levels. Intonation features (TRD1, OPR) and two other pausing features

Table 5.17 Overview of the ANOVA results of the 16 phonological features

Category		Segmental features				Prosodic feature							Fluency features			
		ST	SVT	SCTonset	ICP	OPR	TRD1	IPD	SE	NE	T/Wdur	OST	AR	PF	PFA	PFB	PFC
Adjacent	M-L	√	√						√			√	√	√			
	H-M																
Non-adjacent	H-L	√	√	√	√	√	√		√	√	√	√	√	√	√	√	√
None								√									

Note: √ signifies the role the features played in distinguishing the holistic rating levels.
AR: Articulation rate ICP: Incomplete plosion
IPD: Intonation phrasing deviation NE: Nuclear stress errors
OPR: Overall pitch range OST: Overall stress timing
PF: Silent pause frequency PFA: Clause-boundary silent pause frequency
PFB: Phrase-boundary silent pause frequency PFC: Within-phrase silent pause frequency
SE: Sentence stress errors ST: Phoneme substitution types in stressed syllables
SVT: Vowel substitution types in stressed syllables SCTonset: Onset consonant substitution types in stressed syllables
TRD1: Failure to use rising or level tones at non-default boundaries
T/W dur: Tonic/weak syllable duration ratio

(PFA, PFC) also characterized the high level, though they were found to only distinguish between non-adjacent high and low levels.

As the question of which dimensions of pronunciation (often broadly as segmentals vs. suprasegmentals) have greater impact on L2 pronunciation quality or development (e. g., Anderson-Hsieh et al., 1992; Cucciarini et al., 2000; Jenkins, 2000; Trofimovich & Baker, 2006) has been debated for long, the current findings support Saito et al. (2016) that the relative weight of instructional focus on different dimensions of pronunciation may vary with the learners' pronunciation levels. Besides, the dimensions of pronunciation that different learner levels should focus on need to be further specified, especially in the suprasegmentals, since different suprasegmental aspects seem to characterize different levels.

5.4.1 Features distinguishing all the levels

Two suprasegmental features—articulation rate (AR) and overall stress timing (OST)—were found to successfully differentiate between all the holistic rating levels. This tends to support Harding's recommendation (2017) to "avoid the assumption that suprasegmental information is only important at higher levels" (p. 29).

A faster rate could be a representation of the automaticity of encoding and processing phonological rules, hence an indication of good pronunciation proficiency. However, caution should be applied in the benchmarks, for it is not simply the faster, the better. The students rated high in the current study could speak at a rate of 297.7 syllables per minute (almost five syllables per second), which is a near-native-like rate as shown in Trofimovich and Baker (2007). Also, this speed seems to support what Munro and Derwing (2001) described as the optimal speed for L2 learners, which helps achieve the best effect on listener perception of comprehensibility. According to their justifications, if L2 speech is accelerated to a rate slightly faster than normal L2 speech rates, "listeners may be less inclined to notice phonological errors (because they must process the speech more quickly) and may assign better ratings" (p. 466). Of course, the rate should not be too fast to exceed the listeners' processing capability; otherwise, the listeners would not benefit from the acceleration.

The distinguishing power of OST suggests the importance of English rhythmic patterns in raters' judgment. All the three raters claimed in the interview that rhythm affected their perception of stress, fluency and segmental accuracy. One rater (rater- T) regarded rhythm as the most important feature in her evaluation of the learners' overall pronunciation proficiency, since it reflects the stress realization and vowel articulation in the strong and weak forms. This finding seems to support Chela-Flores (2001), who argued that the English rhythmic pattern should be put at the central position in L2 pronunciation instruction, and the rhythmic instruction should be started from the beginner level, particularly the lengthening of stressed syllables and the shortening of the weak syllable in the meaningful units. One reason that he pointed out is that having a certain control of rhythmic patterns could make it easier to acquire segments and stress.

The raters' interview revealed that rate and rhythm might interrelate with each other in the rating process. According to the raters' comments, when there was a more English-like rhythm and speakers tended to apply liaison and elision, they sounded more fluent. When the speech was too slow, words sounded bullet-like and equally stressed.

The current findings of these two features able to distinguish between all adjacent levels also indicate that it is possible rather than "elusive" (Isaacs et al., 2015, p. 4) to identify common features across all the pronunciation scales when using a smaller number of scales, as opposed to the nine-point scale used in IELTS.

5.4.2 Features distinguishing between the lower levels

The features found to distinguish between the lower levels (M-L) included both segmental and suprasegmental ones, which confirms that suprasegmental information should not be neglected at lower levels.

For one thing, the present study further specifies the saliency of segmental information in the perception of Chinese EFL learners' pronunciation (Crowther et al., 2015) at the lower levels. All the segmental features investigated in the current study—total phoneme substitution (ST), vowel substitution (SVT), onset consonant substitution (SCTonset), and incomplete plosion (ICP)— were found to only distinguish between the adjoining medium and low levels, rather than high and medium levels. This suggests that an accurate segmental production might be a basis for pronunciation proficiency of Chinese EFL learners in raters' minds, and should be given more attention in pronunciation instruction at the low levels.

What is worth noting is that this finding did not concur completely with Saito et al.'s (2016). They found segmental features were able to discriminate between intermediate and high comprehensibility levels and between all the accentedness levels in the picture narratives of Japanese learners of English. The different findings might be attributed to several factors. First, there was a difference in task types, with a narrative task in Saito et al.'s (2016) and a reading-aloud task in this study. With the content of the speech controlled in the reading-aloud, raters might focus more on the form of the language, and segmental accuracy has been reported to be most salient for accentedness ratings (Crowther et al., 2015; Saito et al., 2016). Second, the ways in which segmental accuracy was measured were different in the two studies. In Saito et al.'s (2016), the measurement of segmental accuracy was based on raters' general impression of the frequency of segmental errors, while in the current study, it was based on the segmental annotation in stressed syllables, hence possible that the segmental deviations under investigation were more salient to the raters (Zielinski, 2006). More importantly, the speakers in the two studies were very different, with Japanese speakers in Saito et al.'s (2016) and Chinese EFL learners in the current study. As previous literature suggested, speakers' L1 background (Crowther et al., 2015) could lead to variability in the feature-construct relationship.

Segmental features also included incomplete plosion. This skill has long been incorporated into the language classrooms in China, and students were taught the rules of incomplete plosion explicitly. Therefore, it is reasonable that learners who have received years of English training would have grasped it, and those who could not apply this skill would be perceived as poor in pronunciation.

For another, this study also presents the important role

suprasegmental information plays at the lower levels, particularly sentence stress, measured by the placement errors of sentence stress (SE).

The research on sentence stress placement in L2 speech was limited. While previous literature has presented a cumulative accentuation in Chinese EFL learners' stress production (Chen, 2008a; Chen & Bi, 2015; Yang, 2010), it did not connect sentence stress pattern with pronunciation judgment. This study fills the gap, and suggests the importance of starting the sentence stress instruction and describing sentence stress placement at lower levels. This is not only attributed to the role it plays in the realization of English rhythm, but also to the relatively clear association between sentence stress and word categories (Kingdon, 1958; Pike, 1945; Wells, 2006). As Bi and Chen (2006) found in a longitudinal study, even without explicit instruction, students got improved in sentence stress production over their four years in college.

5.4.3 Features distinguishing between the high and lower levels

The features that characterized the high level of pronunciation are all suprasegmental features, including the features of nuclear stress (NE, T/W dur), intonation (OPR, TRD1), and pausing (PF, PFA, PFB, PFC).

5.4.3.1 Nuclear stress

Among them, the nuclear stress features were able to distinguish the adjoining high and medium levels. Nuclear stresses are information focuses, and are likely to have a close link to comprehensibility. Learners in the high-level groups produced less nuclei errors, and were more capable of using duration contrast to make the information focus more prominent, compared with learners in the medium and low-level groups.

Compared with the placement of sentence stress, nuclear stress distribution seems to be a greater challenge for Chinese EFL students (Bi & Chen, 2006). Students continuously preferred to put nuclei at unmarked locations, which are the last lexical items in the intonation units. Furthermore, the multiple hierarchical systems of stress are not generally recognized in the EFL classrooms. What is taught and emphasized by teachers is usually confined to the difference between sentence stress and unstressed counterparts, and the general relationship between sentence stress and word categories; the nuclear stress and information focus are only studied by researchers and unfamiliar to language teachers and practitioners, hence not being instructed to students. These situations help to explain why nuclear stress placement turned out to be a feature acquired later, and only able to distinguish between the high and medium/low levels. This also supports Chela-Flores' (2001) suggestion that nuclear stress should be instructed later, compared with sentence stress.

Besides placement, nuclear stress was also measured by the feature of tonic/weak duration ratio (T/W dur). This study supports Chen et al.'s (2001) finding that Chinese EFL learners were able to distinguish tonic syllables and weak syllables by duration. Compared with Yang's (2010) findings, the ratios of all the three groups in the current study are much higher than those presented in the freshmen speech, but lower than those in the native speakers' speech. The T/W dur of the low and medium levels in this study is close to the stressed/unstressed duration ratio rather than the tonic/weak duration ratio in the native speech in Yang's (2010); only the high-level group produced the T/W dur higher than the stressed/unstressed duration ratio in native speech, though still lower than the native tonic/weak duration ratio. This seems to suggest that the high-level students are breaking what Hua (2003) called a binary stress hierarchy in Chinese EFL learners' production, and approaching a more native-like multi-level stress hierarchy.

5.4.3.2 Pausing

The finding that less silent pauses only featured the high pronunciation level but could not distinguish lower levels should be interpreted with caution. This might be limited to the particular task type, dialogue reading-aloud. The frequency of silent pauses could be a lot higher in the spontaneous speech and could be caused by various types of difficulties such as vocabulary retrieval, cognitive ability, idea organization, etc. Then pause frequency in the spontaneous speech would most probably play a different role in raters' judgment of pronunciation levels. Conversely, in the read speech, particularly the type of simple dialogue reading-aloud, there was little difficulty in encoding the vocabulary or grammatical structures, hence fewer silent pauses in the production, and mostly at clause- or phrase-boundaries. This could easily lead to a blurred line between low and medium levels.

The significant drop of pause frequency (PF) in the high level can be attributed to the significant decrease in pauses at the phrase boundaries (PFB). Commonly, pauses at syntactic boundaries were not considered to impair fluency (Towell et al., 1996; Skehan, 2009). However, due to the simple reading material in the current study, with a mean length of sentence at 6.4 words, there was no necessity for breathing breaks. Moreover, the decrease in pauses at phrase boundaries might suggest that high-level students paid more attention to the information units rather than small syntactic units in the reading text, while students in medium and low levels still tended to follow syntactic structure, and pause where there was a punctuation accompanying adverbial phrases and adjuncts to the independent clause.

5.4.3.3 Intonation

The two intonation features concerning the non-default rising tone use (TRD1) and overall pitch range (OPR) could characterize a high pronunciation level by distinguishing the high and low levels, but not between the adjoining high-medium levels.

This finding is, to some extent, inconsistent with Saito et al.'s (2016), in which intonation was found to differentiate across all levels of comprehensibility and accentedness. The difference could be a result of the different ways intonation was measured in the two studies. In their study, intonation was measured as a subjective rating of pitch variation from too varied to not varied enough; in the current study, intonation was measured more objectively, both by the overall pitch range and by the deviation of tone choices at specific tone group boundaries.

The finding that intonation features could only discriminate between high and low rather than adjacent levels has several implications. For one thing, it suggests that Chinese EFL learners might have similar difficulties in using the rising or level tone to signify contrast or non-finality in the statements, as reported in the previous literature (Chen & Bi, 2015; Hewings, 1995; Wennerstrom, 1994). Therefore, a more explicit instruction in the use of rising tone might be needed as learners developed from the medium to high levels. For another, it may indicate the less saliency of intonation in the judgment of L2 pronunciation, since the deviated tone choices and a narrower pitch range do not impair intelligibility to a similar extent as segmentals and stress patterns do (Chen, 2008a).

Therefore, this study proposes with caution that the discoursal and attitudinal functions of the rising tone, and the wider pitch range should be included in the descriptors of the high level in the pronunciation rating scale, rather than of the lower levels.

5.4.4 The feature failing to distinguish across holistic rating levels

Intonation phrasing deviation (IPD) is the only feature that could not discriminate across the holistic rating levels of pronunciation. This finding concords with Chen's (2008a), mainly because students tended to have a common problem with intonation phrasing, particularly before the sentence-final vocative and sentence-final reporting clause.

Tonality rules are usually not explicitly instructed in EFL classrooms. Students are likely to break intonation phrases according to where the punctuations are, and put on nuclear tone to the vocative and reporting clauses as well. There seems to be very little awareness that the sentence-final vocative and reporting clause are attached to the preceding main clause as a tail, and they do not carry major information. As Chen and Sun (2010) reported, intonation phrasing could be difficult for Chinese EFL learners to acquire only by listening to the native speech; explicit instruction should be given to students to raise their awareness of the relevant rules.

5.5 Summary

In conclusion, the phonological features played different roles in distinguishing the holistic rating levels. Two features, articulation rate and overall stress timing, were found to differentiate between all the levels. While both segmental features and sentence stress placement could distinguish between the lower pronunciation levels, only suprasegmental features were able to characterize the high pronunciation level, including the nuclear stress features, pausing features, and intonation features.

The findings suggest that in terms of overall pronunciation proficiency, while consistent attention was paid to rate and rhythm across all the rating levels, raters tended to shift their focus gradually from speakers' segmental accuracy and sentence stress placement to more meaning-oriented nuclear stress pattern and intonation.

Chapter Six
RESULTS AND DISCUSSION Ⅲ:
Predicting the Analytic Ratings

This chapter presents the results and discussion of the Phase-Ⅱ study concerning the third research question, which addresses the differential contributions of the phonological features to the analytic ratings of Chinese EFL learners' pronunciation.

The 89 speech samples were also analytically rated in terms of segmentals, prosody, and fluency. To reveal the relative weight of these features on the analytic ratings, three stepwise multiple linear regressions were conducted. The dependent variables were segmental, prosody, and fluency ratings. The independent variables were validated segmental, prosodic, and fluency features.

The results in the three regression analyses are to be reported one by one, each with the checking of the assumptions first, and the regression model next.

6.1 Segmental features

As discussed in Chapter four, five segmental features were found to significantly correlate with the segmental ratings. They were phoneme substitution (ST), vowel substitution (SVT), onset consonant substitution (SCTonset), incomplete plosion

(ICP), and phoneme insertion (PI).

6.1.1 Checking the assumptions for regression

As introduced in 3.4.2.2, there are five assumptions for regression to be checked. The first linearity assumption was satisfied, as all the segmental features had moderately significant correlations with the dependent variable, the segmental rating (Table 6.1).

Table 6.1 The Pearson's correlation coefficients of segmental features and the segmental ratings (n=89)

	ST	SVT	SCTonset	ICP	PI
Segmental rating	0.66**	−0.61**	−0.48**	0.43**	−0.42**
ST		0.84**	0.65**	−0.15	0.34**
SVT			0.32**	−0.22	0.20*
SCTonset				−0.13	0.23*
ICP					−0.11

Note:
** significant at the 0.01 level of probability
* significant at 0.05 level of probability
ST: Phoneme substitution types in stressed syllables
SVT: Vowel substitution types in stressed syllables
SCTonset: Onset consonant substitution types in stressed syllables
ICP: Incomplete plosion
PI: phoneme insertion

Second, the Kolmogorov-Smirnov tests on the standardized residuals proved a normal distribution of the errors between observed and predicted values (i.e., the residuals of the regression) ($p = 0.20$).

Third, as indicated by Variance Inflation Factor (VIF),

no multicollinearity was found in the data (Table 6.4: VIF < 2), which means the predictors were not highly featured with each other.

Fourth, the observations were independent, as can be seen by the Durbin-Watson statistics approaching 1.5 in the regression model for segmental ratings (Tables 6.2).

The last assumption is homoscedasticity which stipulates a similar variance of error terms across the values of the independent variables. A good way to check this assumption is by means of a scatterplot of standardized residuals versus unstandardized predicted values. Figure 6.1 depicts a random scatter of residuals, suggesting no violation of this assumption in the regression.

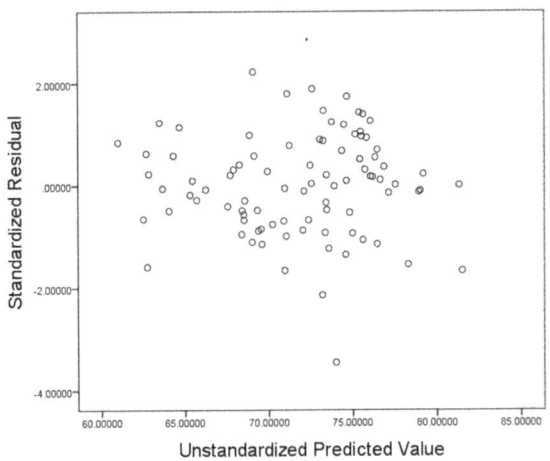

Figure 6.1　A scatterplot of standardized residuals versus unstandardized predicted values (Segmental rating)

6.1.2　The regression model for the segmental ratings

Table 6.2 reveals the model summary of stepwise multiple

linear regression of the segmental features on the segmental ratings of Chinese EFL learners' read speech. Three regression models generated in this analysis were statistically significant. The choice of predictive variables entered was carried out by an automatic procedure in SPSS (20.0). ST, the phoneme substitution in the stressed syllables, was best featured with the oral reading rating, hence entering the model first. This variable alone accounted for 43.3% of the variance in the segmental rating. Adding incomplete plosion (ICP) and phoneme insertion (PI) increased the variance accounted for, to 54.5% and 58.2%, respectively. The other two segmental features, vowel (SVT) and onset consonant substitutions (SCTonset) in stressed syllables, did not enter the model. This is mainly because both SVT and SCTonset played significant roles in the segmental rating, and their combined effects were represented by ST, as ST included both of them and was highly correlated with SVT and moderately with SCTonset (Table 6.1).

Table 6.2　Model summary of stepwise multiple linear regression of the segmental features on the segmental ratings

Model	R	R^2	Adjusted R^2	Std. err. of the estimate	Durbin-Watson
1	0.658[a]	0.433	0.427	4.629	
2	0.739[b]	0.545	0.535	4.170	1.47
3	0.763[c]	0.582	0.567	4.024	

Note: Dependent variable: segmental rating
ST: phoneme substitution in stressed syllables
ICP: incomplete plosion
PI: phoneme insertion
a. Predictors: (Constant), ST
b. Predictors: (Constant), ST, ICP
c. Predictors: (Constant), ST, ICP, PI

Table 6.3 ANOVA of the final model of stepwise multiple linear regression of the segmental features on the segmental ratings

	Sum of squares	df	Mean square	F	Sig.
Regression	1913.928	5	637.976	39.388	0.000
Residual	1376.759	85	16.197		
Total	3290.688	88			

Note: Predictors: (Constant), ST, ICP, PI
Dependent variable: segmental rating
ST: phoneme substitution in stressed syllables
ICP: incomplete plosion
PI: phoneme insertion

Table 6.4 Coefficients of the final model of stepwise multiple linear regression of the segmental features on the segmental ratings

Predictor	B	Std. Error	Beta (β)	t	Sig.	Partial correlation	VIF
(Constant)	73.62	1.26		58.26	0.000		
ST	-0.72	0.10	-0.54	-7.19	0.000	-0.62	1.15
ICP	0.32	0.07	0.33	4.58	0.000	0.45	1.03
PI	-0.36	0.13	-0.20	-2.71	0.008	-0.28	1.14

Note: Dependent variable: segmental rating
ST: phoneme substitution in stressed syllables
ICP: incomplete plosion
PI: phoneme insertion

The R square of the final model, also known as the coefficient of determination, reached 0.582, indicating a relatively good fitness of the model (Table 6.2). The ANOVA of the final model (Table 6.3) also suggested that these three segmental features contributed significantly to the prediction of variance in the segmental rating ($F(5, 85) = 39.39$, $p < 0.001$).

According to the partial correlation coefficients[1] revealed in Table 6.4, phoneme substitution in stressed syllables (ST: partial $r = -0.62$) and phoneme insertion (PI: partial $r = -0.28$) were inversely, while incomplete plosion (ICP: partial $r = 0.45$) was positively proportional to the segmental ratings. This means that the higher segmental ratings were given to those who produced less phoneme substitution types, less phoneme insertions, and more incomplete plosions in the speech. The absolute partial correlation coefficients of the three features showed a stronger effect of phoneme substitutions than incomplete plosion or phoneme insertion on the segmental ratings (ST > ICP > PI).

6.2 Prosodic features

Seven prosodic features were found in Chapter four to significantly correlate with the prosodic ratings. They included three intonation features (TRD1, OPR, IPD), three stress features (SE, NE, T/W dur), and one rhythmic feature (OST).

6.2.1 Checking the assumptions for regression

The first linearity assumption was satisfied on all the prosodic features, except the feature of intonation phrasing deviation (IPD). As Table 6.5 shows, all the prosodic features

---

[1] Compared with the standardized regressive coefficient(β), partial correlation coefficient is preferred when considering the ranking of relative importance of the predictors to the dependent variable, because partial correlation coefficient is computed with the effect of other predictors (Wang, Yang, & Liu, 2006).

significantly correlated with the prosodic ratings, with only IPD having a rather weak correlation with the prosodic rating. A further check of the scatterplot of IPD did not show a linear relationship between this feature and the prosodic ratings; therefore, IPD was removed from the regression analysis in the prosodic dimension.

Table 6.5 The Pearson's correlation coefficients of prosodic features and the prosodic ratings (n=89)

	OST	NE	SE	T/Wdur	TRD1	OPR	IPD
Prosodic rating	-0.67**	-0.59**	-0.58**	0.59**	-0.48**	0.35**	-0.29**
OST		0.51**	0.61**	-0.77**	0.51**	-0.29**	0.35**
NE			0.61**	-0.56**	0.39**	-0.28**	0.50**
SE				-0.61**	0.27*	-0.29**	0.44**
T/Wdur					-0.44**	0.39**	-0.31**
TRD1						-0.20	0.18
OPR							-0.11

Note:
** significant at the 0.01 level of probability
* significant at 0.05 level of probability
OST: Overall stress timing　　　OPR: Overall pitch range
NE: Nuclear stress errors　　　SE: Sentence stress errors
T/W dur: Duration ratio of sampled tonic to weak syllables
TRD1: Failure to use rising or level tones at non-default boundaries
IPD: Intonation phrasing deviation

The other assumptions were met. The Kolmogorov-Smirnov tests on the standardized residuals proved a normal distribution of the errors between observed and predicted values ($p = 0.18$). Besides, no multicollinearity was found between the predictors (Tables 6.8: VIF<2), and the observations were independent as the Durbin-Watson statistics was approaching 1.5 in the regression model for prosodic ratings (Tables 6.6). Finally, the scatterplot of standardized residuals versus unstandardized predicted values illustrates a random scatter of residuals, suggesting no violation of homoscedasticity in the regression.

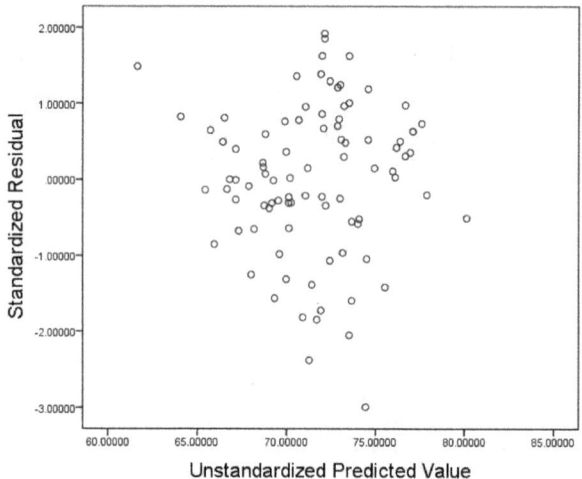

Figure 6.2　A scatterplot of standardized residuals versus unstandardized predicted values (Prosodic rating)

6.2.2　The regression model for the prosodic ratings

As presented in Table 6.6, two regression models were generated in the analysis. In the first model, OST, the feature of overall stress timing, could account for 45.3% of the variance alone in the prosodic rating. Adding nuclear stress errors (NE) increased the variance accounted for to 53.7%. The other prosodic features did not enter the model due to either less contribution to the prosodic rating, such as overall pitch range (OPR) and the rising tone feature (TRD1), or high intercollinearity with OST and NE, such as sentence stress errors (SE) and duration ratio of sampled tonic to weak syllables (T/W dur) (Table 6.5).

Table 6.6 Model summary of stepwise multiple linear regression of the prosodic features on the prosodic ratings

Model	R	R^2	Adjusted R^2	Std. Err. of the estimate	Durbin-Watson
1	0.673^a	0.453	0.446	3.464	1.464
2	0.733^b	0.537	0.526	3.205	

Note: Dependent variable: prosodic rating
OST: overall stress timing
NE: nuclear stress errors
a. Predictors: (Constant), OST
b. Predictors: (Constant), OST, NE

The R square of the final model reached 0.537, suggesting a relatively good fitness of the model (Table 6.6). The ANOVA of the final model (Table 6.7) also suggested that the two prosodic features contributed significantly to the prediction of variance in the prosodic rating ($F (2, 86) = 49.84$, $p < 0.001$).

Table 6.7 ANOVA of the final model of stepwise multiple linear regression of the prosodic features on the prosodic ratings

	Sum of squares	df	Mean square	F	Sig.
Regression	1024.167	2	512.084	49.840	0.000
Residual	883.618	86	10.275		
Total	1907.785	88			

Note: Predictors: (Constant), OST, NE
Dependent variable: prosodic rating
OST: overall stress timing
NE: nuclear stress errors

Table 6.8 Coefficients of the final model of stepwise multiple linear regression of the prosodic features on the prosodic ratings

Predictor	B	Std. Error	Beta (β)	t	Sig.	Partial correlation	VIF
(Constant)	107.13	4.02		26.66	0.000		
OST	−35.87	6.06	−0.50	−5.92	0.000	−0.54	1.34
NE	−0.51	0.13	−0.34	−3.95	0.000	−0.39	1.34

Note: Dependent variable: prosodic rating
OST: overall stress timing
NE: nuclear stress errors

According to the partial correlation coefficients revealed in Table 6.8, overall stress timing (OST: *partial r* = −0.54) had a greater contribution than nuclear stress errors (NE: *partial r* = −0.39) to the prosodic ratings. In other words, the relative importance of the two features to the prosodic rating can be seen as OST>NE. Both features were inversely proportional to the prosodic ratings, indicating that the speakers who produced more stress-timing rhythm and less nuclear stress errors were likely to be rated high in terms of prosody.

6.3 Fluency features

There were five fluency features validated in Chapter four to significantly correlate with the fluency ratings. They included one speed feature (AR) and four breakdown features (PF, PFA, PFB, PFC).

6.3.1 Checking the assumptions for regression

First, all fluency features had moderately significant correlations with the fluency ratings (Table 6.9), indicating a linear relationship between the dependent and independent variables.

Table 6.9 The Pearson's correlation coefficients of fluency features and the fluency ratings (n=89)

	AR	PF	PFA	PFB	PFC
Fluency rating	0.74**	-0.44**	-0.35**	-0.37**	-0.46**
AR		-0.35**	-0.21*	-0.16	-0.39**
PF			0.65**	0.80**	0.84**
PFA				0.46**	0.34**
PFB					0.43**

Note:
** significant at the 0.01 level of probability
* significant at 0.05 level of probability
AR: Articulation rate
PF: Total number of pauses per minute
PFA: Number of clause-boundary pauses per minute
PFB: Number of phrase-boundary pauses per minute
PFC: Number of within-phrase pauses per minute

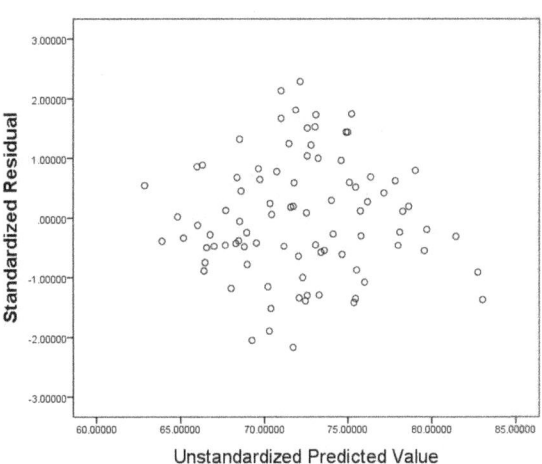

Figure 6.3 A scatterplot of standardized residuals versus unstandardized predicted values (Fluency rating)

Second, the Kolmogorov-Smirnov tests on the standardized residuals proved a normal distribution of the errors between observed and predicted values ($p = 0.20$). Third, a Variance Inflation Factor (VIF) smaller than 2 suggested no multicollinearity in the predictors (Table 6.12: VIF $<$ 2). Fourth, the Durbin-Watson statistics was approaching 2 in the regression model (Tables 6.10), indicating the independence of observations. Last, homoscedasticity was satisfied as a random scatter of residuals can be seen in the scatterplot of standardized residuals versus unstandardized predicted values (Figure 6.3).

6.3.2 The regression model for the fluency ratings

Table 6.10 presents two regression models for the fluency rating. AR, the articulation rate, alone could account for 54.6% of the variance in the fluency rating. Adding silent pause frequency (PF) increased the variance accounted for to 62.5%. The other pause features did not enter the model, because when calculated separately, the pauses at specific locations (PFA, PFB, PFC) had weaker correlations than PF with the fluency rating, and correlated strongly with PF (Table 6.9).

Table 6.10 Model summary of stepwise multiple linear regression of the fluency features on the fluency ratings

Model	R	R^2	Adjusted R^2	Std. err. of the estimate	Durbin-Watson
1	0.739[a]	0.546	0.541	3.658	1.834
2	0.791[b]	0.625	0.616	3.345	

Note: Dependent variable: fluency rating
AR: Articulation rate
PF: Silent pause frequency
c. Predictors: (Constant), AR
d. Predictors: (Constant), AR, PF

Table 6.11 ANOVA of the final model of stepwise multiple linear regression of the fluency features on the fluency ratings

	Sum of squares	df	Mean square	F	Sig.
Regression	1602.988	2	801.494	71.647	0.000
Residual	962.057	86	11.187		
Total	2565.045	88			

Note: Predictors: (Constant), AR, PF
Dependent variable: fluency rating
AR: Articulation rate
PF: Silent pause frequency

Table 6.12 Coefficients of the final model of stepwise multiple linear regression of the fluency features on the fluency ratings

Predictor	B	Std. error	Beta (β)	t	Sig.	Partial correlation	VIF
(Constant)	44.77	4.11		10.90	0.000		
AR	0.12	0.01	0.64	9.04	0.000	0.70	1.14
PF	-0.36	0.09	-0.30	-4.25	0.000	-0.42	1.14

Note: Dependent variable: fluency rating
AR: articulation rate
PF: silent pause frequency

The R square of the final model reached 0.625, suggesting a good fitness of the model (Table 6.10). The ANOVA of the final model (Table 6.11) showed that the two fluency features (AR, PF) contributed significantly to the prediction of variance in the fluency rating ($F_{(2, 86)} = 71.647$, $p < 0.001$).

According to the partial correlation coefficients illustrated in Table 6.12, articulation rate was positively proportional to the fluency ratings (*partial r* = 0.70), while silent pause frequency showed a negative effect on the fluency ratings (*partial r* = -0.42). This means that speakers who spoke faster and paused less tended to have higher fluency ratings. It is clear that articulation rate had a greater weight than silent pause frequency in predicting the fluency ratings (AR > PF).

6.4 Discussion

Since the construct of pronunciation encompasses a few distinct dimensions, such as segmentals, prosody and fluency, it might be "worth using an analytic scale for a finer grained evaluation" (Knoch, 2017, p. 56) of the different aspects of pronunciation. This becomes particularly meaningful when the diagnostic assessment is taken into consideration, with "a goal to provide feedback on strengths and weaknesses" (Knoch, 2017, p. 56). This study investigated the differential contributions of the phonological features to raters' judgments of different dimensions of pronunciation, and provided empirical evidence for the establishment of analytic scales for pronunciation assessment.

6.4.1 Segmental predictors

The study revealed that phoneme substitution best predicted speakers' segmental quality, followed by incompletion plosion and phoneme insertion. The three features combined could account for 58.2% of the variance in the segmental ratings.

The phoneme substitution feature alone could explain 43.3% of the variance in the segmental ratings. The raters tended to give lower segmental scores to speakers who produced more types of phoneme substitutions. The greater contribution of phoneme substitution to the segmental judgment lies in its closer association with accentedness (Crowther et al., 2015;

Saito et al., 2016) as well as intelligibility (e.g., Bent et al., 2007; Rogers & Dalby, 2005; Zielinski, 2006). In the rating rubrics, this feature might be described as *mispronunciations* of sounds (vowels and consonants). Though most rating criteria emphasized the role of the mispronunciations whether to reduce intelligibility or cause more listener efforts, rather than the number of mispronunciations, it is reasonable to suggest that more types of phoneme substitution would require more listener efforts to decode the sounds, hence lowing the segmental ratings. A closer look at the types of phoneme substitution revealed great individual variability, but there seem to be more substitutions of monophthongs for diphthongs in Chinese EFL learners' speech.

Related to phoneme substitution is phoneme insertion, which has been identified by a number of previous studies as a common phenomenon in Chinese EFL learners' speech (Deterding, 2006; Hansen, 2001; Zielinski, 2006); however, its relationship with the judgment of segmental quality has not been studied. The current study revealed that phoneme insertion negatively and significantly predicted raters' evaluation of learners' segmental quality, though less salient than phoneme substitution. Interestingly, phoneme deletion errors did not significantly contribute to the segmental ratings, as there were few cases in Chinese EFL learners' speech.

In addition, the current finding also helps to specify the segmental information that had a positive effect on the segmental evaluation, i.e., the feature of incomplete plosion. This feature has never been measured in the previous literature to relate to any pronunciation construct, to the researcher's knowledge. Also, it has not been formally included in any pronunciation rating scales, though implied as one in the "range of pronunciation features" in IELTS (2018). However, segments are not produced in isolation. Incomplete plosion, as a kind of coarticulation, is very common in connected speech, and should be given attention in both pronunciation instruction and assessment.

6.4.2 Prosodic predictors

With regard to the prosodic scale, among the three subcategories of prosodic features, rhythm and stress features outperformed intonation features in predicting the prosodic ratings. The overall stress timing and nuclear stress errors combined could account for 53.7% of the variance in the prosodic ratings.

Of the two predictors of the prosodic ratings, the stress timing feature enjoyed a relative saliency over nuclear stress placement. A lower stress timing value means greater ability to reduce vowels in the weak syllables, and signifies a more stress-timing rhythm. Its great predicting power might be attributed to the fact that this rhythmic feature also reflected the appropriateness of the learners' stress pattern, since it was measured by the duration ratio of the intended unstressed and stressed syllables, rather than of the actually unstressed and stressed counterparts. Therefore, this feature had a relatively high correlation with sentence stress errors, and for this reason, the sentence stress feature dropped out of the predicting model.

What also needs to be noted is that the regression model dropped the intonation related features completely. This finding poses challenges to the traditional descriptors in the pronunciation rating scales, particularly those used in China, which usually attach great importance to "intonation," or in other words, pitch range or boundary tones, in the descriptors across all the rating levels. It seems that after learners acquire the default tone choices, such as the use of falling tone in the statements and rising tone in yes/no questions, the intonation features concerning the pitch movement become less salient. For one thing, this presents the emphasis of the grammatical function, rather than the discoursal or attitudinal functions of intonation in the Chinese EFL classroom, which leads to a good command of the default tone choice, but a relative difficulty in the non-default rising tone use. For another, the less important role of intonation features in the prosodic ratings showed the less effect intonation had on the conveyance of meaning, compared with rhythm and stress. Since English is a stress-timed language, it is the stressed parts that form the information chain and carry meaning. Therefore, a better command of rhythm and stress patterns helps to convey meaning more efficiently.

6.4.3 Fluency predictors

On the fluency scale, the current finding is in line with Cucchiarini et al. (2002), showing that articulation rate was a better predictor of perceived fluency in read speech, compared with the pause frequency feature. Learners who could read faster were mostly likely to be rated more fluent. However, it should be noted that this might be a result only when the learners' articulation rate did not exceed the optimal speed (as discussed in Section 5.4.1), and when the task was easily controlled (as discussed in Section 4.4.1.3.2).

If the elicitation task is spontaneous speech and even more

difficult read speech which would result in more pauses for a range of reasons, the relative weight of speed and pauses might be different. According to Bosker et al. (2013), the breakdown features (including both silent and filled pauses) accounted for the largest proportion of perceived fluency in spontaneous tasks. It is then reasonable to propose that the relative saliency of the speed and breakdown features might be task-specific. In an easily controlled task, such as the dialogue reading-aloud, raters might prioritize speed over pause frequency.

6.5 Summary

In summary, the differential contributions of the phonological features to the analytic ratings were investigated, respectively. The segmental quality could be accounted for by a combination of phoneme substitution, incompletion plosion, and phoneme insertion, with phoneme substitution as the best predictor. The prosodic ratings were best predicted by overall stress timing and nuclear stress placement, with the rhythmic feature having a greater contribution. The best predictor of perceived fluency was articulation rate, followed by silent pause frequency. The findings provide useful information for the construction of the three analytic rating scales of pronunciation.

Chapter Seven
CONCLUSION

This chapter summarizes the major findings of the present study, provides the theoretical, pedagogical, and testing implications, and discusses the limitations of the study and suggestions for future research.

7.1 Major findings

With its exploratory nature, the current study has served its intended aims to identify and validate a number of criterial features in the assessment of Chinese EFL learners' pronunciation in the reading-aloud task.

7.1.1 The validation of the criterial features

Generally, this study identified some of the intuitively and theoretically derived phonological features as criterial features for either the holistic or analytic pronunciation ratings.

There were 16 phonological features found to significantly contribute to the holistic pronunciation ratings, covering three dimensions of pronunciation, segmentals, prosody, and fluency. The verified features from each dimension also significantly contributed to their corresponding analytic ratings. Only one more feature, phoneme insertion, was found to correlate significantly to the segmental ratings but not to the holistic ratings. The large overlapping of the features correlated to the two types of ratings strengthens the validity of these criterial features in the pronunciation assessment and at the same time, suggests the contribution of all the three dimensions to the overall pronunciation judgment.

First, segmental substitution features and incomplete plosion were found to significantly contribute to both the holistic and segmental ratings, with one more feature—phoneme insertion, specifically to the segmental ratings. The substitution features included both vowel and consonant substitutions, but only consonant substitution at the onset positions contributed to the ratings, and those at the coda positions did not.

Second, the validated prosodic features concerned intonation, stress, and rhythm. To be more specific, the intonation features contributing to both the holistic and prosodic ratings included the deviated intonation phrasing, deviated rising tone use at non-default boundaries and overall pitch range. The stress features were the sentence stress and nuclear stress placement errors, and the duration realization of nuclear stress. Only one rhythmic feature, overall stress timing, outperformed others to contribute significantly to both types of ratings.

Third, the fluency features, such as articulation rate and the features of silent pause frequency, were identified to correlate with both the holistic and fluency ratings significantly; however, all the pause length features and repair features did not.

The failure of other theoretically derived features to significantly contribute to the pronunciation ratings reflects either the shared difficulties of Chinese EFL learners, such as vowel reduction and realization of stress by pitch or intensity, or a good command of particular aspects of pronunciation, for example, the use of falling tones. It might also be attributed to factors that could influence raters' perceptions, such as the position of segments and the task type.

7.1.2 The role of the criterial features in distinguishing the holistic rating levels

The current study revealed the different roles the phonological features played in assessing Chinese EFL learners' overall pronunciation proficiency.

The relative saliency of the phonological features was found to vary with the learners' pronunciation levels. Suprasegmental features seemed to characterize the high pronunciation level, while both segmental and suprasegmental features could distinguish the lower pronunciation levels. Besides, as articulation rate and overall stress timing function well in differentiating between all the levels, other suprasegmental features may characterize different levels, with sentence stress placement distinguishing the lower levels, and nuclear stress, intonation and pausing characterizing the high level.

This suggests that while consistent attention should be paid to rhythm and rate across all the holistic rating levels, raters tended to shift their focus gradually from speakers' segmental accuracy and sentence stress placement to more meaning-oriented nuclear stress pattern and intonation along with the rating levels.

7.1.3 The differential contribution of the criterial features to the analytic ratings

In terms of the different dimensions of pronunciation, the relative weight of the phonological features was found to predict each of the analytic ratings. First, a combination of phoneme substitution, incompletion plosion and phoneme insertion could best account for the variance in the segmental ratings, with phoneme substitution as the best predictor. Second, the prosodic ratings were best predicted by overall stress timing and nuclear stress placement, with the rhythmic feature having a greater contribution. Finally, a combined contribution of articulation rate and silent pause frequency could well predict the perceived fluency, with articulation rate playing a major role.

7.2 Implications

The criterial features revealed in the current study have a number of implications for pronunciation conceptualization, teaching, and testing.

7.2.1 Implications for the conceptualizations of pronunciation

The competing paradigms in the recent pronunciation literature are the two conflicting principles, "nativeness" versus "intelligibility," which have greatly influenced pronunciation rating constructs. The pronunciation rating rubrics, either in high-stakes international exams or in the English tests in China, have abandoned the nativeness principle and tried to be more intelligibility-oriented. This study, though not directly dealing with these two constructs, points out, to some extent, the effect of task type on the rating constructs in assessing pronunciation. The current finding revealed an advantage of many native-like features such as a more stress-timed rhythm, a more native-like articulation rate, intonation, and stress patterns, hence suggesting with caution that in assessing pronunciation in reading-aloud production, intelligibility may not be the only construct in the rating process. When all the grammatical structures and vocabulary were controlled in the reading-aloud task, and when raters did not need to struggle to comprehend the content, raters' attention tended to be paid to accuracy or nativeness for a more discriminative rating, even though this was not clearly instructed. The reading-aloud task, though not often adopted in high-stakes international exams such as TOELF iBT or IELTS, has traversed centuries in the language classrooms and played important roles in various L2 formative assessments from primary schools to colleges in China, and is still now incorporated in the national CET－4 test. The wide application of this task type in various forms of assessment calls for a pronunciation conceptualization that incorporates both intelligibility and accentedness, rather than separating the two completely.

7.2.2 Implications for pronunciation teaching

The relationship between pronunciation scores and phonological properties of L2 reading-aloud speech may contribute to a clearer understanding of the instruction focus in L2 pronunciation teaching.

The question of which phonological dimensions directly

impact L2 pronunciation perception has been debated for decades (e. g., Anderson-Hsieh et al., 1992). While some researchers have proposed that the accuracy of core segmental features has great influence on the successful communication between nonnative speakers (e.g., Jenkins, 2002) and should be given priority in instruction, other researchers argued that prosody and fluency are crucial for comprehensibility (e. g., Derwing, Munro, & Wiebe, 1998) and should be emphasized. The current findings, however, seem to support a view that the focus of pronunciation instructions on segmentals versus suprasegmentals may vary as a function of learners' pronunciation level. Moreover, the relative weight of different features on different levels might be influenced by speakers' L1 background, as the current findings differ from those for Japanese ESL learners (cf. Saito et al., 2016). For Chinese EFL learners, it seems important to pay consistent attention to articulation rate and stress-timed rhythm throughout the L2 pronunciation development; besides, learners need to be encouraged to shift their focus gradually from improving segmental accuracy and sentence stress placement to applying appropriate tone patterns and nuclear stress to convey meaning.

For learners at lower levels, the segmental accuracy, specifically vowels and onset-position consonants in stressed syllables, should be focused. They seemed to be more salient than other features at the lower levels to impact the listeners' perception. Also, the elision of plosives in the consonant sequences (i.e., incomplete plosion) should be emphasized as an efficient way to improve fluidity. Furthermore, suprasegmentals should not be neglected at the lower level, particularly articulation rate and the pattern of sentence stress, including the placement of sentence stress and its duration realization.

For learners at higher levels, more attention should be given to suprasegmentals. It seems that when a speaker reaches a certain threshold of segmental and sentence stress accuracy, listeners tend to require more suprasegmental control for a more fluent and expressive pronunciation in the oral reading production, including the prevention of pauses and a good command of speed, nuclear stress, the use of rising tone, pitch range and the stress timed rhythm. Explicit instruction on suprasegmental for learners at higher levels would be more helpful.

These findings would not only contribute to the textbook writing, but also help Chinese EFL teachers identify individual learners' pronunciation strengths and weaknesses in terms of specific phonological features. Moreover, the findings provide a range of diagnostic information for the development of computer-assisted pronunciation training (CAPT).

7.2.3　Implications for pronunciation testing

In testing, this study promotes the development of pronunciation rating scales and automated scoring.

First, it provides empirically validated criterial features to develop discrete descriptors for the construction of a holistic pronunciation rating scale. The current findings of the phonological features able to distinguish between adjacent levels indicate that it is possible rather than "elusive" (Isaacs et al., 2015, p. 4) to identify common features across all the pronunciation scales when using a smaller number of scales, as opposed to the nine-point scale used in IELTS. However, it is indeed true that it might be impractical to include every feature on different rating levels. As discussed above, at lower levels, the accuracy of segmentals, incomplete plosion, and sentence stress placement might be more salient, while at higher levels, raters might rely more on various suprasegmental features to convey the focal meanings.

Second, the findings of the relative importance of the phonological features in assessing different dimensions of pronunciations help the construction of analytic scales in the pronunciation assessment. The analytic scales are particularly helpful in formative or diagnostic assessment, which can provide useful information on the strengths and weaknesses of a particular aspect of pronunciation.

In addition to the implications for rating scale development, the differential contribution of the phonological features revealed in the study also provide crucial information for the development of automated pronunciation scoring. All the three dimensions of pronunciation should be taken into consideration, with a relatively higher weight given to segmental accuracy, rhythm, and articulation rate, respectively.

7.3 Limitations

The present study suffers from a number of limitations due to its corpus-driven nature and the difficulty in speech coding.

One limitation has to do with the task used to elicit the speech samples. The speech samples applied in the present study were dialogue reading-alouds taken from RESCCL. Though the findings of this study contribute to the construction of pronunciation rating scales for the reading-aloud task, they should be applied with caution in assessing pronunciation in spontaneous oral tasks. Munro and Derwing (1994) reported no difference in raters' accentedness rating between the controlled reading-aloud task and the spontaneous picture description task; however, Foote and Trofimovich (2016) reported differences in the dimensions underlying listeners' perception of L2 read speech and interview speech. Considering the different natures of controlled and spontaneous tasks, the impact of the phonological features on raters' judgment of overall pronunciation proficiency could be task specific. Moreover, the reading material used in the task is both lexically and syntactically simple for college students, with very few multisyllabic words; thus, it is impossible to investigate the effect of word stress errors on the pronunciation rating. Considering that word stress has been widely researched, and proved to have great impact on intelligibility (Field, 2005), comprehensibility and accentedness (Saito et al., 2015), the lack of such a feature made the current study incomplete.

Second, the pronunciation ratings were taken from the corpus directly. The researcher only got the chance to interview the three Chinese raters but had no access to the four native English-speaking raters, hence difficult to look into the raters' real-time rating process, and identify the criterial features from the raters' perspective.

Finally, due to the complexity of speech coding and the large number of phonological features identified in the literature, the sample size in the Phase-I study was relatively small. Also, for the same reason, the speech samples were coded by the researcher alone. Though most coding was based on the existing annotation in the corpus to ensure accuracy, the lack of a second coder might cause reliability issues.

7.4 Suggestions for future research

The present study is the first of its kind to explore the relationship between holistic as well as analytic pronunciation ratings and a large quantity of discrete phonological features in the reading-aloud production of Chinese EFL learners. However, due to the limitations discussed above, future research can be carried out to answer a few more questions.

The first is the extent to which task type might affect the relationship between pronunciation ratings and phonological features. This comparison will better our understanding of the pronunciation constructs raters follow in different tasks, and help construct task-specific pronunciation rating scales.

Also, while this study focused on the features of the speech samples with shared holistic pronunciation judgments of both native and nonnative raters, future research can examine the phonological features of those rated differently in terms of overall pronunciation quality by native and nonnative raters.

Moreover, qualitative research examining the pronunciation rating process can be carried out to explore the impact of various phonological features on the raters' judgments. This will serve as a supplement to the present study, and reveal, hand in hand, the differential contribution of phonological features in pronunciation assessment.

References

Abercrombie, D. (1967). *Elements of general phonetics*. Edinburgh: Edinburgh University Press.

Anderson-Hsieh, J., Johnson, R., & Koehler K. (1992). The relationship between native speaker judgments of nonnative pronunciation and deviance in segmentals, prosody, and syllable structure [Electronic version]. *Language Learning*, 42(4), 529–555.

Anderson-Hsieh, J., & Koehler, K. (1988). The effect of foreign accent and speaking rate on native speaker comprehension [Electronic version]. *Language Learning*, 38, 561–613.

Anderson-Hsieh, J., & Venkatagiri, H. (1994). Syllable duration and pausing in the speech of Chinese ESL speakers [Electronic version]. *TESOL Quarterly*, 28(4), 807–812.

Bachman, L. F. (2004). *Statistical analyses for language assessment*. Cambridge, UK: Cambridge University Press.

Barnwell, D. (1989). 'Naive' native speakers and judgments of oral proficiency in Spanish [Electronic version]. *Language Testing*, 6, 152–163.

Bartels, C. (1999). *The intonation of English statements and questions*. New York & London: Garland Publishing, Inc.

Beckman, M.E. (1986). *Stress and non-stress*. Foris: Dordrecht.

Bent, T., & Bradlow, A. R. (2003). The interlanguage speech

intelligibility benefit. *Journal of the Acoustical Society of America*, *114*(3), 1600-1610. doi: 10.1121/1.1603234

Bent, T., Bradlow, A. R., & Smith, B. L. (2007). Segmental errors in different word positions and their effects on intelligibility of non-native speech: All's well that begins well. In O. S. Bohn & M. J. Munro (Ed.), *Language experience in second language speech learning. In honor of James Emil Flege* (pp. 331-347). Amsterdam: John Benjamins Publishing Company.

Bergeron, A., & Trofimovich, P. (2017). Linguistic dimensions of accentedness and comprehensibility: Exploring task and listener effects in second language French. *Foreign Language Annals*, *50*(3), 547-566. doi: 10.1111/flan.1228

Bernstein, J. (1999). *PhonePass testing: Structure and construct*. Menlo Park, CA: Ordinate Corporation.

Bernstein, J., Van Moere, A., & Cheng, J. (2010). Validating automated speaking tests. Language Testing, 27, 355-377. doi: 10.1177/0265532210364404

Binghadeer, N. (2008). An acoustic analysis of pitch range in the production of native and nonnative speakers of English [Electronic version]. *The Asian EFL Journal Quarterly*, *10*, 96-113.

Bolinger, D. (1958). A theory of pitch accent in English. *Word*, *14*, 109-149. doi: 10.1080/00437956.1958.11659660

Bolinger, D. (1972). Accent is predictable (if you're a mind-reader). *Language*, *48*, 633-644. doi: 10.2307/412039

Bond, Z. S., & Small, L. H. (1983). Voicing, vowel, and stress mispronunciations in continuous speech. *Perception and Psychophysics*, *34*(5), 470-474. doi: 10.3758/BF03203063

Bongaerts, T., van Summeren, C., Planken, B., & Schils, E.

(1997). Age and ultimate attainment in the pronunciation of a foreign language [Electronic version]. *Studies in Second Language Acquisition*, *19*, 447–465.

Bosker, H. R., Pinget, A., Quené, H., Sanders, T., & De Jong, N. H. (2013). What makes speech sound fluent? The contributions of pauses, speed and repairs. *Language Testing*, *30*(2), 159–175. doi:10.1177/0265532212455394

Bosker, H. R., Quené, H., Sanders, T., & De Jong, N. H. (2014). The perception of fluency in Native and nonnative speech. *Language Learning*, *64*(3), 579–614. doi: 10.1111/lang.12067

British Council, IDP: IELTS Australia and University of Cambridge ESOL Examinations. (n.d.). IELTS speaking band descriptors (public version). Retrieved from https://www.ielts.org/-/media/pdfs/speaking-band-descriptors.ashx?la=en

Brown, A. (2000). An investigation of the rating process in the IELTS Speaking Module. *Research Reports 1999*, *3*, 49–85.

Brown, A., Iwashita, N., & McNamara, T. (2005). *An examination of rater orientation and test-taker performance on English-for-academic-purposes speaking tasks*. (TOEFL Monograph No. 29). Princeton, NJ: Educational Testing Service.

Brown, A., & Taylor, L. (2006). A worldwide survey of examiners' views and experience of the revised IELTS Speaking Test [Electronic version]. *Research Notes*, *26*, 14–18.

Browne, K., & Fulcher, G. (2017). Pronunciation and intelligibility in assessing spoken fluency. In T. Isaacs & P.

Trofimovich (Ed.), *Second language pronunciation assessment*, (pp. 37 – 53). Bristol: Multilingual Matters.

Buchman, L. F. (1990). *Fundamental considerations in language testing*. Oxford: Oxford University Press.

Buck, G. (1989). Written tests of pronunciation: Do they work? [Electronic version] *ELT Journal*, 43(1), 50 – 56.

Cambridge English. (2016). *Cambridge English first for schools: Handbook for teachers for exams from 2016*. Cambridge, UK: Author.

Canale, M., & Swain, M. (1980). Theoretical bases of communicative approaches to second language teaching and testing [Electronic version]. *Applied Linguistics*, 1(1), 1 – 57.

Cao, R. L. (2010). A study of factors affecting Chinese EFL learners' production of English onset consonant clusters. (Doctoral dissertation, Nanjing University).

Carey, M. D., Mannell, R. H., & Dunn, P. K. (2011). Does a rater's familiarity with a candidate's pronunciation affect the rating in oral proficiency interviews? *Language Testing*, 28(2), 201 – 219. doi: 10.1177/0265532210393704

Carroll, S. E. (2004). Segmentation: Learning how to 'hear words' in the L2 speech stream. *Transactions of the Philological Society*, 102(2), 227 – 254. doi: 10.1111/j.0079 – 1636.2004.00136.x

Cesar-Lee, B. V. (1999). *Quantification of accented pronunciation by American-English speakers in French-as-a-foreign language setting* (Doctoral dissertation, University of Florida).

Chang, J. (2001). Chinese speakers. In M. Swan & B. Smith (Eds.), Learner English. A teacher's guide to interference and other problems (pp.310 - 324). Cambridge: Cambridge University Press.

Chang, L. A. (2008). *Understand me or not? Accent, acceptability and intelligibility in international English: The case of Singapore.* (unpublished Master's thesis). National University of Singapore.

Chen, Y., Robb, M. P., Gilbert, H. R., & Lerman, J. W. (2001a). A study of sentence stress production in Mandarin speakers of American English. *Journal of the Acoustic Society of America*, *109*, 1681 - 1690. doi: 10. 1121/1. 1356023

Chen, Y., Robb, M. P., Gilbert, H. R., & Lerman, J. W. (2001b). Vowel production by Mandarin speakers of English. *Clinical Linguistics & Phonetics*, *15*(6), 427 - 440. doi: 10.1080/0269920011004480

Chela-Flores, B. (2001). Pronunciation and language learning: An integrative approach [Electronic version]. *International Review of Applied Linguistics*, *39*, 85 - 101.

Cicchetti, D. V. (1994). Guidelines, criteria, and rules of thumb for evaluating normed and standardized assessment instruments in psychology. P*sychological Assessment*, *6* (4): 284 - 290. doi:10.1037/1040 - 3590.6.4.284

Cincarek, T., Gruhn, R., Hacker, C., Nöth, E., & Nakamura, S. (2009). Automatic pronunciation scoring of words and sentences independent from the non-native's first language. *Computer Speech and Language*, *23*, 65 - 88. doi:10.1016/j.csl.2008.03.001

Cole, M. W., Dunston, P. J., & Butler, T. (2017). Engaging English language learners through interactive read-alouds: A literature review. *English Teaching Practice & Critique*,

16(1), 97-109. doi: 10.1108/ETPC-11-2015-0101

Council of Europe. (2001). *Common European Framework of Reference for languages: Learning, teaching, assessment.* Cambridge: Cambridge University Press.

Couper-Kuhlen, E. (1986). *An introduction to English prosody.* London: Edward Arnold.

Cruttenden, A. (2001).《吉姆森英语语音教程》.北京:外语教学与研究出版社.

Crowther, D., Trofimovich, P., Saito, K., & Isaacs, T. (2015). Second language comprehensibility revisited: Investigating the effects of learner background. *TESOL Quarterly*, *49*, 814-837. doi: 10.1002/tesq.203

Crowther, D., Trofimovich, P., Saito, K., & Isaacs, T. (2016). Linguistic dimensions of second language accent and comprehensibility: Nonnative listeners' perspectives. *Journal of Second Language Pronunciation*, *2*(2), 160-182. doi: 10.1075/jslp.2.2.02cro

Crowther, D., Trofimovich, P., Saito, K., & Isaacs, T. (2018). Linguistic dimensions of L2 accentedness and comprehensibility vary across speaking tasks. *Studies in Second Language Acquisition*, *40*, 443-457. doi:10.1017/S027226311700016X

Crystal, D. (1969). *Prosodic systems and intonation in English.* Cambridge: Cambridge University Press.

Crystal, D. (2003). *A dictionary of linguistics and phonetics.* Malden, MA: Blackwell Publishing.

Cucchiarini, C., Strick, H. & Boves, L. (2000). Different aspects of expert pronunciation quality ratings and their relation to scores produced by speech recognition algorithms [Electronic version]. *Speech Communication*,

30, 109–119.

Cucciarini, C., Strick, H., & Boves, L. (2002). Quantitative assessment of second language learners' fluency: Comparisons between read and spontaneous speech. *Journal of the Acoustical Society of America*, *111*, 2862–2873. doi: 10.1121/1.1471894

Cutler, A. (1984). Stress and accent in language production and understanding. In Gibbon & Richter (Ed.), *Intonation, accent and rhythm: Studies in discourse phonology* (pp. 77–90). Berlin & New York: W de Gruyter.

Cutler, A. (2005). Lexical stress in English pronunciation. In M. Reed & J. M. Levis (Ed.), *The handbook of English pronunciation* (pp. 106–124). Wiley Blackwell.

Cutler, A., & Carter, D. M. (1987). The predominance of strong initial syllables in the English vocabulary. *Computer Speech and Language*, *2*(3/4), 133–142. doi: 10.1016/0885-2308(87)90004-0

Dauer, R. M. (1983). Stress-timing and syllable-timing reanalyzed. *Journal of Phonetics*, *11*(1), 51–62. doi: 10.1515/jlsc.1983.12.2.54

De Jong, N. H. (2016). Predicting pauses in L1 and L2 speech: The effects of utterance boundaries and word frequency. *Iral*, *54*(2), 113–132. doi: 10.1515/iral-2016-9993

De Jong, N. H. (2018). Fluency in second language testing: Insights from different disciplines. *Language Assessment Quarterly*, *15*(3), 237–254. doi: 10.1080/15434303.2018.1477780

De Jong, N. H., & Bosker, H. R. (2013). Choosing a threshold for silent pauses to feature second language fluency. *Proceedings of Disfluency in Spontaneous Speech 2013*, 17–

20. Retrieved from https://www.isca-speech.org/archive/diss_2013/papers/dis6_017.pdf

De Jong, N. H., Groenhout, R., Schoonen, R., & Hulstijn, J. H. (2015). Second language fluency: Speaking style or proficiency? Correcting measures of second language fluency for first language behavior. *Applied Psycholinguistics*, *36* (2), 223–243. doi:10.1017/S0142716413000210

De Jong, N. H., Steinel, M. P., Florijn, A., Schoonen, R., & Hulstijn, J. H. (2013). Linguistic skills and speaking fluency in a second language. *Applied Psycholinguistics*, *34* (5), 893–916. doi:10.1017/S0142716412000069

Dellow, V. (2006). Rhythm and speech rate: A variation coefficient for Delta C. In P. Karnowski & I. Szigeti (Ed.), *Language and language processing: Proceedings of the 38th linguistic colloquium* (pp. 231–241). Piliscsaba 2003, Frankfurt: Peter Lang.

Derwing, T. M., & Munro, M. J. (1997). Accent, intelligibility, and comprehensibility: Evidence for four L1s [Electronic version]. *Studies in Second Language Acquisition*, *20*, 1–16.

Derwing, T. M., & Munro, M. J. (2005). Second language accent and pronunciation teaching: A research-based approach [Electronic version]. *TESOL Quarterly*, *39* (3), 379–397.

Derwing, T. M., & Munro, M. J. (2009). Putting accent in its place: Rethinking obstacles to communication [Electronic version]. *Language Teaching*, *42*, 1–15. doi: 10.1017/S026144480800551X

Derwing, T. M., Munro, M. J., & Thomson, R. I. (2008). A longitudinal study of ESL learners' fluency and comprehensibility development. *Applied Linguistics*, *29*, 359–380. doi: 10.1093/applin/amm041

Derwing, T. M., Munro, M. J., & Thomson, R. I. (2009). The relationship between L1 fluency and L2 fluency development. *Studies in Second Language Acquisition*, *31*, 533–557. doi: 10.1017/S0272263109990015

Derwing, T. M., Munro, M. J., & Wiebe, G. E. (1998). Evidence in favor of a broad framework for pronunciation instruction [Electronic version]. *Language Learning*, *48*, 393–410.

Derwing, T. M., Rossiter, M. J., Munro, M. J., & Thomson, R. I. (2004). Second language fluency: Judgments on different tasks. *Language Learning*, *54*, 665–679. doi: 10.1111/j.1467-9922.2004.00282.x

Deterding, D. (2001). The measurement of rhythm: A comparison of Singapore and British English. *Journal of Phonetics*, *29*, 217–230. doi.10.006/jpho.2001.0138

Deterding, D. (2006). The pronunciation of English by speakers from China. *English World Wide*, *27*(2), 175–198. doi: 10.1075/eww.27.2.04det

Ding, Y. X. (2017). *A study on the intonation features of English interrogative sentences by the Chinese EFL learners: A case study of learners from Shandong dialectal region* (Master's thesis, Shandong Agricultural University).

Douglas, D. (1994). Quantity and quality in speaking test performance [Electronic version]. *Language Testing*, *11*(2), 125–144.

Douglas, D., & Selinker, L. (1992). Analysing oral proficiency test performance in general and specific purpose contexts. *System*, *20*, 317–328. doi: 10.1016/0346-251X(92)90043-3

Duez, D. (1982). Silent and non-silent pauses in three speech styles [Electronic version]. *Language and Speech*, *25*(1), 11-28.

Duez, D. (1993). Acoustic features of subjective pauses. *Journal of Psycholinguistic Research*, *22*(1), 21-39. doi: 10.1007/BF01068155

Educational Testing Service. (2014). Independent speaking rubrics/integrated speaking rubrics. Retrieved from http://www.ets.org/s/toefl/pdf/toefl_speaking_rubrics.pdf

Ejzenberg, R. (2000). The juggling act of oral fluency: A psycho-sociolinguistic metaphor. In H. Riggenbach (Ed.), *Perspectives on fluency* (pp. 287-313). Ann Arbor: The University of Michigan Press.

Evans, J. D. (1996). *Straightforward statistics for the behavioral sciences*. Belmont, CA, US: Thomson Brooks/Cole Publishing Co.

Fear, B. D., Cutler, A. & Butterfield, S. (1995). The strong/weak syllable distinction in English. *Journal of the Acoustical Society of America*, *97*, 1893-1904. Retrieved from https://pure.mpg.de/rest/items/item_68835_4/component/file_68836/content

Field, A. (2000). *Discovering statistics using SPSS for Windows*. London: SAGE Publications.

Field, A. P. (2005). Intraclass Correlation. In *Encyclopedia of Statistics in Behavioral Science* (Vol. 2, pp. 948-954). New York: John Wiley & Sons Inc. doi: 10.1002/0470013192.bsa313

Field, J. (2005). Intelligibility and the listener: The role of lexical stress [Electronic version]. *TESOL Quarterly*, *39*(3), 399-423.

Flege, J. E. (1995). Second language speech learning: Theory, findings, and problems. In W. Strange (Ed.), *Speech perception and linguistic experience: Issues in cross-language research* (pp. 233-277). Timonium, MD: York Press.

Flege, J. E., Bohn, O. S., & Jang, S. (1997). Effects of experience on non-native speakers' production and perception of English vowels. *Journal of Phonetics*, 25(4), 437-470. doi: 10.1006/jpho.1997.0052

Flege, J. E., Munro, M. J., & MacKay, I. R. A. (1995). Factors affecting strength of perceived foreign accent in a second language. *Journal of the Acoustical Society of America*, 97, 3125-3134. dio: 10.1121/1.413041

Flege, J. E., Schirru, C., & MacKay, I. R. A. (2003). Interaction between the native and second language phonetic subsystems. *Speech Communication*, 40, 467-491. doi:10.1016/S0167-6393(02)00128-0

Foster, P., Tonkyn, A., & Wigglesworth, G. (2000). Measuring spoken language: A unit for all reasons. *Applied Linguistics*, 21(3), 354-375. doi: 10.1093/applin/21.3.354

Frando, H., Neumeyer, L, Digalakis, V., & Ronen, O. (2000). Combination of machine scores for automatic grading of pronunciation quality [Electronic version]. *Speech Communication*, 30, 121-130.

Fry, D. B. (1958). Experiments in the perception of stress [Electronic version]. *Language and speech*, 1, 126-152.

Fulcher, G. (1996). Does thick description lead to smart tests? A data-based approach to rating scale construction. *Language Testing*, 13(2), 208-238. doi: 10. 1177/026553229601300205

Fulcher, G. (2003). *Testing second language speaking*. London: Pearson Education.

Galaczi, E. D., Ffrench, A., Hubbard, C. & Green, A. (2011). Developing assessment scales for large-scale speaking tests: A multiple-method approach. *Assessment in Education: Principles, Policy & Practice, 18*(3), 217 - 237. doi: 10.1080/0969594X.2011.574605

Galaczi, E. D., Post, B., Li, A. K., Barker, F. & Schmidt, E. (2017). Assessing second language pronunciation: Distinguishing features of rhythm in learner speech at different proficiency levels. In T. Isaacs & P. Trofimovich (Ed.), *Second language pronunciation assessment* (pp. 157 - 182). Bristol: Multilingual Matters. doi: 10.21832/ISAACS6848

Ghanem, R., & Kang, O. (2018). Pronunciation features in rating criteria. In O. Kang & A. Ginther (Ed.), *Assessment in second language pronunciation* (pp. 115 - 136). New York: Routledge.

Ginther, A., Dimova, S., & Yang, R. (2010). Conceptual and empirical relationships between temporal measures of fluency and oral English proficiency with implications for automated scoring. *Language Testing, 27*(3), 379 - 399. doi:10.1177/0265532210364407

Goldman-Eisle, F. (1968). *Psycholinguistics: Experiments in spontaneous speech*. New York: Academy Press.

Grabe, E., & Low, E. L. (2002). Durational variability in speech and the rhythm class hypothesis. In C. Gussenhoven & N. Warner (Ed.), *Laboratory phonology 7* (pp. 515 - 546). Berlin: Mouton de Gruyter.

Guillot, M.-N. (1999). *Fluency and its teaching*. Clevedon,

England: Multilingual Matters.

Gut, U. (2009). *Non-native speech: A corpus-based analysis of phonological and phonetic properties of L2 English and German*. Frankfurt am Main: Peter Lang.

Gut, U. (2012). Rhythm in L2 speech [Electronic version]. *Speech and Language Technology*, *14/15*, 83–94.

Hadden, B. L. (1991). Teacher and nonteacher perceptions of second language communication [Electronic version]. *Language Learning*, *41*, 1–20.

Hahn, L. D. (2004). Primary stress and intelligibility: Research to motivate the teaching of suprasegmentals. *TESOL Quarterly*, *38*(2), 201–223. doi:10.2307/3588378

Halliday, M. A. K. (1967). *Intonation and Grammar in British English*. Mouton: The Hague.

Halliday, M. A. K. (1970). *A course in spoken English: Intonation*. London: Oxford University Press.

Hansen, J. G. (2001). Linguistic constraints on the acquisition of English syllable codas by native speakers of Mandarin Chinese. *Applied Linguistics*, *22*(3), 338–365. doi: 10.1093/applin/22.3.338

Harding, L. (2013). Pronunciation assessment. In C. A. Chapelle (Ed.), *The encyclopedia of applied linguistics* (pp. 1–6). Hoboken, NJ: Wiley-Blackwell.doi: 10.1002/9781405198431.wbeal0966.

Harding, L. (2017). What do raters need in a pronunciation scale? The user's view. In T. Isaacs & P. Trofimovich (Ed.), *Second language pronunciation assessment*, (pp. 12–34). Bristol: Multilingual Matters.

Harding, L. (2018). Validity in pronunciation assessment. In O. Kang & A. Ginther (Ed.), *Assessment in second language pronunciation* (pp. 30 - 48). New York: Routledge.

Hawkey, R., & Barker, F. (2004). Developing a common scale for the assessment of writing. *Assessing Writing*, *9* (2), 122 - 159. doi:10.1016/j.asw.2004.06.001

Hawkins, P. R. (1971). The syntactic location of hesitation pauses [Electronic version]. *Language and Speech*, *14*(3), 277 - 288.

Hawkins, J. A., & Filipovik, L. (2012). *Criterial features in L2 English: Specifying the reference levels of the Common European Framework*. Cambridge: Cambridge University Press.

He, D., & Zhang, Q. (2010). Native speaker norms and China English: From the perspective of learners and teachers in China. *TESOL Quarterly*, *44* (4), 769 - 789. doi: 10.5054/tq.2010.235995

Hewings, M. (1995). Tone choice in the English intonation of nonnative speakers [Electronic version]. *International Review of Applied Linguistics*, *33*, 251 - 265.

Hieke, A. E., Kowal, S., & O'Connell, D. (1983). The trouble with "articulatory" pauses [Electronic version]. *Language and Speech*, *26*(3), 203 - 214.

Hilton, H. (2008). The link between vocabulary knowledge and spoken L2 fluency. *The Language Learning Journal*, *36*, 153 - 166. doi: 10.1080/09571730802389983

Hincks, R., & Edlund, J. (2009). Transient visual feedback on pitch variation for Chinese speakers of English. *Proceedings of FONETIK 2009*. Retrieved from http://www.speech.kth.se/prod/publications/files/3354.pdf

Hua, T. F. (2003). The acquisition of English speech rhythm by adult Chinese ESL and EFL learners (*Doctoral* dissertation, University of Hawaii).

IELTS. (2018). IELTS Guide for teachers: Test format, scoring and preparing students for the test. Retrieved from https://www.ielts.org/-/media/publications/guide-for-teachers/ielts-guide-for-teachers-uk.ashx

Isaacs, T. (2008). Towards defining a valid assessment criterion of pronunciation proficiency in non-native English-speaking graduate students [Electronic version]. The Canadian Modern Language Review, 64, 555–580.

Isaacs, T. (2014). Assessing pronunciation. In A. J. Kunnan (Ed.), *The companion to language assessment* (pp. 140–155). Hoboken, NJ: Wiley Blackwell.

Isaacs, T. (2018). Shifting sands in second language pronunciation teaching and assessment research and practice. *Language Assessment Quarterly*, 15(3), 273–293. doi: 10.1080/15434303.2018.1472264

Isaacs, T., & Harding, L. (2017). Research timeline: Pronunciation assessment. *Language Teaching*, 50(3), 347–366. doi: 10.1017/S0261444817000118

Isaacs, T. & Thomson, R. I. (2013). Rater experience, rating scale length, and judgments of L2 pronunciation: revisiting research conventions. *Language Assessment Quarterly*, 10(2), 135–159. doi: 10.1080/15434303.2013.769545

Isaacs, T., & Trofimovich, P. (2012). Deconstructing comprehensibility. *Studies in Second Language Acquisition*, 34, 475–505. doi:10.1017/S0272263112000150

Isaacs, T., & Trofimovich, P. (2017). Key themes, constructs and interdisciplinary perspectives in second language pronunciation assessment. In T. Isaacs & P. Trofimovich (Ed.), *Second language pronunciation assessment* (pp. 3–

11). Bristol: Multilingual Matters. doi: 10. 21832/ISAACS6848

Isaacs, T., Trofimovich, P., & Foote, J. A. (2018). Developing a user-oriented second language comprehensibility scale for English-medium universities. *Language Testing*, *35*, 193–216. doi:10.1177/0265532217703433

Isaacs, T., Trofimovich, P., Yu, G., & Chereau, B. M. (2015). Examining the linguistic aspects of speech that most efficiently discriminate between upper levels of the revised IELTS pronunciation scale. In *IELTS research reports* (online series Vol. 4, pp. 1–48). British Council, Cambridge English Language Assessment and IDP: IELTS Australia.

Iwashita, N., Brown, A., McNamara, T., & O'Hagan, S. (2008). Assessed levels of second language speaking proficiency: How distinct? *Applied Linguistics*, *29* (1), 24–49. doi:10.1093/applin/amm017

Jang, T. Y. (2008). Speech rhythm metrics for automatic scoring of English speech by Korean EFL learners. *Malsori Speech Sounds*, *66*(1), 41–59.

Jenkins, J. (2000). *The phonology of English as an international language*. Oxford: Oxford University Press.

Jenkins, J. (2002). A sociolinguistically based, empirically researched pronunciation syllabus for English as an international language [Electronic version]. *Applied Linguistics*, *23*(1), 83–103.

Jin, T., & Mak, B. (2012). Distinguishing features in scoring L2 Chinese speaking performance: How do they work? *Language Testing*, *30*(1), 23–47. doi: 10. 1177/0265532212442637

Kahng, J. (2014). Exploring utterance and cognitive fluency of L1 and L2 English speakers: Temporal measures and stimulated recall. *Language Learning*, *64* (4), 809 – 854. doi:10.1111/lang.2014.64.issue – 4

Kang, O. (2010). Relative salience of suprasegmental features on judgments of L2 comprehensibility and accentedness. *System*, *38*, 301 – 315. doi:10.1016/j.system.2010.01.005

Kang, O., Rubin, D. L., & Pickering, L. (2010). Suprasegmental measures of accentedness and judgmets of language learner proficiency in oral English. *The Modern Language Journal*, *94*(4), 554 – 566. doi: 10.1111/j.1540 – 4781.2010.01091.x

Kang, O., & Ginther, A. (2018). Introduction. In O. Kang & A. Ginther (Ed.), *Assessment in second language pronunciation* (pp. 1 – 7). New York: Routledge.

Kang, O., Vo, S. C. T., & Moran, M. K. (2016). Perceptual judgments of accented speech by listeners from different first language backgrounds [Electronic version]. *The Electronic Journal for English as a Second Language*, *20*, 1 – 24.

Kennedy, S., & Trofimovich, P. (2008). Intelligibility, comprehensibility, and accentedness of L2 speech: The role of listener experience and semantic context [Electronic version]. *Canadian Modern Language Review*, *64*, 459 – 489.

Kettemann, B., & Wieden, W. (1993). *Current issues in European second language acquisition*. Tubingen: Gunter Narr Verlag.

Kim, Y.H. (2009). An investigation into native and non-native teachers' judgments of oral English performance: A mixed methods approach. *Language Testing*, *26*(2), 187 – 217. doi:10.1177/0265532208101010

Kingdon, R. (1958). *The groundwork of English intonation*. London: Longmans.

Knoch, U. (2011). Rating scales for diagnostic assessment of writing: What should they look like and where should the criteria come from? *Assessing Writing*, *16*, 81 – 96. doi:10.1016/j.asw.2011.02.003

Knoch, U. (2017). What can pronunciation researchers learn from research into second language writing? In T. Isaacs & P. Trofimovich (Ed.), *Second language pronunciation assessment* (pp. 54 – 71). Bristol: Multilingual Matters. doi: 10.21832/ISAACS6848

Koren, S. (1995). Foreign language pronunciation testing: A new approach [Electronic version]. *System*, *23*(3), 387 – 400.

Kormos, J., & Denes, M. (2004). Exploring features and perceptions of fluency in the speech of second language learners. *System*, *32*(2), 145 – 164. doi: 10.1016/j.system.2004.01.001

Krashen, S. (1982). *Principles and practice in second language acquisition*. Oxford: Pergamon Press.

Ladd, D. R. (1980). *The structure of intonational meaning. Evidence from English*. Bloomington: Indiana University Press.

Ladd, D. R. (1983). Phonological features of intonational peaks [Electronic version]. *Language*, *59*, 721 – 759.

Lado, R. (1961). *Language testing: The construction and use of foreign language tests*. London, UK: Longman.

Lee, O., & Kim, J. (2005). Syllable-timing interferes with

Korean learners' speech of stress-timed English. *Speech Sciences*, *12* (4), 95 – 112. Retrieved from http://cms.kangwon.ac.kr/user/kimjm/publication/13 _ 05timing _ KASS_r90718.pdf

Lennon, P. (1990). Investigating fluency in EFL: A quantitative approach. *Language Learning*, *3*, 387 – 417. doi:10.1111/ j.1467 – 1770.1990.tb00669.x

Levis, J. M. (2005). Changing contexts and shifting paradigms in pronunciation teaching [Electronic version]. *TESOL Quarterly*, *39*(3), 369 – 377.

Levis, J. M. (2006). Pronunciation and the assessment of spoken language. In R. Hughes (Ed.), *Spoken English, TESOL and applied linguistics: Challenges for theory and practice* (pp. 245 – 270). New York: Palgrave Macmillan.

Li, A. K., & Post, B. (2014). L2 acquisition of prosodic properties of speech rhythm. *Studies in Second Language Acquisition*, *36*, 223 – 255. doi: 10.1017/S0272263113000752

Liberman, M. Y. & Prince, A. (1977). On stress and linguistic rhythm. *Linguistic Inquiry*, *8* (2), 249 – 336. Retrieved from https://linguistics.ucla.edu/people/hayes/251English/Readings/LibermanAndPrince1977.pdf

Low, E. L., Grabe, E. & Nolan, F. (2000). Quantitative characterizations of speech rhythm: Syllable-timing in Singapore English. *Language and Speech*, *43*(4), 377 – 401. doi: 10.1177/00238309000430040301

Low, E. L. (2006). A review of recent research on speech rhythm: Some insights for language acquisition, language disorders and language teaching. In R. Hughes (Ed.), *Spoken English, TESOL and applied linguistics: Challenges for theory and practice* (pp. 99-125). Houndmills, Hampshire: Palgrave Macmillan.

Luoma, S. (2004). *Assessing Speaking*. Cambridge: Cambridge University Press.

Major, R. C., Fitzmaurice, S. F., Bunta, F., & Balasubramanian, C. (2002). The effects of nonnative accents on listening comprehension: Implications for ESL assessment. *TESOL Quarterly, 36*, 173-190. doi: 10.2307/3588329

Makarova, V., & Zhou, X. (2006). Prosodic characteristics in the speech of Chinese EFL learners [Electronic version]. *Speech Prosody, May, 2-5*.

Marslen-Wilson, W. D. (1989). Access and integration: Projecting sound onto meaning. In W. D. Marslen-Wilson (Ed.), Lexical representation and process (pp. 3-24). Cambridge, MA: MIT Press.

McNamara, T. (1996). *Measuring second language performance*. Harlow, Essex: Pearson Education.

Miller, M. (1984). On the perception of rhythm [Electronic version]. *Journal of Phonetics, 12*, 75-83.

Munro, M. J., & Derwing, T. M. (1994). Evaluation of foreign accent in extemporaneous and read material [Electronic version]. *Language Testing, 11*, 253-266.

Munro, M. J., & Derwing, T. M. (1995). Foreign accent, comprehensibility, and intelligibility in the speech of second language learners [Electronic version]. *Language learning, 45*(1), 73-97.

Munro, M. J., & Derwing, T. M. (2001). Modeling perceptions of the accentedness and comprehensibility of L2 speech: The role of speaking rate [Electronic version]. *SSLA, 23*,

451-468.

Munro, M. J., & Derwing, T. M. (2006). The functional load principle in ESL pronunciation instruction: An exploratory study. *System*, *34*, 520-531. doi: 10.1016/j.system.2006.09.004

Munro, M. J., & Derwing, T. M. (2008). Segmental acquisition in adult ESL learners: A longitudinal study of vowel production. *Language learning*, *58*(3), 479-502. doi: 10.1111/j.1467-9922.2008.00448.x

Munro, M.J., Derwing, T.M., & Morton, S. L. (2006). The mutual intelligibility of L2 speech. *Studies in Second Language Acquisition*, *28*, 111-131. doi: 10.10170S0272263106060049

Munro, M. J., Derwing, T. M., & Thomson, R. I. (2015). Setting segmental priorities for English learners: Evidence from a longitudinal study. *IRAL*, *53*(1), 39-60. doi: 10.1515/iral-2015-0002

Neumeyer, L., Franco, H., Digalakis, V., & Weintraub, M. (2000). Automatic scoring of pronunciation quality [Electronic version]. *Speech Communication*, *30*, 83-93.

North, B. (2000). *The development of a common framework scale of language proficiency*. New York: Peter Lang.

O'Brien, M. G. (2016). Methodological choices in rating speech samples. *Studies in Second Language Acquisition*, *38*, 587-605. doi: 10.1017/S0272263115000418

O'connor, J. D., & Arnold, G. F. (1973). *Intonation of colloquial English*. London: Longman.

O'Sullivan, B., Saville, N., & Weir, C. (2002). Using observation checklists to validate speaking-test tasks. *Language Testing*, *19*(1), 33-56. doi: 10.1191/

02655322021t2190a

Pearson. (2011). *Versant English test: Test description and validation summary*. Menlo Park, CA: Pearson. Retrieved from http://www.versanttest.com/technology/Versant FrechTestValidation.pdf

Piccardo, E. (2016). Phonological scale revision process report. *Common European framework of reference for languages: Learning, teaching, assessment*. Retrieved from https://rm.coe.int/phonological-scale-revision-process-report-cefr/168073fff9

Pickering, L. (2001). The role of tone choice in improving ITA communication in the classroom [Electronic version]. *TESOL Quarterly, 35*(2), 233-255.

Pierrehumbert, J. (1980). *The phonology and phonetics of English intonation*. (Doctoral dissertation, MIT).

Pierrehumbert, J., & Hirschberg, J. (1990). The meaning of intonational contours in the interpretation of discourse. In P. Cohen, J. Morgan, & M. Pollack (Eds.), *Intentions in communication* (pp. 271-311). Cambridge MA: MIT Press.

Pike, K. L. (1945). *The intonation of American English*. Ann Arbor, MI: University of Michigan Press.

Quirk, R., Greenbaum, S., Leech, G., & Svartvik, J. (1985). *A comprehensive grammar of the English language*. New York: Longman.

Rajadurai, J. (2007). Intelligibility studies: A consideration of empirical and ideological issues. *World Englishes, 26*, 87-98. doi: 10.1111/j.1467-971X.2007.00490.x

Ramus, F., Nespor, M., & Mehler, J. (1999). Correlates of linguistic rhythm in the speech signal [Electronic version].

Cognition, *73*, 265–292.

Rau, D. V., Chang, H.-H. A., & Tarone, E. E. (2009). Think or sink: Chinese learners' acquisition of the English voiceless interdental fricative. *Language Learning*, *59*, 581–621.

Reed, M., & Levis J. M. (2015). Introduction. In M. Reed & J. M. Levis (Ed.), *The handbook of English pronunciation* (pp. xii-xviii). Wiley Blackwell.

Révész, A., Ekiert, M., & Torgersen, E. N. (2016). The effects of complexity, accuracy, and fluency on communicative adequacy in oral task performance. *Applied Linguistics*, *37*(6), 828–848.

Riazantseva, A. (2001). Second language proficiency and pausing a study of Russian speakers of English. *Studies in Second Language Acquisition*, *23*(4), 497–526. doi: 10.1017/S027226310100403X

Riney, T. J., Takada, M., & Ota, M. (2000). Segmentals and global foreign accent: The Japanese flap in EFL [Electronic version]. *TESOL Quarterly*, *34*(4), 711–737.

Riney, T. J., Takagi, N., & Inutsuka, K. (2005). Phonetic parameters and perceptual judgments of accent in English by American and Japanese listeners, *TESOL Quarterly*, *39*(3), 441–466.

Robinson, P. (2001). Task complexity, task difficulty, and task production: Exploring interactions in a componential framework. *Applied Linguistics*, *22*, 27–57. doi: 10.1093/applin/22.1.27

Rogers, C. L. (1997). *Intelligibility of Chinese-accented English*. (Doctoral dissertation, Indiana University, Bloomington Indiana)

Rogers, C. L. & Dalby, J. (2005). Forced-choice analysis of segmental production by Chinese-accented English speakers. *Journal of Speech, Language, and Hearing Research*, *48*, 306 – 322. doi: 10.1044/1092 – 4388 (2005/021)

Rossiter, M. J. (2009). Perceptions of L2 fluency by native and non-native speakers of English. *Canadian Modern Language Review*, *65*, 395 – 412. doi: 10.3138/cmlr.65.3.395

Saito, K., & Brajot, F. (2013). Scrutinizing the role of length of residence and age of acquisition in the interlanguage pronunciation development of English /r/ by late Japanese bilinguals. *Bilingualism: Language and Cognition*, *16*, 847 – 863. doi: 10.1017/S1366728912000703

Saito, K., & Plonsky L. (2019). Effects of second language pronunciation teaching revisited: A proposed measurement framework and meta-analysis. *Language Learning*, *2019*, 1 – 57. doi: 10.1111/lang.12345

Saito, K., Trofimovich, P., & Isaacs, T. (2015). Using listener judgments to investigate linguistic influences on L2 comprehensibility and accentedness: A validation and generalization study. *Applied Linguistics*, *38* (40), 439 – 462. doi: 10.1093/applin/amv047

Saito, K., Trofimovich, P., & Isaacs, T. (2016). Second language speech production: Investigating linguistic correlates of comprehensibility and accentedness for learners at different ability levels. *Applied Psycholinguistics*, *37*, 217 – 240. doi: 10.1017/S0142716414000502

Sangwan, A. & J. H. L. Hansen. (2012). Automatic analysis of Mandarin accented English using phonological features [Electronic version]. *Speech Communication*, *54*, 40 – 54.

Segalowitz, N. (2010). *Cognitive bases of second language fluency*. New York, NY: Routledge.

Shah, A. P. (2004). Production and perceptual features of Spanish-accented English. *From Sound to Sense*, June, C79-84. Retrieved from http://www.rle.mit.edu/soundtosense/conference/pdfs/fulltext/Friday% 20Posters/FA-Shah-STS.pdf

Skehan, P. (1998). *A cognitive approach to language learning*. Oxford: Oxford University Press.

Skehan, P. (2003). Task-based instruction. *Language Teaching*, *36* (1), 1-14. doi: https://doi.org/10.1017/S026144480200188X

Skehan, P. (2009). Modelling second language performance: Integrating complexity, accuracy, fluency, and lexis. *Applied Linguistics*, *30* (4), 510 - 532. doi: 10.1093/applin/amp047

Slowiaczek, L. M. (1991). Stress and context in auditory word recognition [Electronic version]. *Journal of Psycholinguistic Research*, *20*(6), 465-481.

Sluijter, A. (1995). *Phonetic correlates of stress and accent*. (Doctoral dissertation, Holland Institute of Generative Linguistics).

Spada, N., & Tomita, Y. (2010). Interactions between type of instruction and type of language feature: A meta-analysis. *Language Learning*, *60*, 263 - 308. doi: 10.1111/j.1467-9922.2010.00562.x

Stevens, J. P. (2009). *Applied Multivariate Statistics for the social sciences* (5th ed.). New York: Routledge.

Suenobu, M., Kanzaki, K., & Yamane, S. (1992). An experimental study of intelligibility of Japanese English.

International Review of Applied Linguistics in Language Teaching, *30*(2), 146 - 153. doi: 10.1515/iral.1992.30.2. 121

Syllabus for TEM 4-Oral. (2014). Shanghai: Shanghai Foreign Language Education Press.

Szpyra-Kozlowska, J. (2014). *Pronunciation in EFL instruction: A research-based approach*. Bristol, UK: Multilingual Matters.

Taniguchi, M. (2001). Japanese EFL learners' weak points in English intonation. In paper presented at the 2001 Phonetics Teaching and Learning Conference, London.

Tarone, E. (1983). On the variability of interlanguage systems [Electronic version]. *Applied Linguistics*, *4*, 142 - 164.

Tench, P. (1996). The intonation systems of English. London: Cassell.

Thomson, R. (2018). Measurement of accentedness, intelligibility, and comprehensibility. In O. Kang & A. Ginther (Ed.), *Assessment in second language pronunciation* (pp. 11 - 29). New York: Routledge.

Thomson, R. I. & Derwing, T. M. (2015). The effectiveness of L2 pronunciation instruction: A narrative review. *Applied Linguistics*, *36*(3), 326 - 344. doi:10.1093/applin/amu076

Toivanen, J. (2004). Pitch dynamism of English produced by proficient non-native speakers: Preliminary results of a corpus-based analysis of second language speech. *Fonetik*. Dept. of Linguistics, Stockholm University.

Towell, R., Hawkins, R., & Bazergui, N. (1996). The development of fluency in advanced learners of French. *Applied Linguistics*, *17*(1), 84 - 119. doi:10.1093/applin/17.1.84

Trinity College London. (2015). Integrated Skills in English (ISE) specifications: Speaking & listening. ISE Foundation to ISE III. Retrieved from http://www.trinitycollege.com/resource/? id=6298

Trofimovich, P., & Baker, W. (2006). Learning second language suprasegmentals: Effect of L2 experience on prosody and fluency characteristics of L2 speech. *Studies in Second Language Acquisition*, *28*, 1 - 30. doi: 10.1017/S0272263106060013

Trofimovich, P., & Baker, W. (2007). Learning prosody and fluency characteristics of second language speech: The effect of experience on child learners' acquisition of five suprasegmentals. *Applied Psycholinguistics*, *28*, 251 - 276. doi: 10.1017.S0142716407070130

Trofimovich, P., & Isaacs, T. (2012). Disentangling accent from comprehensibility. *Bilingualism: Language and Cognition*, *15*(4), 905 - 916. doi:10.1017/S1366728912000168

Van den Doel, R. (2006). *How friendly are the natives? An evaluation of native-speaker judgments of foreign-accented British and American English*. Utrecht, the Netherlands: LOT.

Vanderslice, R. & Ladefoged, P. (1972). Binary suprasegmental features and transformational word-accentuation rules [Electronic version]. *Language*, *48*, 819 - 838.

Van Katwijk, A. (1974). *Accentuation in Dutch: An experimental linguistic study*. Amsterdam: Van Gorcum.

Watanabe, Y. (2013). The national center test for university admissions. *Language Testing*, *30*, 565 - 573. doi: 10.1177/0265532213483095

Weigle, S.C. (2002). *Assessing Writing*. Cambridge: Cambridge

University Press.

Weir, C. J., Vidaković, I., & Galaczi, E. (2013). *Measured constructs: A history of Cambridge English language examinations 1913 – 2012*. Cambridge, UK: Cambridge University Press.

Weisberg, S. (1985). *Applied linear regression*. New York: Wiley.

Wells, J. C. (1990). Syllabification and allophony. *Studies in the pronunciation of English-A commemorative volume in honour of A.C. Gimson* (pp. 76 – 86). London and New York: Routledge. Retrieved from https://www.phon.ucl.ac.uk/home/wells/syllabif.htm

Wells, J. C. (2005). *Longman English pronunciation dictionary*. London: Longman.

Wells, J. C. (2006). *English Intonation*. New York: Cambridge University Press.

Wennerstrom, A. (1994). Intonational meaning in English discourse: A study of nonnative speakers [Electronic version]. *Applied Linguistics, 15*, 399 – 421.

Wennerstrom, A. (1998). Intonation as cohesion in academic discourse: A study of Chinese speakers of English [Electronic version]. *Studies in Second Language Acquisition, 42*, 1 – 13.

White, L., & Mattys, S. L. (2007). Calibrating rhythm: First language and second language studies. *Journal of Phonetics, 35*, 501 – 522. dio: 10.1016/j.wocn.2007.02.003

Wild, C. & Seber, G. (2000). *Chance encounters. A first course in data analysis and inference*. New York: John Wiley & Sons, Inc.

Xi, Y. (2013). ProsodyPro-A tool for large-scale systematic

prosody analysis. In *Proceedings of tools and resources for the analysis of speech prosody* (pp. 7 – 10). Aix-en-Provence, France. Retrieved from http://www.homepages.ucl.ac.uk/~uclyyix/ProsodyPro/

Yates, L., Zielinski B., & Pryor, E. (2011). The assessment of pronunciation and the new IELTS pronunciation scale. *IELTS Research Reports*, *12*, 1–46. Retrieved from http://www.ielts.org/PDF/vol12_report1.pdf.

Zhang, Y., Nissen, S. L., & Francis, A. L. (2008). Acoustic characteristics of English lexical stress produced by native Mandarin speakers.*The Journal of the Acoustical Society of America*, *123*, 4498–4513. doi: 10.1121/1.2902165

Zhong, W. J. (2019). Pronunciation rating scale I second language pronunciation assessment: A review. *Journal of Language Teaching and Research*, *10*(1), 141–149. doi: 10.17507/jltr.1001.16

Zielinski, B. W. (2006). *Reduced intelligibility in L2 speakers of English* (Doctoral dissertation, La Trobe University, Australia).

Zielinski, B. (2008). The listener: No longer the silent partner in reduced intelligibility. *System*, *36*(1), 69–84. doi: 10.1016/j.system.2007.11.004

Zielinski, B. (2015). The segmental/suprasegmental debate. In M. Reed & J. M. Levis (Ed.), *The handbook of English pronunciation* (pp. 397–412). Wiley Blackwell.

毕冉,陈桦,2006.中国英语专业学生英语朗读口语中陈述句语调模式的纵贯研究.第七届中国语音学学术会议暨语音学前沿问题国际论坛,1–10.

陈桦,2006.英语学习者朗读口语中的调核位置.解放军外语学院学报,29(6):32–38.

陈桦,2008a. 中国学生英语语调模式研究.上海:上海外语教育出版社.

陈桦,2008b. 学习者英语朗读中重音复现的节奏归类研究.外语与外语教学,228(3):35-37. doi:10.3969/j.issn.1004-6038.2008.03.009

陈桦,毕冉,2015. 中国英语语调音系结构研究.北京:外语教学与研究出版社.

陈桦,李景娜,2017. 英语语音评测的现状与思考———项对标准化口试评分员的调查.外语与外语教学,296(5):81-87. doi:CNKI:SUN:WYWJ.0.2017-05-009

陈桦,梁茂成,House,J.,2004. 学习者英语朗读的无声停顿模式.语料库语言学的研究与应用.何安平编,108-112. 长春:东北大学出版社.

陈桦,孙兴平,2010. 输入、输出频次对英语韵律特征习得的作用.外语研究,122(4):1-8. doi:10.3969/j.issn.1005-7242.2010.04.001

陈桦,文秋芳,李爱军,2010. 语音研究的新平台:中国英语学习者语音数据库.外语学刊,152(1):95-99.

陈桦,吴奎,李景娜,2019. 英语口语自动评测新方法———中国学生英语朗读自动评测系统.外语电话教学》185(2):72-77.

陈文凯,2002. 英语语音语调学习主要问题分析及对策.河南教育学院学报,21(3):126-127. doi:10.3969/j.issn.1006-2920.2002.03.043

陈晓湘,郭兴荣,2017. L2水平对中国学习者英语词重音产出的影响.湖南大学学报,31(5):76-83.

程春梅,何安平,2008. 高级英语学习者口语音段错误分析———项基于语料库的研究.解放军外国语学院学报,31(1):38-42.

程欣,2020. 二语朗读中不当停顿的感知研究.外语与外语教学,310(1):81-90.

戴峥峥,陈桦,2010. ESCC 朗读语音库音段标注与研究. 中国二语语音习得研究的现状及发展趋势,264 – 271. 北京:外语教学与研究出版社.

窦艳,2003. 英汉语调特点对比及英语语调教学. 佳木斯大学社会科学学报,21(3):120 – 121. doi: 10.3969/j.issn.1007 – 9882.2003.03.058

高霞,2007. 朗读评分方案评析及设计. 国外外语教学,4:15 – 20.

高霞,朱正才,杨惠中,2006. 朗读在外语教学和测试中的作用. 外语界,2:64 – 71.

高莹,樊宇,2011. 基于语料库的中美大学生口语叙述中停顿现象比较研究. 解放军外国语学院学报,34(4):71 – 75.

何莲珍,张洁,2008. 多层面 Rasch 模型下大学英语四、六级考试口语考试(CET – SET)信度研究. 现代外语,31(4):15 – 20.

蒋同海,张俊博,潘复平,颜永红,2011. 英语篇章朗读质量的自动评分. 应用声学,30(6):418 – 426.

李爱军,2005. 语调研究中心里和声学等价单位. 声学技术,24(3):13 – 17.

李艳玲,颜永红,2012. 多特征融合的英语口语考试自动评分系统的研究. 电子与信息学报,34:2098 – 2102.

李萌涛,杨晓果,冯国栋,吴敏,陈纪梁,胡国平,2008. 大规模大学英语口语测试朗读题型及其阅卷可行性研究与实践. 外语界,4:88 – 95.

马冬梅,2014. 英语专业学生阐述性口语产出停顿特征及其与口语成绩的相关性. 外语与外语教学,276(3):42 – 48.

缪海燕,2009. 第二语言口语非流利产出的停顿研究. 解放军外国语学院学报,32(4):56 – 60.

田朝霞,金檀,2015. 英语语音评估与测试实证研究——世界发展趋势及对中国教学的启示. 中国外语,12(3):80 – 86. doi:10.13564/j.cnki.issn.1672 – 9382.2015.03.011

王桂珍,2011.英语语音语调教程(第二版).北京:高等教育出版社.
王海贞,2008.全国英语专业四级口试评分员对评分标准的理解和使用.外语教学理论与实践,2:33-39.
巫玮,肖德法,2011.基于语料库的中国英语学习者加音现象研究.外语学刊,159(2):80-83
徐鹰,曾用强,2015.基于概化理论和多层面 Rasch 模型的计算机化英语听说考试评分研究.课程与教学,263(3):89-95.
徐鹰,曾用强,2017.中国英语学习者朗读语音特征和分数预测模型研究.西安外国语大学学报,25(2):69-74.
杨晋,2010.反复聆听模仿和中国英语学生重音模式习得研究.外语研究,122(4):9-16.doi:10.13978/j.cnki.wyyj.2010.04.013
杨军,陈桦,2005.二语口语产出的韵律——与朗读相关的文献研究.外语研究,93(5):46-50.doi:10.13978/j.cnki.wyyj.2005.05.010
余红梅,罗艳虹,萨建,艾永梅,2011.组内相关系数及其软件实现.中国卫生统计,28(5):497-499.
袁咏,2010.英语附加疑问句的语调模式.湖北第二师范学院学报,27(9):24-26.
张文忠,吴旭东,2001.第二语言口语流利性发展定量研究.现代外语,94(4):341-351.
周卫京,宋会萍,2010.中国大学生产出性英语语音素质管窥.外语与外语教学,282(3):1-7.

Appendix A
Text of the read dialogues

Dialogue 1:

A: Tell me the story about the clever monkey, mummy.

B: We had that one last night. Here's another story. Once upon a time, there's a foolish monkey.

Dialogue 2:

A: I don't think Mary likes swimming.

B: I'm sorry. Mary does like swimming.

Dialogue 3:

A: How many seasons are there in a year?

B: There are four.

A: What are they?

B: They are spring, summer, autumn, and winter.

Dialogue 4:

A: "Will they come tomorrow?" Betty asked.

B: "No, they will come two days later," Bob answered cheerfully.

Dialogue 5:

A: Something's wrong with my computer. I don't know what I can do with it.

B: Take it back to the shop where you bought it.

Dialogue 6:

A: What do you want to buy?

B: I want a pound of meat, a box of chocolates, and a loaf

of bread.

Dialogue 7:

A: Do you know that boy?

B: Which one?

A: The handsome boy who is on his bicycle.

Dialogue 8:

A: They went to London, didn't they?

B: I don't think so. They must have gone to New York.

Dialogue 9:

A: Do you want to go to the cinema tonight, or have you got to stay late at work again?

B: No, I'd love to. But only if there's something good on.

A: I've heard that that film from the United States is really good. I think it's called *Gone with the Wind*.

B: Oh Yes! Somebody told me that it's a famous tragedy.

A: Well, let's have a look at the newspaper.

Appendix B
Categorization of the within-sentence pauses

Category	Specific Location
A) clause-boundary pauses	01. between coordinate clauses, before the linking conjunction such as *or*; 02. in coordinate clauses, after the linking conjunction such as *or*; 03. before the restrictive pronoun which introduces a restricted attributive clause such as *who*; 04. after the restrictive pronoun which introduces a restricted attributive clausesuch as *who*; 05. before the first word or the binding conjunction *that* in an object clause; 06. before the binding conjunction *what* in an object clause; 07. after the binding conjunction *that* or *what* in an object clause; 08. between the direct speech and the final reporting clause; 09. between the main clause and the tag question.
B) phrase-boundary pauses	10. between the NP and the VP, most often between the initial subject and the predicative verb phrase; 11. before the sentence-final vocative; 12. before a clause-final adverbial phrase or complement; 13. between listing lexical items (before or after the binding conjunctions if there is any); 14. after other sentence-initial adjuncts such as the sentence-initial discourse marker *well* and affirmative expression *yes/no*; 15. after the sentence-initial adverbial phrases

Continued

Category	Specific Location
C) within-phrase pauses	16. within a noun phrase, mostly between the modifier and the modified noun/NP; 17. within a verb phrase, between the modifier and the modified verb/adjective; 18. within a verb phrase such as *don't* | *think* or phrasal verb such as *stay* | *up*, or within the infinitive structure 19. within a verb phrase, between a verb/VP and its object or predicative; 20. within an adverbial or predicative or attributive phrase, often after a preposition; 21. within a word; 22. between, before or after the repetition (repeated words or syllables) or reformulation (repeats while making some grammatical, lexical or phonetic changes); 23. elsewhere at word boundaries within phrases, for example, the one before the preposition within the nominal partitives (*a loaf* | *of*)

Appendix C
Locations of boundary tones examined for tone deviation

Note: The parentheses signal the 13 intonation phrases with a rising (H-H%) or level (L-H%) boundary tone, while the square brackets the 22 intonation phrases with a falling (L-L%) boundary tone. The marked boundary tones were agreed by at least nine native American speakers. The intonation phrases in bold are those whose boundary tones were examined for tone deviation.

Dialogue 1:

A: (Tell me the story about the clever monkey, mummy).

B: [We had that one last night]. Here's another story. **(Once upon a time)**, [**there's a foolish monkey**].

Dialogue 2:

A: [I don't think Mary likes swimming].

B: **(I'm sorry)**. [**Mary does like swimming**].

Dialogue 3:

A: [**How many seasons are there in a year**]?

B: [**There are four**].

A: [**What are they**]?

B: (They are spring), **(summer)**, **(autumn)**, [and winter].

Dialogue 4:

A: ("Will they come tomorrow?" Betty asked).

B: ("No, they will come two days later," Bob answered

cheerfully).

Dialogue 5:

A: [Something's wrong with my computer]. [I don't know what I can do with it].

B: [Take it back to the shop where you bought it].

Dialogue 6:

A: [**What do you want to buy**]?

B: (**I want a pound of meat**), (**a box of chocolates**), [and a loaf of bread].

Dialogue 7:

A: (**Do you know that boy**)?

B: [**Which one**]?

A: [The handsome boy who is on his bicycle].

Dialogue 8:

A: [They went to London], (**didn't they**)?

B: [I don't think so]. [**They must have gone to New York**].

Dialogue 9:

A: (**Do you want to go to the cinema tonight**), [**or have you got to stay late at work again**]?

B: [No, I'd love to]. But only if there's something good on.

A: I've heard that that film from the United States is really good. I think it's called *Gone with the Wind*.

B: [Oh Yes]! [Somebody told me that it's a famous tragedy].

Appendix D
Syllables possible to be stressed in the read text

Dialogue 1:

A: **Tell** me the **story** about the **clever monkey**, **mummy**.

B: We **had that** one **last night**. Here's a**nother story**. **Once** upon a **time**, there's a **foolish monkey**.

Dialogue 2:

A: I **don't** think **Mary likes swimm**ing.

B: I'm **sorry**. **Mary does** like **swimm**ing.

Dialogue 3:

A: **How** many **seasons** are there in a **year**?

B: There are **four**.

A: **What are** they?

B: They are **spring**, **summ**er, **autumn**, and **winter**.

Dialogue 4:

A: "Will they **come tomorrow**?" **Betty asked**.

B: "**No**, they will **come two** days **later**," **Bob answered cheer**fully.

Dialogue 5:

A: **Something's wrong** with my com**pu**ter. I **don't know what** I can **do** with it.

B: **Take** it **back** to the **shop** where you **bought** it.

Dialogue 6:

A: **What** do you **want** to **buy**?

B: I want a **pound** of **meat**, a **box** of **choco**lates, and a **loaf** of **bread**.

Dialogue 7:

A: Do you **know that boy**?

B: **Which one**?

A: The **hand**some **boy** who is on his **bi**cycle.

Dialogue 8:

A: They **went** to **London**, **didn't** they?

B: I **don't** think **so**. They **must** have **gone** to **New York**.

Dialogue 9:

A: Do you **want** to **go** to the **cinema tonight**, or have you **got** to **stay late** at **work** again?

B: **No**, I'd **love** to. But **only** if there's something **good** on.

A: I've **heard** that **thatfilm** from the **United States** is **really good**. I **think** it's **called** *Gone with the Wind*.

B: **Oh Yes**! **Some**body **told** me that it's a **famous trage**dy.

A: **Well**, **let's have** a **look** at the **news**paper.

Appendix E
Possible locations for accented syllables and sampled tonic/weak syllables

Note: Possible locations for accented syllables are in uppercase; the sampled tonic syllables are marked with *, and the sampled weak syllables underlined.

Dialogue 1:

A: Tell me the story about <u>the</u> clever * MONKey, mummy.

B: We HAD THAT <u>one</u> last night. Here's anOTHer story. Once upon <u>a</u> TIME, there's a * FOOLish monkey.

Dialogue 2:

A: I DON'T think Mary likes swimming."

B: I'm * SORRy. Mary * DOES like swimming.

Dialogue 3:

A: How many SEAsons are there in a YEAR?

B: There are * FOUR.

A: What * ARE they?

B: They are * SPRING, * SUMmer, * AUTumn, <u>and</u> * WINTer.

Dialogue 4:

A: "Will they COME toMOrrow?" Betty asked.

B: "NO, <u>they</u> will come TWO days LATer," Bob answered cheerfully.

Dialogue 5:

A: Something's WRONG with my comPUTer. I don't know what I can * DO with it.

B: Take it back to the shop where you * BOUGHT it.

Dialogue 6:

A: What do you want to * BUY?

B: I want a * POUND of meat, a * BOX of chocolates, and a loaf of * BREAD.

Dialogue 7:

A: Do you know that * BOY?

B: WHICH ONE?

A: The handsome boy who is on his * BICycle.

Dialogue 8:

A: They went to * LONDon, * DIDN'T they?

B: I DON'T thinkso. They MUST have gone to NEW YORK.

Dialogue 9:

A: Do you want to go to the CINema toNIGHT, or have you got to STAY LATE at WORK again?

B: NO, I'd * LOVE to. But only if there's something * GOOD on.

A: I've heard that that film from the United States is REALLy GOOD. I think it's CALLED *GONE with the WIND*.

B: Oh, * YES! Somebody told me that it's a famous TRAGedy.

A: Well, let's have a look at the NEWSpaper.